iWant

My JOURNEY from ADDICTION and OVERCONSUMPTION to a SIMPLER, HONEST LIFE

JANE VELEZ-MITCHELL

Health Communications, Inc.
Deerfield Beach, Florida

www.hcibooks.com

Disclaimer: some names have been changed to protect the privacy of certain individuals.

Library of Congress Cataloging-in-Publication Data

Velez-Mitchell, Jane.
   iWant : my journey from addiction and overconsumption to a simpler, honest life / Jane Velez-Mitchell.
     p. cm.
   Includes bibliographical references.
   ISBN-13: 978-0-7573-1371-4
   ISBN-10: 0-7573-1371-X
   1. Velez-Mitchell, Jane.   2. Velez-Mitchell, Jane—Philosophy.   3. Women television journalists—United States—Biography.   4. Television journalists—United States—Biography.   5. Recovering addicts—United States—Biography. 6. Conduct of life.   7. Lifestyles—United States—Case studies.   8. Alcoholism—United States—Case studies.   9. Compulsive behavior—United States—Case studies.   I. Title.   II. Title: I want.
   PN4874.V45A3 2009
   070.92—dc22
   [B]

2009023435

Publisher: Health Communications, Inc.
   3201 S.W. 15th Street
   Deerfield Beach, FL 33442–8190

Cover photo ©Toky Photography
Cover design by Larissa Hise Henoch
Interior design and formatting by Lawna Patterson Oldfield

For my dad,
Pearse Mitchell

Dad, you were so smart, funny, handsome, and hardworking. I only wish you had made it into recovery. It hurts that I never really knew you, the real Pearse who would have emerged in sobriety. I'm sure you know that when you died, I was headed along the very same path. But I just happened to find a different way. I got sober. I got to know myself. Dad, I wish I could have shared this journey with you. This is for you.

Contents

*"Peace is present right here and now,
in ourselves and in everything we do and see.
The question is whether or not we
are in touch with it."*

—**Thich Nhat Hanh** from
*Peace Is Every Step: The Path of
Mindfulness in Everyday Life*

Acknowledgments

This book would not be what it is were it not for my fabulous editor at HCI, Carol Rosenberg. Carol took a leap of faith in me, and for that, I will always be grateful. With patience and great judgment, she expertly guided me through the process of telling an honest, personal story. HCI President and Publisher Peter Vegso and his entire team also offered tremendous support. My literary agent, Sharlene Martin, is a buoyant spirit who encouraged me to pursue my dream of telling this story.

There have been many other amazing guides and gurus in my life, people who generously and patiently shared their wisdom and pointed me in the right direction. My news agent, Carole Cooper, and I go back decades. She has always been there for me, with humor and understanding. My dear friend and mentor *Celebrity Justice* and TMZ creator Harvey Levin has also given me crucial breaks and taught me so much. Nancy Grace, and her executive producer Dean Sicoli, also changed my life by having confidence in me and giving me incredible opportunities. Ken Jautz, executive vice-president of CNN Worldwide, gave me the shot of a lifetime by asking me to host *Issues* on HLN. I will always be indebted to him. My amazing *Issues* executive producers, Conway Cliff and Stephanie Todd, have assembled an extraordinary staff and made hosting the show a delightful experience. Janine Iamunno, CNN's brilliant public relations director, is also a blast to work with.

Jane Langley is a very patient, wise, and compassionate friend who has shared with me her wealth of knowledge about how to navigate daily life. Stephen Doran has also been someone to whom I've turned for help and for a laugh. He always has a fascinating observation that puts things in their proper perspective. Debbie Merrill will always be one of my gurus. She has led the way, showing me through example, how to let go of things that aren't good for me and replace them with joyous adventures. My dear friend Abbott Andresen, who tragically passed away, was an angel who guided me to sobriety and with whom I shared so many fun times. Sandra Mohr will always be family to me. She is one of the most compassionate and evolved people I've ever encountered.

And then there's the rest of my fantastic family. My sister, Gloria Vando, is an accomplished poet who is also a true friend. My niece Lorca Peress now a successful director, started me on my journey to self-awareness by getting me into therapy and has always been a caring shoulder to lean on. My nephew, Paul Peress, is an amazing musician who has embraced a vegan lifestyle and—with his wife Teresa—has raised a beautiful and smart vegan daughter, Nicole. Anika Peress, my other niece, a superb songwriter and composer, is a creative and uplifting presence in my life, whose positive spirit is contagious.

Finally, my mom, Anita, has experienced almost a century of adventures and is still going strong thanks to her astounding attitude and vegetarian lifestyle. She is the one who taught me that life is a journey filled with sharp turns and unexpected bumps but that, no matter what, it can still be a fun and joyful ride.

Introduction

I Want My Experiences to Serve a Purpose

This is the story of my ch . . . ch . . . changes, which took me from insanity to clarity, from egocentricity to altruism, from alcoholism to activism. These changes have marked an evolution in what I want from this life. I *am* what I *want*. What I seek to consume, possess, and achieve is a mirror that reflects my lusts and cravings, values and priorities, and moral boundaries or lack thereof. I am happy to say that what I want today is much less toxic and self-centered than what I used to want. It's taken decades of self-examination to peel back the layers and figure out what really makes me happy. And while I'm still searching for my ultimate bliss, I know for sure it's not what I once thought it was. It's not alcohol, cigarettes, money, food, sugar, or status symbols: I've consumed all of those in massive quantities, and they've just made me miserable. Now, I want what can't be tasted, smoked, worn, seen, or counted. It's the opposite of material. As sappy as it might sound, what I want is spiritual.

The shift from material to spiritual is a particular challenge in our culture. We have allowed ourselves to be defined by our consumption, instead of by our ability to move beyond it. To keep consumers consuming, the corporate culture has brainwashed us into thinking we can change ourselves by changing what we buy, which pills we pop, what type of booze we swill, what gated community we join, what kind of golf clubs we swing, and what kind of cancer sticks we dangle between our lips. We've been told that certain consumer choices say a lot about us, that they reveal our character. If we've stepped up to a more prestigious brand, we've changed for the better. Nonsense! We cannot consume our way into personal growth. Yet, millions of us have bought into this cynical concept of faux identity. If you keep buying the "latest and the greatest" but feel like you're stuck in the same place, you're just changing labels, and that's not changing. That's rearranging. *Real* change occurs on the emotional, psychological, and spiritual levels, not in a shopping mall, a car dealership, online, at the drugstore, at the liquor store, or at the fast-food joint.

For too long, we have allowed ourselves to be manipulated by forces whose sole purpose is PROFIT and POWER. We have given advertisers leave to claim that inanimate objects have spiritual qualities. One ad, in perhaps the world's most prestigious newspaper, urges us to buy an expensive diamond by insisting that such a purchase will feed the soul, lift the spirit, and increase our resolve to achieve whatever we wish. *Really?* How exactly does a diamond feed the soul? It's absurd! This is false advertising. Today, as a culture, we are awash in false advertising.

As a society, we've lent legitimacy to these patent lies by literally buying into them. As a result of this unnecessary, self-indulgent consumption, we've gone a long way toward destroying our natural environment with our waste. Perhaps most important, by obsessing about material things, we've cheated ourselves out of the most fundamental aspect of the human experience: *real* experiences that result in *real* growth.

Unlike diamonds, meaningful experiences can actually feed the soul, resulting in self-development and self-knowledge. *Authentic* change has allowed me to gradually learn why I'm here experiencing this existence as well as what I am destined to contribute during my lifetime.

For me, meaningful change has been about getting sober, becoming honest, and adopting a new attitude. Sobriety has allowed me to shift the criteria I use for all the decisions I make from an ego-based formula of *what's in it for me* to a more evolved formula based on compassion for other people, other living creatures, and our environment. It's an ongoing struggle, and there are many times when I fail. But I keep trying.

This book is my story of how I've progressed from self-obsession to a life that I hope will count. In the tradition of the Twelve Steps* created by Alcoholics Anonymous, I'm going to lay out what it was like, what happened to change me, and what it's like now. For thirty years as a television news reporter, I've been recounting other people's mostly sordid stories. Frankly, the prospect of airing my own dirty laundry scares the wits out of me. The very thought of this sparks a flood of memories, primarily featuring the many stupid and embarrassing things I've done over the years, especially before I got sober. My face burns at the prospect of sharing some of these memories with you.

I know we're all only *as sick as our secrets**. By pouring out the intimate details of my personal history, I am trying to get healthier through honesty. Still, I can't help but wonder if you really have to know every single one of my secrets. Is that what is meant by *rigorous honesty**? These thoughts swirl through my mind as I huddle under my covers unable to sleep.

Suddenly, I pop out of bed and I'm at my computer, my sleep mask still affixed to my forehead. Am I having a bout of inspiration? Or is it just a spell of insomnia brought on by my Chihuahuas, Cabo and Foxy, who keep scratching and burrowing under the covers, trying to find a more comfortable spot? The recovering *people pleaser** that I am, I could learn something from these two. They have an innate self-esteem that borders on haughtiness. They crack me up. I'm so glad these two little rescues are with me on this leg of my journey. I tell *them* everything . . . and they don't judge.

I am fifty-three, and I feel like parts of me are disappearing into the ether. Like most boomers, I've convinced myself that I don't look my age. Still, as my mom says, "The body is like soap. It gets used up." My eyesight is getting fuzzier, so I have to set the point size of the type at 14 so that I can actually read what I'm writing on the computer screen. But the good news is my increasingly used-up body is feeling less weighed down to this earth as I continue to lighten my load spiritually and psychologically. I am feeling more and more that, when my time comes, I will be ready to take off and see what's next.

The biggest leap in my personal evolution was getting sober. I was a drunk. I was what you would call your garden-variety lush. I didn't kill or maim anyone. I didn't leave a baby or a dog to suffocate in a hot car. I didn't even get a DUI. But believe me, I was a blackout drinker who did many bizarre things while under the influence. I am not proud of those times. However, like many drunks, I also have a few fond memories of the silly, kooky things I'd done and the wild, decadent parties I'd attended. Even in darkness, there is *some* light.

I finally put down my last drink in 1995 on April Fools'Day (yes, I got sober on April Fools' Day). At the time, I thought any possibility of fun was gone forever. I also thought my problems were finally over. I was wrong on both counts. Now that I'm actually in touch with my feelings, because I'm no longer covering them up with inauthentic substances, I cry more than I ever have, but I also laugh more, much more. Why, just earlier this evening, I got a serious case of the giggles after losing my shoe upon leaving a fancy charity gala in Bel Air. My high heel simply slipped off my foot, tumbled down a flight of stairs, and into a gully. I limped along to the parking lot on one high heel, sparking stares from people who must have thought I was quite tipsy. But I wasn't concerned. At this point in my sobriety, I'm always relatively relaxed because I know there's absolutely nothing I can do sober that's as embarrassing as what I used to do drunk. Not even if I tried hard!

Sometimes I get so giddy in sobriety that someone will ask me if I'm okay to drive. I love that! I laugh and assure them that I'm okay. There's still a goofy teenager inside me, and I don't think she's going anywhere. That's okay. I like her. But I do believe that virtually everything else about me has metamorphosed and continues to do so thanks to finally ridding myself of my drug of choice—alcohol— and getting into recovery.

Becoming sober was a profound shift that occurred in my psyche.

I've placed an asterisk (*) beside certain lingo so you can learn the language of those in recovery as well as the language of vegans. An explanation and discussion of these terms can be found in the glossary on page 254.

Just about everything about me has changed these last fourteen years. My attitude, my expectations, my thoughts, my feelings, my behavior, my sexuality—it's all different. There's a sober saying: *The only thing that has to change is everything.* How true that is!

Once I got sober, I was slammed with a host of new challenges I hadn't expected. I quickly learned that addictions jump! Without alcohol, I began craving food—particularly refined sugar and carbohydrates. Junk food that I'd never even noticed before—like Oreos—suddenly became *very* seductive. It's very common for recovering alcoholics to crave sugar. I was relatively lucky because I also became a vegan and that automatically knocked a ton of junk food off of my plate. But I still managed to find the sweets, like Oreos, that had no butter, milk, or other animal products. I also gorged on high-tech gadgets as my addiction hopped to shopping. My work became an obsession as well, and I over-did it there too until I hit bottom. That happened when my workaholism destroyed a very important love relationship.

Alcoholic thinking*—a black-and-white/all-or-nothing view—often remains even in sobriety. For many *dry drunks** this type of thinking never gets resolved. I recognized this, and so, once the obsession to drink was lifted, I began working on my *emotional sobriety**.

When I was still *in my disease**, I had been devoting huge amounts of energy trying to escape from unpleasant emotions. In other words, I was *stuffing my feelings**. When I finally *surrendered to my powerlessness** over alcohol, I had tons of energy that needed a new outlet. I looked at the world around me and realized that there were things about it I desperately wanted to change. With this newfound energy, I began to take action to effect change and make my life count. But there was still more to come internally.

Without alcohol, my unresolved personal issues—which I had grappled with in therapy for many years—resurfaced with a vengeance. I no longer had a way to drown my innermost secrets. I could no longer drink my way into denial. With nowhere to hide, I finally admitted my true sexual orientation to myself. I am gay. I also had to take a fresh look at how I interacted with people. I began to examine my *codependent** behavior and realized that I, alone, must take full responsibility for my life and my happiness and not try to find self-esteem or fulfillment through another person.

There's so much to tell. But would you *want* to know *everything* about my personal struggles? You may simply be reading this book because you're interested in my life, and for that I thank you. But if you *identify with my story**, then we will both learn from my experience. That is the essence of all recovery programs. Many of the battles I'm fighting, the compulsions I'm struggling to conquer, are the same as those experienced by many of my friends, relatives, co-workers, and neighbors. Some struggle with overeating, with alcohol or drugs, with workaholism, with codependency, with compulsive spending, with gambling, with *sex addiction**, or with facing the truth about themselves—whatever that truth may be. And virtually everyone I know, including myself, suffers from generic overconsumption—a chronic craving for more of everything that is poisoning our lives, not to mention our oceans, skies, and forests. My friend once called himself a tornado of consumption. That description fits most Americans. Sadly, we're a nation of addicts. For a multitude of reasons—our health, our finances, and our environment, among them—we need to take immediate action to reduce our collective consumption levels. Unfortunately, addicts don't respond to reason or rationality. Just as you can't reason with a drunk who is on a binge, we are not going to lecture our way out of America's consumption mess. Fortunately, there are proven recovery methods out there that can help us get a handle on our addictive consumption. I've used them to deal with my plethora of addictions, and I will share these techniques with you while I tell you my story.

The clearest path to overcoming any addictive behavior is to listen to somebody else talk about having that same addiction and what they did to deal with it. The reason this works is there is no judgment or blame. When you and I *share** our experience about an addiction or a secret behavior, you are neither above me nor below me. We are the same. And we are both on the way to getting better.

Virtually every one of us has some addiction or compulsion or secret urge with which we are grappling. This even applies to those recovering alcoholics call *normies**. Those are the so-called normal people who don't seem to be under the sway of weird or uncontrollable urges, the annoyingly perfect people who never seem to lose it or go off the deep end. Normies can be the worst closet addicts! They can have some of the most crippling addictions, namely the ones you can't see, hear, or consume.

Addiction appears in many disguises, from ambition to neurosis. Obsessive-compulsive behavior can turn life into a giant game of avoiding the cracks in the pavement. Such compulsive disorders often have an addictive component. *Workaholism** makes one so obsessed with his or her career that family and friends become irrelevant.

Shopaholics—or overconsumers—buy uncontrollably, to the point of accumulating massive debt. *Drama addicts** are people who seem to thrive on creating chaos and emotional conflict wherever they go. There are also *rage-aholics**, people who erupt into tantrums at the drop of hat. You also have the "professional victims,"—people for whom life is one giant *pity party**! We like to say these folks are "married to their martyrdom." And, of course, there are *love addicts**, people who are so hooked on the romance of courtship that they never learn to endure the nitty-gritty of a long-term partnership. And my personal favorite, codependency, is when someone is essentially addicted to somebody else and goes into *withdrawal** if they're not around. In one way or another, it would seem we're all addicts—the only difference is the *drug of choice**.

In sobriety, I've been given some amazing recovery tools, which I try to use in all aspects of my life. These tools are the *Twelve Steps.* They help me mend all manner of dysfunctional, addictive, compulsive, and irrational behaviors. Originally developed to help alcoholics achieve and maintain sobriety, they've since been applied to every addiction under the sun. And, you know what, they work! At times they seem like magic. Actually, they're gems of wisdom that crystallize timeless and fundamental spiritual principles into a modern format that's easy to put to use. Some call it religion without the mumbo jumbo. As you take in my story, you will get a thorough knowledge of the Twelve Steps and how to apply them to your own life, if you so choose.

The Twelve Steps have guided me through a whole maze of mind-blowing changes that have formed the true adventure of my life, a journey of self-discovery that is still in full throttle. As a recovering drama addict, I try to react to each new challenge with all the serenity I can muster, though the sharp turns and bumps keep coming.

"Foray, foray, come what may!" I sometimes cry out, only half joking. I am striving to experience the ultimate joy and freedom that lies in compassion and *being of service** to other people and other living beings. It's my hope that, as you read my story, you will relate. Let's change ourselves and the world for the better!

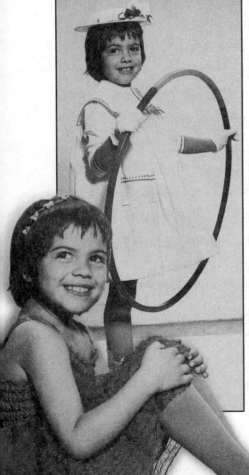

I was performing from the get-go.

1

Growing Up:
I Want to Fit In

"You'll always be behind the eight ball," the principal, Miss M., hissed at me with deadly certainty, her eyes flashing as she delivered this omen.

As a sixth grader, having spent little time hustling in pool halls, I had no idea what an eight ball was or why it was so awful to be behind one. However, based on Miss M.'s facial expression, I knew exactly what she meant.

That evening, I casually asked my dad, "What does it mean when someone says 'you'll always be behind the eight ball'?"

"*Who* said that to you?!" Dad responded, his Irish temper rising like a surface-to-air missile.

"Miss M.," I replied with faux innocence.

It wasn't long before I switched schools . . . again. That was my parents' solution. Trouble at school? Find a new school. I went through six schools by the time I graduated high school.

This was part of my early education in being *terminally unique**, an outlook particularly prevalent among alcoholics. I was taught that I was special and the rules didn't apply to me. When my father—a very charming, though alcoholic, advertising executive—wanted to go on vacation, he would just pull me out of school and take me along. Given that he never had opportunities to travel abroad when he was a Depression-era youngster growing up on Long Island, he saw his decision as the mark of a generous and doting father.

When he was warned that I would miss classwork, he'd reply, "What Janie will learn travelling will be far more educational than what she could ever learn in class."

Good point. Probably true. But it did result in my regarding school (and homework in particular) as an optional activity.

I went to Europe, the Caribbean, and Mexico and bragged to my classmates that I was a jet-setter. Needless to say, they resented my swaggering. My grades and attitude reflected my father's alcoholic belief system that he, and by extension I, was special and that all those boring rules were for the dull people he regarded as sleepwalkers. I never repeated a grade, but I suspect I was promoted on several occasions on the condition that I would not return to that school the following year. I was an erratic student and a showoff, which is not an endearing combo. Hence, I left, in my wake, a half a dozen schools and a collection of traumatized educators. My saving grace, at least educationally, was that I was an only child. My half sister, Gloria, was already married when I came along. With few friends my own age, I read voraciously to pass the time.

As is the case with most of us, my parents have been my greatest influences. Certainly, they had their *character defects**, but they also left a few indelible messages that have served me very well throughout my journey. Somewhere in all that *acting special* was also buried a very positive message: "Don't ever let anybody else define you. Whatever label they choose to give you is going to reflect that particular person's values, prejudices, and agendas, not yours."

Because my parents themselves were creatures of their own invention, it was natural for them to send me the message "Invent yourself!" In fact, the whole message was "Reinvent yourself *over and over* again." And that's exactly what I've been doing all my life. A boyfriend of mine once told me, "Dating you is like dating a different person every month." (I wasn't quite sure if he meant it as a compliment.) As it turns out, he didn't know the half of it. For a time, I was stuck in the quicksand of ever-shifting *false personas**. It took years of work for me to make changes that were more than just new window dressings for old problems. Now, on the days when I get it right, I continue to discover more about who I am and why I am here.

My gravitation toward false personas came about partly because of my inability to be like the other kids. It's not that I chose *not* to conform. On the contrary, I desperately wanted to fit in, like most kids do, but I had no idea *how* to conform. Because my parents were wildly eccentric, I had no template for standard behavior. For example, my parents were vitamin nuts and took megadoses of vitamins daily. As

I child, I organized the empty vitamin bottles into warring armies. The B12's would ally themselves with the niacins and the folic acids and wage complex strategic maneuvers against the vitamin Cs, Ds, and Es. One of my earliest memories is sitting on the couch, pretending it was a boat, while watching my mother—in a wildly theatrical outfit—rehearsing with her dance partner to the 1950s hit song "Mack the Knife." Perhaps I could have fit in if I had watched more programs like *The Andy Griffith Show*, but I preferred fantasies such as *The Wild Wild West* and *Star Trek*. Then again, my parents always discouraged TV watching and sent me back to my books. Some of my favorite memories are of going with my mother to the bookstore, where we would spend at least an hour just going up and down the aisles looking at titles and skimming through various works. What I chose to read didn't model "normal" behavior either. When you think about it, what good literature does? My youthful tastes included the surreal works of Franz Kafka and Hermann Hesse's mystical adventures.

With no model for fitting in, though it was what I desperately wanted, I figured my next best option was to be radically different and revel in my distinctiveness. For a period during my teens, I wore a nurse's cape and a Sherlock Holmes hat. I was a misfit á la Ally Sheedy in *The Breakfast Club*.

My dare-to-be-different streak dovetailed with defiance toward adults, stoked by my father's strong distaste for authority figures. He had contempt for teachers and often used the old cliché *those who cannot do . . . teach*. This was especially strange because my grandmother, his mother, was a teacher. Whatever their reasoning, my parents gave me the sign-off to challenge authority. If I talked back to one of my teachers, Mom and Dad would back me, just as long as I didn't challenge *their* authority. This was a mixed message, but parental messages usually are. Perhaps my father was unconsciously encouraging me to articulate his own rage at something that happened to him during his impressionable school years.

Today, I understand why Miss M. (and other principals after her) seemed to despise me as if I were demonically possessed. To say I was a bit of a prankster is like saying Hurricane Katrina was an overcast day. I regarded sixth grade as my own Second City comedy workshop, with an emphasis on improv. Among my escapades, I catapulted tapioca pudding from my fork into the ceiling fixture, and I turned the school's hallowed Christmas play into a bawdy farce. I also used a wire hanger to transform my two long braids into a pair of antenna. For a while, that was my signature look.

One day, when I had goaded our teacher into throwing me and two of my friends out of class, we passed the time until the bell rang by playing tag in the halls. The boys' bathroom was "base." When Miss M. caught me sliding into home plate at a urinal, she lost her normally steely composure. In a rage, she grabbed me by one of my elevated braids and dragged me out of the bathroom. To humiliate me and my two cohorts, she made us stand in the lunchroom facing the wall in front of the whole school during lunch hour, which conveniently was about to begin.

The three of us faced the wall side by side. At first, Miss M., carefully chewing her food and observing us from a few feet away, seemed to have regained the upper hand. Then, I began my loud multilingual sneezing. "GeeeeSSSUNDheit!" I shouted, faking a loud sneeze. This caused a trio of giggling. "Kaaaa-BOO-ki!" I sneezed again, trying to sound Japanese.

Soon, the three of us had lost all control and were weeping with laughter. I collapsed on the floor, writhing in a fit of hysteria. The entire lunchroom burst into a chorus of laughter. Miss M. shook with anger, but I didn't care. I felt like a star in a hit Broadway show. That was the day I realized that I craved attention, and, if I couldn't get it the right way, I'd get it any way I could.

What the adults around me should have been asking was, *Why is Jane acting out so much? Is Jane angry about something? What's going on in Jane's home that makes her so defiant at school?* Could it be that my dad's alcoholic mindset was rubbing off on me? After all, defiance is the hallmark of addiction. Perhaps I was so defiant at school and elsewhere because I knew that I could be defiant anywhere *but* home. Perhaps defying my dad with his fierce temper was just too scary. (It would take years of therapy for me to sort it all out, but I still had a lot of acting out to do before I would throw myself on *that* couch.)

Though not big on boundaries, structure, or rules, my parents were avid readers. (My mother, who is now in her nineties, still takes pleasure in reading, and I take pleasure in that.) My parents' taste tended toward titles like *Art in the Light of Mystery Wisdom, The Secret Life of Plants,* and *The Shape of Thought.* Would they have been interested in reading a chapter or two from the famed parenting expert Dr. Spock? Not so much. They were pleased with their own unique parenting style.

Both of my parents had traumatic upbringings that affected who they were and how they parented me. By the time they met in the early 1950s, they had both completely reinvented themselves. My dad—the son of humble Irish immigrants—had transformed himself into a bon vivant and entrepreneur, living on Central Park South. Similarly, my mother had metamorphosed into a glamorous, exotic sexpot who reduced every man she met to a blubbering fool. They did their best to be good parents, and I wouldn't trade them in for a million Dr. Spocks. Anita and Pearse's unconventional attitudes and their heightened appreciation of the absurd prepared me to withstand the many bizarre turns life invariably takes. For them, life amounted to a never-ending performance-art piece. They never committed the "ultimate sin" in our world: being boring.

On several occasions, my mother, who'd volunteered to teach dance at one of the many schools I attended, was scolded by the prudish academics for making her routines too sexy for kids. One dance routine she choreographed when I was in first grade had me tied up to a large pole in the gym while the boys did some kind of jungle dance around me. (Needless to say, I revisited that skit later in therapy.)

Alcoholics often talk about their earliest memories centering on their inability to fit in. In that sense, I'm classically alcoholic. I was defiant toward teachers, but frankly terrified of kids my own age. I could crack a joke in front of the whole class without breaking a sweat, but became totally freaked out at the prospect of going over to a friend's house and just hanging out and doing nothing in particular. When I wasn't performing, I had no idea what my role was or even *who* I was. This confusion dragged on into adulthood. For years, it was much easier for me to do a live television show or make a speech in front of five hundred people than to have dinner with two.

As a kid, I felt most comfortable talking to, amusing, and essentially performing for adults at cocktail parties, where my parents would often take me when they couldn't find a babysitter. "We'll just throw her in with the fur coats," my dad would joke, chuckling at his own cleverness. As a result, I saw *a lot* of fur coats. (Later in life, I'd become an animal-rights activist, and I wonder if my time spent with the fur was partly a result of that.) When I managed to crawl out of the coatroom at those parties, I would walk around and chat up the big people, often finishing up their cocktails when they weren't looking.

My earliest memory of having an alcoholic drink was at one of the many big parties my parents threw. I must have been about nine or ten. As the evening wore on, I noticed that many of the abandoned martini glasses still had alcohol in their hollow stems. I just walked around and finished them off. The burning sensation as the clear liquid went down was exquisite. Unfortunately, I never experienced that "I hate the taste" phase. No one ever seemed to notice that I was little tipsy. They must have just chalked it up to "Janie's performing again . . . how cute!"

Since my mother was a performer, I got the message early on that I was *supposed* to perform. I was programmed by my parents to be a human *doing*, not a human *being*. A human just *being* was lazy and uninteresting, unless—of course—she was earnestly meditating or quietly experiencing a past-life regression. I was seven the first time I was on stage. My big debut was at Little Carnegie Hall in New York City, which was right next to the big one. I sang a song that sounded like it had been written by a pedophile. Imagine a little girl belting out a song about licking and licking an apple on a stick that's covered with molasses candy. This was an apple that cost a nickel yet tasted better than a sour pickle. Yikes! These truly unforgettable lyrics will haunt me forever.

Aside from performing, I also took a multitude of after-school classes. I studied elocution, painting, and sculpture; suffered through years of classical piano instruction; and even learned how to play castanets. I also took Hindu dance classes and the inevitable ballet. But the classes I remember most? Tap dancing!

My old-tap dancing routines, which I learned at Charlie Lowe's Tap Dancing Studio near Times Square after school, still reverberate in my mind like a Buddhist chant. Uncle Charlie, a tough but kindly man who looked like Jimmy Durante, would consult with the stage mothers, as we future stars of America watched ourselves in a giant wall mirror (getting an early jump-start on narcissistic personality disorder) going through our paces . . . over and over again.

A rough old broad leaning into a rickety upright piano would bang out hoofer tunes as Uncle Charlie shouted orders: "Hop, two taps, step, brush out, stamp, stamp. Hop, brush out, stamp, stamp. Hop, two taps, buffalo. Hop, two taps, buffalo. Change toe, change toe."

Incidentally, Uncle Charlie and his wife were friends of the family and babysat for me from the time I was toddler. They were just two of the many who would have the dubious honor of having me, a bed wetter, in their home.

In addition to my tap-dancing lessons, Mom also took me to classes with a legendary jazz dance teacher who went simply by "Luigi." Mom called him the original Bob Fosse.

With my parents, self-improvement (theirs and mine) was a constant underlying theme that has stuck with me my entire life. The never-ending campaign was admirable . . . but only to a point. It may be what led to my developing workaholic tendencies in later years and also to my acting out alcoholically—in revolt—by partying way too much. After one too many dance, elocution, guitar, painting, and sculpture classes, I became suspicious. What was the motive for all this frenetic self-improvement? Were they trying to fix me? If not, what *were* we trying to prove? Why was it not okay just to hang out and chill like the other kids? I almost felt like a candidate campaigning for election. The other kids didn't seem so programmed to go out and prove something. While I was constantly mugging and speaking in a stage voice, my peers seemed quietly inscrutable. That intimidated me. Years later, I would experience the same thing dining with Hollywood heavyweights who seemed very withholding about the personal details of their lives, leaving me compelled to fill up the dead air with personal details of my life. I didn't interact with people. Rather, I had an audience and tried to win them over. This is classic "people pleasing" behavior. I've spent most of my life trying to get a handle on this through therapy and recovery programs. The part that deals with codependency has been a real eye-opener. Now, I have much less of a need to perform for anyone.

This need to perform didn't come only from my mother. It came from both of my parents. The World War II generation *sold themselves* a lot more. Fuller Brush men and Encyclopedia Britannica salesmen were always coming to the door hawking their wares. Personal salesmanship was a huge part of the culture, which faded with the rise of television. Did my parents' childhood traumas and their resulting insecurities make them feel *less than**, leading them to compensate by *selling themselves* more? Or were they just trying to give me every opportunity—precisely what they wished they had gotten as kids themselves?

My mom is Puerto Rican. She came to New York on a boat all by herself in 1928, at the age of twelve, just in time for the stock-market crash and the Great Depression. But she didn't let any of *that* stop her. Her credo? "We are not poor. We simply have no money!" In high school, she worked as an usherette in a movie house in Times Square, studying dance by watching musicals on the big screen. While the other Puerto Rican girls were steered toward professions like . . . housekeeping, Mom said, "To hell with that! How dare you try to pigeonhole me?" Anita Velez had perfect features and a knockout body. She quickly taught herself to dance, briefly joined the circus and then formed her own Latin dance troupe. Anita Velez Dancers toured across the Caribbean, the United States, and Canada. She capped her career by playing Manhattan's famous Palace Theater during the waning days of vaudeville. To help preserve evidence of my mother's role in that pivotal time in showbiz, I made a documentary called *Anita Velez: Dancing through Life* that's available on the Internet at movieflix.com. It's filled with extraordinary photos of her and her dance troupe in full Latin regalia.

Eventually, Mom teamed up with a Russian ballerina, Marina Svetlova, who was always billed as a "prima ballerina." Together they were quite a team . . . on and off stage. These two stunning women attracted a lot of male attention.

One of Marina and Anita's best pals was the famous Russian aviator Boris Sergievsky, whom my mother always said was as great as
Lindbergh but never got the credit. His obituary says he was "an aviator with the Imperial Russian Air Force in World War One," and went
on to " . . . set 18 world records for speed and altitude."

When I was a child, the wealthy Boris was always somehow in the
background, sending Mother giant baskets of fruit for the holidays
and flying us to his home in Connecticut. He was a mysterious but
extremely benevolent figure. Dad sometimes seemed jealous. Still, he
ate the fruit, at least the fruit that was in season (by that time, he had
gone macrobiotic, a type of diet that was all the rage at that time and
stressed seasonal food choices).

Because of her Russian connections, my mother was very involved
in the Russian Nobility Association. Even though the Association,
which was founded in 1938, limits its membership to those rare individuals who are heirs to those listed in the nobility archives of the
former Russian empire, my Puerto Rican mom had become very
popular with the Ruskies. She tells me that when she was first invited
to join the Association, she said, "But I don't have a title." Their
reply? "We'll give you one."

I'd return home from school to find a variety of overdressed,
bejeweled people assembled in our living room drinking sherry and
eating fondue. This was around the same time that my parents
decided, after much huddling and sotto voce chatter, that I should
curtsy when meeting visitors. Generally, I went along with their
kooky schemes, but at this I revolted. My two best friends (one of
whom was Alessandra Greco, the daughter of the famous flamenco

dancer José Greco) told me they would physically beat me up if I ever curtsied, their primary fear being that the curtsy contagion would spread to their households. While my parents couldn't see how strange their request was, they finally gave up trying to make me curtsy because I was so adamantly against it and they knew I rarely put my foot down.

Sans curtsy, I would be introduced to these anachronistic, but friendly, characters who actually did have titles.

"Jane, say hello to Countess Boxhovenden," my mother would intone, leading me around the group. *Who are these counts and countesses . . . and why are they in our apartment?* I would wonder, trying to figure out how to get my paws on the sherry in their glasses. Later, I would grab whatever drink was left lying around and finish it off.

My parents didn't seem to notice my habit. Then, when I was about ten, they took me to Europe and allowed me to drink the wine served with some of the meals. I threw up in the lobby of a very fine hotel in Vienna, Austria. I distinctly remember I had been listening to a quartet of violins minutes earlier. This was an early foreshadowing of future behavior.

In my early teens, my dad would ask me to run errands. "Janie, run downstairs, will you, and get me a carton of Pall Malls and two quarts of Gordon's Gin."

That was back in the days when kids could pick stuff like that up without the Department of Child and Family Services being called in. While at the liquor store, where Dad had a running account, I would pick up a bottle or two of wine for myself. Nobody ever noticed. I was the only teenager I knew with my own wine closet.

As awful as this sounds, alcohol was really the way I began making friends my own age and having a social life. When I started ninth grade at a new school, I didn't know anybody and they were all divided up into cliques. I was still suffering from my preference of talking to adults rather than kids my own age. I felt the other kids at school were looking at me like I was a freak. I was frightened that I was on the verge of becoming a weirdo loner. So, I decided drastic action was necessary. I began inviting kids over to share my booze. It was astounding how rapidly my status changed. Soon, I had friends. I remember the night it all came together. I was at a dimly lit bar on the Upper East Side of Manhattan, which was known to cater to underage drinkers. I was wearing my cool elephant bell bottoms from a hippie store called The Different Drummer. I was in a tight circle of friends, and we were all drinking Harvey Wallbangers, which are made of vodka, orange juice, and Galliano liqueur. Rod Stewart's "Maggie May" was playing, as I sucked on a Tareyton cigarette. It was all working for me at that moment. I spent years drinking to try to recapture that initial moment of bliss, when alcohol makes all your social anxieties dissolve and life suddenly feels smooth and carefree. That futile effort to recapture the initial euphoria that alcohol brings is called *chasing the high**. Ironically, even though my dad smoked, he urged me not to. When I pointed out his double standard, he would explain that he didn't inhale. But I observed him smoking and could've sworn he did inhale. Apparently, I was right because, tragically, he died in his late sixties of lung cancer.

I have a genetic predisposition to alcoholism on my father's side, as do some of my relatives. Not only was my dad an alcoholic, but one of his very handsome nephews, Billy, died of cirrhosis of the liver and is buried in the Veteran's Cemetery in Los Angeles. Another cousin was, and possibly still is, an alcoholic street person somewhere in Southern California. He once contacted me for help, after seeing me on television back when I was a news anchor in Los Angeles. Sadly, he never showed up to meet me as planned.

Of course, it wasn't just drinking that set my family apart, as you now understand. It seemed we always cha-cha-cha'd to a different drummer. My mother's distant cousin Raquel hit the mother lode in the eccentricity department, quirks made possible by her marriage to the wealthy Mr. Campbell. Mr. Campbell was elderly and worked on very large jigsaw puzzles in his living room. I never knew how he made his money. Suffice it to say, I knew how Raquel spent it. Perhaps another precursor to my fascination with animal rights, Raquel was a kindhearted but misguided person who inappropriately kept wild animals as pets. She had various animals in her sprawling Midtown apartment, including a very large chimpanzee and a parrot who called people dirty names in Spanish.

As the story goes, a few years before I was born, someone gave Raquel the chimp as a gift when it was a tiny infant, probably ripped from its mother grasp very prematurely. Raquel immediately fell in love and considered the animal her baby. Raquel would dress the chimp in expensive baby clothes and put him in a fancy stroller. She and my mom would walk down Fifth Avenue and encourage people to say hello to the baby and would laugh at their startled reactions.

As the chimp matured, he became increasingly jealous of Mr. Campbell and began having violent tantrums. Eventually, although

Raquel clearly adored the chimp, she had to confine the animal to one room and affix wire mesh across the doorway. Apparently, this broke her heart. When I visited Raquel and saw the chimp sitting unhappily in his room, I bore witness to the sadness animals kept as prisoners endure and became determined to help them. Eventually, Raquel and Mr. Campbell moved to Connecticut and bought land where the chimp could roam free, which is how he lived out his life.

Shortly after they moved out of their apartment . . . we moved into the same building. Mom had long had her eye on this building—now called the Briarcliffe—which stands across from Carnegie Hall. We'd vacated a smaller apartment a block away for this more prestigious one. Although our ninth floor apartment was smaller than the Campbell's, it was still a lot bigger than what I had been used to. In a classic early 1960s move, my parents converted the dining room into what they called the Jungle Room, complete with bongos and faux leopard-skin curtains. Dad had served in Africa during World War II. He often bragged that not only did he never see action, he actually played polo much of the time. This comment came from the very same man who later wanted to bomb anything that moved in Vietnam or Laos. He returned from his playful military experience with a fondness for making African curry, which was one of three dishes in our household culinary repertoire.

My parents were intellectually adventurous. Nothing was too strange for their examination. (Except hippies. My father detested hippies.) When Scientology rolled into town for an introductory seminar, the three of us headed over to the Waldorf Astoria to check it out. I remember peering into various contraptions and being told all about "getting clear." Both of my parents were fascinated by the controversial psychoanalyst Wilhelm Reich and orgone boxes. These boxes, which came in various sizes, were said to be accumulators of orgone energy, using metal coils to harness the universal life force responsible for everything from the ozone layer to orgasms.

My mother claimed she only became pregnant with me at the age of thirty-nine after sitting in a giant orgone box and getting radiated with the orgone energy. One of my father's best friends was either a brilliant analyst or a quack, depending on your view of these sorts of things. Dr. P., said to be a disciple of Reich's, built a large orgone box in his apartment where he lived a couple of blocks from us. It was a glass case, several times the size of a coffin, affixed with all sorts of wires and coils. You had to climb a short set of stairs to get into it. My dad kept a smaller orgone box, the size of a cooler, in our house. It was connected to a short hose that fed into what looked like a bullhorn. Once, when I was sick, he tried to use it on me.

"This'll do the trick," he explained, as if trying to sell me the product. He leaned over and began lowering the giant suction cup onto my stomach. But I was having none of it. Dad seemed perplexed that I wasn't enthusiastic about his unorthodox treatment plan.

Unfortunately, while Dad took a dilettante's crack at every fad that came to town, he neglected to try the two things that really would have helped him: Alcoholics Anonymous and regular old therapy with a licensed psychiatrist. I do not blame him. As the *Alcoholics Anonymous Big Book* says, there are those who are constitutionally incapable of self-honesty. "They are not at fault; they seem to have been born that way. They are naturally incapable of grasping and developing a manner of living which demands rigorous honesty." That sums up my father. He lacked the necessary humility to admit he had a problem and surrender to it. He never got sober, and he died before I got sober. I often wonder what kind of relationship we could have had if we both had gotten sober in time.

Dad was extremely smart and managed to become very successful in the ad business despite his drinking. One can only imagine what he might have achieved in sobriety. My fondest memories are of going to the offices of the ad agency he and two partners had founded and visiting the art department. There I would be given a variety of magic markers and a giant pad to execute my visions. I'd create my own story boards complete with my own ad slogans.

At the office, everything seemed cheerful and rosy. And Dad was always in great spirits. I think this was part of the reason I longed to have a career. People behaved themselves on the job. They didn't get drunk and argue about nonsense, like we did at home. At work, there were clear boundaries. (Of course, I was still too young to pick up on the three-martini lunch syndrome, although I'm sure it existed.)

Although my childhood was steeped in alcoholic thinking and drinking, my parents' sense of adventure and their creativity inspired me to push beyond the boundaries that might have otherwise constrained me. The best thing about my parents is that they were always curious about life. They continually strove to learn more and create something beautiful, be it an ingenious new product, a poem, or a play. When my mother became too old to dance professionally, she became a playwright and wrote a series of quirky plays, including my personal favorite, *A Cave Named Ego*. Our home was often filled with the sounds of actors rehearsing. I'd wake up from a deep sleep to hear someone shouting something like, "Give me the knife, dammit!" For a moment, I'd be frozen in fear, until I realized it was just another line from a scene they were rehearsing.

Dad always loved to say, "Third-class minds talk about people, second-class minds talk about things, first-class minds talk about ideas"—and he lived by it. Dad had a lot of those sayings. In fact, a boyfriend of mine once asked me to please stop repeating all the clichés I'd grown up hearing. He said it sounded like I was raised on them. And you know what? It's true. I was raised on them. My dad's inability to go within and find himself left him with a "persona" as opposed to a really grounded, genuine identity. It follows that he would spew clichés as opposed to our having true communication. Real conversations are often messy and emotional and that was a big no-no. Clichés are neat.

Another one of Dad's favorite lines was, "Throw your hat over the fence. Then, you'll have to follow it." I've done that a lot. Where it's taken me is where he feared to go, into the heart of darkness, to the core of my being, which I feared confronting, which I feared embracing. But I did it anyway. In large respects, I did it for him.

So, although I wanted to fit in as a child, there was no fitting in for me, not with parents like Anita and Pearse. I always stood apart from the crowd . . . or in front of it.

Mom, center, with her troupe.

**My stage debut at
Little Carnegie Hall.**

2

Career:
I Want to Be Somebody

My very first story as a cub reporter during college was the 1977 premiere of The Who's movie *Tommy* at the Ziegfeld movie theater. Before the show, I earnestly interviewed an Ann-Margret male impersonator, completely convinced that it was her, only to watch in amazement as the real Ann-Margret showed up a bit later.

"Make sure to make a fool of yourself at least once every day," my dad would advise me as a way of encouraging me to be adventurous and not take myself so seriously. I tend to think I have surpassed his wildest dreams in that department. But how do you make a fool of yourself and build self-esteem at the same time?

Want self-esteem? Try doing esteemable things.

I once heard that comment from a sober person, and it really struck me. It sums up everything that was wrong with my early ambition. It was all about me! When I stopped thinking just about myself and started using my skills to make this world a more compassionate place, that's when I really began feeling like I had a meaningful career. But that shift in thinking happened *only* after I got sober and learned a spiritually sound way of living.

While I was still drinking, I had the best of intentions. But my ego, fueled by the terrible alcoholic twins of grandiosity and paranoia, often got in the way. It's fine to dream big, but when those big dreams are all about you, then it's just mental masturbation.

Now, I still dream big, but my dreams are about changing the world and getting important ideas, like the much maligned concept of peace, out there and into the discussion of how to deal with society's problems. In 2008, as the race between Barack Obama and John McCain entered its final stretch, I was able to do a whole segment on the HLN TV show I host, *Issues with Jane Velez-Mitchell*, about the proposal to create a Department of Peace, which antiwar activists would like to see as a Cabinet-level position. One of the conservatives we had on the show was incensed, calling the idea "ridiculous" and "an embarrassment." Seemingly indignant that I would give air time to this proposal, the conservative huffed, "We have a Department of Peace and it's called the Defense Department." The other pundit, who was a Democrat, also disagreed with the idea, saying that's the State Department's job. Oh really? Well, if both of those departments are supposed to work for peace, then I give them both an F. "Peace" is not a dirty word or a ridiculous concept. To *have* a world without war, we first have to *imagine* a world without war. For some people, just imagining that is extremely threatening. That's why I believe that just having a conversation about the proposed Department of Peace is, if not revolutionary, certainly evolutionary.

That's the kind of dialogue I am most proud of when it comes to my career. But it took me three decades of grueling work to get to a place where I could make a conversation like that happen on national television.

Toward the end of high school, I was confronted with two agonizing challenges. Both turned out to be blessings, however, in that they inspired me to pursue a career in journalism—where I can make a real difference.

These experiences still serve to remind me that, when circumstances take an unexpected turn, you rarely can predict the outcome. What seems like the worst news can often be the best news. It's taken me years of self-exploration to get to the point where I can, usually, just relax and let the river's current take me where it wants and enjoy life as the adventure it is.

The first challenge occurred in my senior year of high school. My parents sat me down and with big smiles informed me, "You are going to be a debutante."

They cheerfully explained how I would have two escorts, one a West Point cadet and the other a civilian escort in white tie and that all this would all happen at the Waldorf-Astoria during the International Debutante Ball. I was quietly horrified.

At the time, I was trying my darndest to be a hippie . . . to my father's horror. ("Why must you dress like a farmer's daughter?" he would ask me repeatedly.) The early 1970s marked the crescendo of the counterculture movement and being a debutante was the antithesis of everything anybody my age wanted to stand for—unless you came from Texas, as many of the debs did. The Texas girls were famous for their deep curtsies. For some reason, my parents were still obsessed with getting me to curtsy.

How could I get out of it? I couldn't. This 1950s-style family unit was not a democracy. It was a dictatorship, mostly benevolent, but sometimes not. Almost all decisions were handed down by my father and were not open for discussion. This was one of them. To have protested too much would have been regarded as an example of how ungrateful I was for the wonderful opportunities my parents afforded me.

Once again, hovering in the background, was that famous Russian aviator Boris Sergievsky. Many years later, I learned that he had paid for the whole thing. It makes sense, since Dad—undoubtedly traumatized by his experiences during the Great Depression—was very tight with a buck. I always wondered why he decided to spring for that. Turns out he didn't. He was, however, a master at self-promotion.

One of Dad's society friends was a lady I will call Blondie. She appeared to harbor a long-standing crush on my father, which drove my mother to distraction. Blondie was contacted by a local TV news station, looking to do a three-part series profiling a typical debutante. So, undoubtedly to win favor with my dad, she suggested I would be the ideal profile subject.

You could stretch your imagination from here to Hong Kong and still not justify the conclusion that I was your typical deb. First of all, most of the other girls came from genuinely wealthy families, whose fortunes often went back for generations. Second, I was destined to "come out" in a very different way years later. Suffice it to say, even as a repressed teenager, I was never a frilly, satin-and-lace kind of girl. I hated shopping for clothes and loved to talk politics. And, I'm Puerto Rican. Not a typical deb profile.

None of this appeared to give my parents second thoughts. Looking back, these factors may have even been the subconscious impetus behind this whole debutante operation, part of a campaign to both legitimize and feminize me!

Soon, a camera crew was following me around for gown fittings and even videotaping my hair being shampooed! Then came the sit-down on-camera interview. It seemed to go on forever, with me—secretly the world's most reluctant debutante—in the uncomfortable position of debating this female reporter who was grilling me about how anachronistic this whole coming-out business was. Of course, she was right. However, in a foreshadowing of the TV puppetry I would later become very good at, I argued with her that this was a wonderful tradition. She didn't let up. She seemed more like a prosecutor trying a case than a reporter.

Finally I said, "Look, it's just like a bar mitzvah," which is sort of true. Turns out, that was just about the only sound bite she used of mine in her series.

Watching myself on the news was an eye-opener. I suddenly saw myself in a totally different context, namely as somebody worthy of being on television. I marveled at how the news report made me seem, somehow, important. Suddenly, watching this person who was me on TV, a new possibility dawned on me. I'd always had a compulsion to perform, but my acting career never took off. The biggest role I'd ever snagged was when I was eight and got the juvenile lead on one episode of the old TV legal drama called *The Defenders*. The truth is, I never really yearned to be an actress. The stage was my mother's passion. I was more interested in politics and current events. Bingo! I decided right then and there that I would love to try my hand at TV reporting, which combined both of my passions: performing and real life issues. My original ambition was to become a newspaper columnist in the hope of someday becoming a writer, but thanks to my up-close-and-personal encounter with TV news, when it came time to fill out my college application, I checked off the box marked BROADCAST JOURNALISM.

This debutante experience also taught me not to believe everything you read in the paper. My boyfriend at the time was a tall, sexy Brazilian with shaggy blond hair and olive skin. I met him while I was waitressing over the summer at an ice-cream parlor on Manhattan's East Side. He was the busboy! Louie became my coming-out arm candy and was described in a newspaper clipping, planted by Blondie, as being a medical intern.

This deception left me a little bitter. It seemed that getting ahead was all about hiding who you really are. (This would be another one of the issues that drove me into therapy.) While I ended up enjoying certain aspects of the experience of coming out, and all the attendant attention, I also felt very inauthentic throughout the process, as if I were pretending to be someone I was not. Why was it *not* okay to have a boyfriend who was a busboy? Luckily, Louie didn't seem to mind being upgraded to med student. My Brazilian squeeze was a party animal just like me and happy to be along for the ride.

Louie and I got into a lot of adventures together. One night, we were driving around town in his car, which was quite the jalopy. Because I was a budding hippie, forever honing my eccentricities, I was wearing an all-white outfit, featuring an authentic Nehru jacket, which I topped off by wearing a genuine pith helmet. I was sitting in the passenger seat when, suddenly, a limo lurched toward us, crossing the yellow dividing line at Park Avenue and 79th Street. Louie slammed on the brakes, but it was too late. Though we were the tipsy teenagers, it was actually not our fault. The limo slammed head-on into us. My head went into the windshield. Had I not been wearing a genuine pith helmet, I might have had a very serious, even disfiguring, injury. However, since I was wearing a metal hat that was hard as rock, I emerged relatively unscathed. After getting out of the car, I wandered around in shock until I noticed something familiar about the people hastily exiting the limo. It turns out that Ari Onassis, Jackie Kennedy Onassis, and her sister Lee Radziwill were the passengers in the limo. I approached them, still reeling from the accident.

"I know you from somewhere, but I can't place you," I said to them.

They silently observed me, before disappearing into the night.

A few days later, sporting a pair of black eyes from the head bump, I got a call from a British tabloid that had tracked me down, probably through the emergency-room records. They were on the street outside my building and asked if I would come down and tell them about the accident. I grabbed my trusty pith helmet and went out to meet them, where I gleefully posed for photos. As they snapped away, I tilted my pith helmet at a jaunty angle. Another bizarre moment of exposure to my future profession.

Many of my adolescent experiences were educational in unintended ways. The debutante episode was just one of many times that I was exposed, through my dad's social climbing, to people who supposedly counted—that is, people who came from old money and who had pedigrees because of their family names. Dad was very intent on being accepted by "society." I now realize that it was to compensate for his own humble origins as a Depression-era Irish Catholic who learned to play golf by being a caddy, who went to public school, and who survived polio, which was akin to being diagnosed with AIDS in the 1980s. I give Dad a lot of credit for how he rose above his origins and became as successful as he did.

Today, I feel compassion for people who buy into the whole notion that there is a "society" that is somehow special and superior. What a horrible burden to have to go around representing the premise: *I'm better than you because of the family and the fortune into which I was born.* Of course, on some level, they have to know the entire concept is absurd. Yet, since so many of them have predicated their self-esteem on this flawed notion, it's something they ferociously defend, which accentuates their snobbery. I much prefer people who are arrogant because of their accomplishments! That, I can respect.

Society characters are very good at sniffing out pretenders in a blink. Every stitch of clothing, every accessory, and every article of furniture are viciously scrutinized. The interrogations about where you went to school and where in the Hamptons your summerhouse was located, were swift and to the point. It can all be summed up by the comment made to me by one member of the Southampton private beach-club set at the end of a date. He was driving me home to my parents' summer place in the less exclusive Hampton Bays, which my father insisted on calling Southampton or Shinnecock Hills. We were talking about trees. I told him I had maple trees and weeping willows in my backyard.

"You don't have trees," he corrected me, rolling his eyes. Apparently, even my trees weren't good enough.

I now see that being on the receiving end of that kind of condescension was all part of the Divine plan to steer me away from a life of competitive socializing and status seeking. It taught me that too much money is like too much food. It can make you very ugly. My mother's artist friends, most of whom were struggling actors, dancers, painters, or sculptors, always seemed a million times happier than Dad's set. They would laugh and sing while they cooked paella and drank sangria in the kitchen. They didn't sit around drinking martinis and waiting for someone to leave the room so they could make cutting remarks about them, the way Dad's gossipy friends often did.

I mentioned earlier that two nightmarish situations inspired me to pursue a career in journalism. My debutante experience was the first—it sparked the idea. The other, a different sort of trauma, helped propel my career into existence.

Most news anchors are stalked *after* they begin appearing on television. I was stalked before I even made an appearance. During my last year of high school, I went to a party that was totally out of my age league at Columbia University—as always a hotbed of hipster cool. I was drinking and popping NoDoz (caffeine pills) when I met a guy who I thought was interesting. He was in his thirties and had long black hair. Although he drove a cab, he said he was a graphic artist. On one of our few dates, when he left me in his cab to go buy something, I put the meter on and drove around the block. I'd never driven a car before, so fortunately, nothing terrible happened. But the truth is, water finds its own level. Had I not been drinking at the tender age of seventeen and had I not been "acting out," I would have known better than to hook up with this chucklehead.

I dated him only a few times (we didn't get any further than making out) before I realized that he was a major-league whack job. His "portfolio" consisted of a series of pencil drawings that would embarrass a ten-year-old. *Check please!* Of course it wasn't just his lack of drawing skills that turned me off, he was just clearly not right. Upon discovering that there was something very wrong with him, I immediately broke it off, but he knew where I lived and where I went to school and that my favorite bar, Denton's, was on Lexington and 79th Street.

From the end of high school all the way through college, the stalker followed me around the streets of New York and called my house repeatedly. It was one of the most frightening experiences of my life. He would tape-record his voice and then play it back over the phone in slow motion to give it that added demonic quality. He'd scrawl letters to me that would terrify a handwriting analyst and leave them in the lobby of our apartment building. These letters were almost impossible to read but seemed to revolve around the theme of his having been removed from his mother's womb with forceps.

Although there was clearly a need for it, my father wouldn't change our phone number because he was worried that old friends in for a visit wouldn't be able to look him up. He did offer to get me my own line so I wouldn't have to pick up theirs.

This situation was so unnerving that I finally convinced my dad to let me go to college in Mexico, as part of a junior-year-abroad program. Quite by accident, I picked what turned out to be an infamous party school. It was attended by some of Mexico's elite along with a bunch of Americans who didn't have anything in particular in common except perhaps a desire to learn Spanish, which I spoke, but not well. The school was surrounded by discotheques that had been built to accommodate the hard-partying student body. This junior year was one long lost weekend for me. Although I have to say I had lots of fun, being away from home with no supervision whatsoever gave my alcoholism license to really take off. When my parents sent me the tuition money for the second semester, I took some friends on a jaunt to Acapulco and blew it all. My parents had to be convinced there was a teacher uprising at the school and they needed to send more money to cover suddenly higher tuition.

I dated a Mexican student, and we spent lots of time tooling around Mexico in his yellow Volkswagen. One morning, at around 4:00 AM, we pulled into a tiny town and woke up a man who was literally sleeping on the reception desk of a rundown hotel. We'd been drinking. But we'd run out of booze and were starting to get hungover and dehydrated. I couldn't drink the tap water. Everything was closed.

I was deliriously thirsty, and when we went to sleep, I had this incredibly vivid dream about orange juice. There was a container of orange juice in a store window but the store was closed and I couldn't get to it. I don't think I've ever wanted anything so desperately. It was one of those dreams that felt so incredibly real. What was the significance of the orange juice that I couldn't reach? Given that OJ is non-alcoholic, I think it was an early sign of how I subconsciously felt about sobriety. I would grow to crave it desperately. But it just seemed out of reach for me. My junior year in Mexico was a wild adventure, but I'm glad it ended when it did. With no supervision or boundaries, had I stayed on, I could've turned out like the woman in *The Sheltering Sky*, who finds herself alone in a foreign continent and first loses her bearings and then her mind.

When I got back to New York, the stalker was waiting for me. He had used the time I'd been away to insinuate himself into my bar scene. When I walked into Denton's, I was shocked to see him sitting at a table with a few people I knew. He looked up and smiled at me ominously, as if to say, "See, you just never know where I'll turn up, do you?" I was terrified. I immediately headed toward the bartender, a friend of mine, and told him to eighty-six the creep after explaining that he was a stalker.

As the bouncer physically dragged him out of the bar, the stalker let out a primal scream that rivaled anything you'd hear from Led Zeppelin. Someone called the cops.

"I'll get you for this!" he shouted at me right in front of a uniformed officer. Despite his threat, they refused to arrest him. The cop just stood there. Well, that was New York in the 1970s. Back in the bar, I found out that my stalker had been carrying a gun. That's the moment I became deathly afraid.

It's amazing what you can accomplish when you think it's a matter of life and death. Until that point, I had been a typical college party animal—getting up late, studying as little as possible, and going out to clubs as often as I could, and I had been fine with that. But suddenly, life didn't seem like a party anymore.

It was late September of my senior year at NYU, and I was celebrating my twenty-first birthday. That night, I lost complete control. One minute I was dancing and laughing and the next minute I just blacked out. I woke up with an apology note pinned to my shirt from my niece, Lorca, who was just a few years younger than me. Apparently, I had screamed at her for coming to the party too late.

With the note still pinned to my T-shirt, I rolled out of bed, feeling the kind of remorse and demoralization that only alcoholics and drug addicts can truly understand. I was a total mess. I looked in the mirror and, in a flash of clarity, I saw myself for who I was—a lush, a party girl, and someone who had no idea who she was or where she was going. On top of that, there was somebody out there with a gun who had it out for me. It was a college coed's perfect storm. It motivated me to change. And I actually quit drinking for a while.

Within days of forsaking alcohol, I experienced a personality change on a radical scale, the kind you often see when alcoholics get sober. In a sense, I reverted to the person I was before I had started drinking, the bookworm who was always studying something and working on a project. Now, with a newly clear head, I contemplated my dilemma. I knew if I continued living at home, this crazy stalker could hurt or even kill me. I also knew my parents weren't going to let me move out and move on until I had a decent job in my chosen profession. Since I was a broadcast journalism major, that meant getting a job on television as a reporter and/or anchor. Everybody, including my college professors, told me it was virtually impossible to get an on-camera reporting job straight out of college. However, not everybody thought they would be killed if they failed to do so. It wasn't just the fear of death; I also really wanted to get away from home and start my adult life. I was almost a split personality. When drinking, I seemed to care only about having fun, but when sober, I became intensely ambitious and studious.

As if my life depended on it, which I felt it did, I launched a campaign. When it came to jump-starting my career, I'm happy to say my dad was right there with me. In short order, we got stationery printed up and fashioned a résumé. I also put together a demo video reel of my reporting and anchoring. I had been doing an internship in Greenwich Village with a fabulous older photographer who limped around with a cane. He told us he used to work with Jacques Cousteau until he got the bends during an underwater shoot—hence, the limp. He had all sorts of film equipment and recruited kids with an emphasis on cute coeds from NYU to put on shows for the local public access channel. Somehow, this old bohemian managed to get funding from vanilla organizations like the Boy Scouts. Anyway, he helped me put together my audition tape. I told him I needed to include a sample of reporting and asked him to suggest a story idea.

"It doesn't matter. Do anything. Go downstairs to the florist shop and do a story on the rising price of flowers."

And that's exactly what I did. Somewhere in my many boxes of old tapes, I still have that story.

"A rose at any price would smell as sweet," I concluded in my standup close, having already repurposed every line of poetry and cliché involving flowers I could think of. It was a cute little report that holds up over time. Beginner's luck.

Then, I bought some magazines with famous people in them; one of them was Princess Caroline of Monaco. I pasted several celebrity cutouts onto lime-green poster boards, using them as backdrops for my anchor segment. The anchor script I'd written was about three minutes long. Since we certainly didn't have a teleprompter, I had to memorize it. Also, since we were using my mentor's expensive film stock, I was only given two takes. I nailed it on the first one! Three minutes without a flub. It's shocking how a credible threat can improve your memory.

Once I was armed with a jazzy letterhead, a résumé, and an audition tape, Dad placed an ad for me. We worked on the copy together and put it in *Broadcasting* magazine under "seeking positions." It was a big ad for that section, taking up a nice chunk of the page. On each line was one word: BEAUTIFUL, INTELLIGENT, BILINGUAL, MOTIVATED BROADCAST JOURNALISM GRADUATE SEEKS REPORTER POSITION. WILL MOVE ANYWHERE. MONEY NO OBJECT.

I got two job offers out of it. One was in Raleigh-Durham, North Carolina, and the other in Fort Myers, Florida. I chose Fort Myers, because it essentially involved moving to a vacation resort with great beaches just a bike ride away.

I learned I'd gotten the job when the news director told me, "I never answer those ads, but yours was so intriguing." That comment made me feel like I had beaten the odds for a reason. I tell this story when I talk to students. There's a very simple moral: Imagine what you could accomplish if you thought your life depended on it? The perceived threat of possible death was an amazing motivator. I guess I have to thank that nut job who scared me straight . . . at least for a while.

My mom and dad took me to the airport for the flight to Fort Myers. Mom found the tragedy in the moment and wept dramatically. But I also know that she was thrilled for me, happy that her little girl was following—with a slight deviation—in her footsteps. I too was going *on the road* as she had with her troupe. But instead of vaudeville, it was local news. There are some commonalities. For one thing, my mom taught me well that no matter what, the show must go on. That showbiz ethos has always kept me going through the invariable roller-coaster ride of ratings, management changes, and sheer exhaustion. It was bittersweet leaving my parents behind at the gate. I knew I would have a hard time finding anyone half as interesting.

So, there I was, sitting in a bar in Fort Myers with one of the reporters from the station. He was the bureau chief of one of the outer counties, which basically meant he did it all. He shot, reported, and edited all of his own stories. He lived on a boat and tooled around in a sports car. I thought he was very cool. He was tall, had long blond hair, and loved doing stand-ups in his Speedos. (It was a beach town so he could get away with it.)

"Have a drink," he said.

"I don't drink," I replied, having vowed to stay away from the stuff and excited enough over my brand-new job to keep it that way so far.

"Oh, come on, just have one drink," he repeated.

Every alcoholic has experienced this moment. It's like the devil is sitting on one shoulder and an angel is sitting on the other. A part of me desperately wanted to be responsible. But I didn't have any kind of a program to help me understand my cravings. I had no sober friends to offer moral support. I also didn't have any spiritual beliefs to help me cope with the emotional pain that had begun surfacing because I had stopped using alcohol to numb myself. The only philosophy I had was classic alcoholic nihilism, which reassured me that there was really no good reason to tow the straight and narrow since life is meaningless and we're going to die in the end anyway. You know this parlor game? If you were certain you were going to die tonight, what would you do? The answer is usually something wild and crazy. Well, that's how most alcoholics actually live their daily lives. There's a lot of pride in one's ability to maintain this devil-may-care attitude. One of the stunning aspects of all addiction is the horrible attitudes that we cling to when we're in our disease. It's an upside-down world, and we are most proud of the very traits the rest of the world most abhors in us. By asking me to have a drink, this new friend was sparking within me a ferocious war over my entire belief system. Intellectually, I knew I had many excellent, practical reasons to stay away from the bottle. But my twisted outlook on life and my emotional fragility, combined with the physical cravings of my body for alcohol were no match for the more reasonable arguments in my head. The devil won.

After a couple of drinks, he asked me, "So what kind of furniture do you have?"

"I don't have any," I replied.

"Well, let's get you some," he chortled.

We got into his Datsun 280ZX and took off with the wheels screeching. We headed over to a construction site and he hopped out.

"We're here." he said.

I was confused. My new buddy started picking up some of the two-by-fours that were scattered around on the dirt. He piled those in his trunk, the ends sticking out. Then he went back for about half a dozen extra-large construction blocks. We brought them back to my place, and he made a book case and a coffee table for me.

Clearly, I'd always had a mischievous side that led to me push the envelope, and this wasn't much different. Still, I'd never stolen anything in my life before, and I never would again. However, it doesn't mean I was some innocent little thing. In fact, while I was still in college, I explored CBS and ABC by pretending to deliver coffee. (This was long before 9/11 and our current security obsession.) In the predawn hours, I would show up at the CBS broadcast center with a brown bag and a to-go cup of coffee from a Greek diner and would confidently bark, "Delivery!" while walking past the security checkpoint.

I walked around the halls of CBS, sneaking into the studios where people were doing live shows. I think some of them thought I worked there. Once when I was watching Hughes Rudd doing the news, he looked over at me quizzically during a break.

"I'm watching because I'm planning on becoming a journalist,"

I explained cheerfully, hoping he wouldn't get me tossed out. Fortunately, he was very charming.

"Why the heck would you want to get involved in this crazy business?" he replied with a rasp, while wielding a fly swatter at something on his anchor desk. He was your classic gruff-but-benevolent newsman and I was thrilled to be chatting with him.

"I think journalism is very exciting," I replied.

"You'll see how exciting it is," he shot back, adding, "Get out now while you still can. Take it from me."

There was also a very sweet man in a wheelchair, who took a special liking to me. Perhaps he recognized a fellow underdog trying to make her way against the odds. He gave me some pointers on putting together a résumé and tried to get me an internship at CBS, but no-go. I didn't have the connections. Still, I fondly recall sneaking in and traipsing around in awe, the coffee in my hand getting colder and colder. Years later, I would end up working in the very same building, as a reporter for WCBS-TV.

After that first drink with my fellow reporter, I was off to the races. The news director, who was a very decent, married, clean-living guy, had suggested I move into an apartment complex just a few blocks from the station, where many of the other young staffers lived. I'll never forget my fast times at the Richardson Arms. My boss's concept was that he could mobilize us quickly when a really big story hit. Well, a really big story never hit little old Fort Myers, then the 144th media market. To give you an idea of how small the town was back then, New York is the number one market, LA the number two, and so forth. What did hit the 144th market? Quite a few wild parties among his staff. We basically lived in a glorified dorm and did our best *Animal House* impressions.

I was the weekend anchor, reporter, and producer, not to mention morning photographer and afternoon assignment editor. Basically, in a small town like that you get to do everything, which is great training. I always tell journalism students to go work in a small market and make their mistakes there, so they can learn from them and not repeat them when they get to a big market, where they would probably get fired for the same goof-up.

I made a major mistake on the very first day of my first job. Generally, nothing newsworthy happened in Fort Myers, but that day there was a train derailment. I was standing in the newsroom when my new news director handed me a camera and a sheet of paper with an address and yelled, "Roll on it!"

I took this to mean I was to leave the building immediately and head toward the train wreck, which I did. I was a horrible driver. Up until then I had lived in Manhattan and *never* drove. That I had even gotten my license was a tribute to the kindness of the man who gave me my road test and must have felt sorry for me. I was unable to parallel park and just kept repeating that I desperately needed a driver's license to qualify for a job I'd been offered. Not only did I not really know how to drive, but I had no idea how to use a camera. This was back in the days when we still used film. During my job interview, my boss had asked me if I shot film and I said, "Of course!" I should have added the word "not."

Somehow I managed to drive to the scene of the train derailment. I rolled on some shots and headed back. The record light had gone on so how bad could it be? I soon learned I had held the camera the wrong way and had shot the train derailment sideways, so our viewers would see a derailed train aiming toward the top of their televisions. Now with today's editing techniques you can just rotate a shot however many degrees you want. But film is on sprockets and doesn't just flip. Thankfully, my boss didn't flip out, although I got a few dirty looks from the film editor who muttered something about incompetent women. (Funny that sexism reared its ugly head on my very first day of work.)

Of course, I soon got the hang of it. Every Saturday and Sunday morning, I would head out with my silent-film camera and a battery-powered tape recorder. First, I would film the subject of my story, always careful to avoid showing a tight shot of their lips. Then I would interview them on my tape recorder. I then transferred that sound to an eight-track cart, which would play on the air while the film of the person rolled. Since we didn't see their lips moving, it was as if they were talking while on camera. This was very primitive stuff, but some of the reports were very entertaining. One of my favorite stories was the disco wedding I covered in 1978, where the bride and groom disco danced to the altar and then disco danced away as man and wife. I think Donna Summer's "Love to Love You Baby" was playing.

Another memorable report was the one I did on this dashing pilot who had landed a small plane right in the middle of Fort Myers's Miracle Mile, within a stone's throw from Denny's and other fast-food joints. I interviewed him and reported that he was having engine problems. I would have been on my way, but this guy was just too fascinating to pass up. I ended up accepting a date—one of the only times I actually dated someone I did a story on. Later, in confidence, he told me he had purposely landed on the highly traveled roadway to make a phone call. This guy had some kind of survivalist complex. He owned a huge swath of land about a hundred miles north of Fort Myers upon which he'd built a totally self-sufficient compound. I went to visit him and he warned me his cryptic directions functioned as an IQ test. I finally found his lair in the middle of a vast orange grove. He had about fifteen Mercedes sedans in different colors sitting there, but told me his license had been revoked for unrepentant speeding. Once he took me flying in a sea plane, landing in the very lake Busch Gardens used for their jet skiing shows, while a show was in progress nearby. (I had no idea he was going to do that.) We tooled around the lake for a while, stealing the show as it were, and then took off again.

I would stumble upon characters like this as I drove around town, hoping to turn anything or anyone who caught my eye into a news story. I shot stories on film in the morning, typed up my script, and recorded it on a cart, then ran the assignment desk in the afternoon, picked the wire service stories to read, typed them up, and then put on a jacket and read the whole thing on the air.

Despite my alcoholism, work was very important to me. There are many different types of alcoholics and each behaves by his or her own set of rules, usually learned from a parent or mentor in alcoholism. My dad taught me to be the work hard/play hard kind of alcoholic. Dad was what they call a *high-functioning alcoholic**. To his credit, he struggled mightily to keep his drinking under control with certain rather strict rules. He never drank while at the office and he generally did not go out for the three-martini lunches. Dad never missed a day at work as the result of his drinking and neither did I. It was our family credo. You go to work no matter how hungover you are. Period. Now, there are days when I wish I had stayed home. The idea that drinking doesn't affect your work is a fantasy that alcoholics maintain so they can keep drinking.

One Friday night a bunch of us from the news station were invited to a party on a boat. The boat took off. We all got plastered. The boat got lost. We ended up sailing around all night and finally arrived back on land the next afternoon, but not at the same dock from which we left. I was in a swimsuit, a T-shirt, and flip-flops, as was another reporter assigned to the weekends. We had no idea where we were or where our cars were. The Saturday 6:00 PM show that we should have been preparing for all day was fast approaching. Frantically, we hitch-hiked back to the station in a mad scramble to get something ready by airtime.

Still in my bikini, I tried to jot down a rundown of what stories I was going to report in what order. Thank God for the long roll of national, state, and local news copy from the wire service machine that constantly printed Associated Press stories. There was also another news service we subscribed to that offered up prepackaged video reports with the introductions already written. I grabbed what I could, put the stories in one-two-three order and told the technician to fasten his seat belt, it would be a bumpy ride. He knew to roll the readymade reports as I tossed to them. I raced to the anchor desk, pulled my hair back in a ponytail, and put a knot in my T-shirt to make it look intentional. The news jingle announced the start of the show and it quickly faded, leaving a tight shot of me. I was very nervous. I feared this bikini newscast could be my last. It's not exactly what you want to be wearing when you get fired.

With a super serious face, I took a deep breath and started reading. Nobody ever said a word. I don't think anybody noticed. After all, the viewers couldn't see below the desk and didn't know I was wearing just a bikini. I learned a lot from that experience. When it comes to live television, even when it's hitting the fan, just keep on talking. While there's certainly a difference between a show that's put together in five minutes and one that's put together over hours, sometimes television is just television.

After a little over a year, I knew I had to get out of Fort Myers. Even though I was thrilled to have been chosen to do our station's first live report *ever*, with what was in 1978 very newfangled technology, I knew it was simply time to move on. I was having way too much fun: the beach, the outer islands like Captiva and Sanibel, the parties, the fast drive across Alligator Alley to the nightlife in Fort Lauderdale. It was all so seductive, and I knew that if I didn't leave soon, I might never get out. So, I sold my candy-apple red MG Midget, the most fabulous car I've ever owned (even though it spent most of its time in the shop). My logic was that by selling my car, I was challenging myself to move forward. Once again, I took Dad's advice—and threw my hat over the fence.

But now, I had no ride to work. The prim receptionist in the main lobby at the station clearly thought I was a loose woman, since I'd hitch a ride to work with a different neighbor almost every day. One morning, I'd arrive on the back of a Harley. The next day, I'd pop out of "The Thing." The day after that, my chariot was a pickup truck. Other times I rode my bike or walked the half mile. All the while, I was sending audition tapes to my agent, a crusty old lady named Shirley. Finally, in the winter of 1979, it paid off.

"My name's Ted. I saw your tape. How'd you like to come and work in Minneapolis?" said the deep voice on the other end of the phone.

Crank call, I thought at first. But the voice turned out to belong to a legendary news consultant, and it took me only a few more moments to realize his offer was genuine.

"I'd love to!" I replied.

There was no job interview or audition. I was told to give my notice and hop on the next plane to Minneapolis. They were in the middle of revamping the station and were in the process of hiring a whole bunch of people. I immediately thought of Mary Tyler Moore striding down the streets of Minneapolis and imagined myself, like her, tossing my hat high into the air. *Bigger city, here I come! Fourteenth news market, I'm on my way!* What I didn't consider when I packed my wardrobe—shimmery disco outfits, miniskirts, bathing suits, and pumps—was the below-zero windchill factor that blasted me as I stepped out of the airport. I didn't even own a coat. *Culture shock!*

I bought a new car with money from my dad. His only condition was that I buy an American brand, which I did. Unfortunately, it turned out to be a lemon, but I had no idea it was unsafe to drive. Who knew you shouldn't have to spin the steering wheel around twice to make a turn? I didn't even know defrosters existed. I drove around with a fogged-up windshield until a passenger in my car freaked out and showed me how to use the defroster.

I moved into a downtown neighborhood, which I thought looked quaint and safe, only to find out that it was virtually the only slum in the Twin Cities. Turns out, I was simply ahead of my time. From what I hear, Loring Park is now the "cool" area to live.

It wasn't long after I started my new job that I met my Prince Charming, Jim, a fellow reporter with whom I'm still good friends. One night I was certain someone had followed me back to my quaint but dangerous ground-floor brownstone apartment. Once inside, I literally pushed a chest of drawers against the door.

I called Jim, even though we'd only gone on a few dates. "I'm really scared," I told him. "I think somebody followed me home. Can you come over?"

Jim flew to my rescue, and not long after that, I moved in with him. We had a lot of fun for two years. Jim was a very grounded, meticulous guy. He opened my eyes to how to live a more organized life. Up until that time, I had no idea how to balance a checkbook or do my taxes. He taught me these and other basic, but vital, life skills. Jim also introduced me to the woman who would become my agent and remains so today. Carole chuckles that she discovered me when I was just a young, pigtailed hippie. (That's a pretty good description!)

Thanks to Carole, my next stop was Philadelphia. Again, I had a new job offer. I was more than ready to hop on the next plane and head to a bigger news market. As fond as I was of Jim, I was relatively detached emotionally from all the men who came into my life.

I could pick up and leave without so much as a tear. That should have been a huge red flag that there was something *off* about my romantic life. As much as I tried to connect, the depth of feeling just wasn't there. What a sharp contrast to a time, later in my life, when I was more honest about my true sexual inclinations and my tears flowed like a fountain.

I spent a year and a half in Philadelphia, working six days a week, reporting and anchoring. It was a grueling schedule and left relatively little time for drinking, carousing, or dating. While I enjoyed the many challenges that came with filing daily news reports for a news market that stretched from the suburbs of Philly to Atlantic City, on a personal level I felt lost and lonely.

One day, while covering a raging, out-of-control forest fire in the Pine Barrens of New Jersey, I met a guy who first became my good buddy and eventually my first and only husband. We divorced after about four years and are friends to this day. Michael was a producer for WABC-TV, Channel 7, in New York City. Each of us had raced to the scene of the fire in a helicopter. Soon after landing, we found ourselves joking around and laughing. Michael began calling me and coming down from New York to Philly to visit. He kept telling me that I needed to move to New York City and get a reporting job in my hometown, which also happens to be the center of the universe. I couldn't have agreed more. That was already my plan, but Michael was very encouraging and kept pushing me to make the move. I credit him with giving me the gumption to walk in and beg Bill, my Philadelphia news director, to take me with him when he was promoted to the New York-owned and operated CBS station, WCBS-TV, Channel 2.

I literally walked in and said, "Please take me with you. I'm begging you. It's my hometown. I have to get back!"

Bill, another sweetheart of a boss, did take me along.

So, finally, in 1982, I arrived in New York City to work at WCBS-TV, in the very building where I used to roam as a college student pretending to deliver coffee. My dream had always been to be a reporter in my hometown, so that my mom and dad could watch me on TV. It took me five long years to get back. I was elated. But this is where the road suddenly got narrower. While I had learned a lot about reporting as I scrambled to meet deadlines and come up with stories in these smaller markets, there was a glaring gap in my education. I had worked so hard to get ahead that I had forgotten to work on myself. And it showed.

Me with my escort, the busboy turned med student.

I really feared my bikini newscast would be my last.

3

Therapy:
I Want to Be Myself

"I don't know any other way to put this. You reek of insincerity," the very young, very smart Channel 2 news director said.

He waited for my response. I didn't have one. I felt humiliated by this dressing-down, but I knew he had a point. I had just been completely inauthentic on television. A popular reporter was celebrating a big anniversary at the station. We ran a compilation of the many notable stories she had done over the years, and when the report ended, up came a two-shot of her and me, the anchor. The moment called for some lighthearted banter, precisely something I had yet to excel at in this phase of my development.

Cameras rolling, I turned to her and said, "Look up the word 'professional' in the dictionary and your photo's right there."

Lame! I wanted to smack myself. She laughed for the camera, but I could just imagine the groans back in the main newsroom.

I felt very comfortable reporting out in the field, and people would often compliment me. I was especially thrilled when legendary CBS News anchor Walter Cronkite ran into me in the cafeteria and told me *he* thought I was an excellent reporter. That was a moment I will always treasure. Being good at my job was perhaps my biggest source of self-esteem.

Out in the field, I would be so engrossed in relaying the information I'd gathered to the viewers that I had no time to think about myself. As an anchor, however, my primary role was to introduce other reporters' stories, serving as a glorified traffic cop, switching from sports, to weather, to a feature story, or to a special report. I often felt like window dressing and didn't really know why anchoring was considered so prestigious. To me, reporting was the most important role. As an anchor, I knew I needed to connect with the viewers so that they would regard me as their friend, someone who would give them the straight story. In this job, I needed to be my true self, and this is where I flunked. I didn't have the faintest clue about what it meant to be authentically me. I watched other news anchors and copied what they did. I simply didn't have an authentic concept of myself to fall back on. At this point, I didn't even know I should be trying to figure out who I was. The closest I came to understanding how to be myself could be summed up by the old showbiz saying, *The key to success is knowing how to "fake" being "real."* My parents were often larger-than-life, as befits a theatrical couple who came of age during vaudeville. But television was a more discerning medium. No need to "throw your voice" or "belt out" a line of copy. It called for different skills. Television was a dichotomy. The trick was to be as comfortable and genuine on TV as you were off.

Years on a therapist's couch would eventually help me uncover a genuine identity, where I could define myself as a being shaped by certain core values, experiences, passions, philosophies, and goals. Given that one's identity is not static and that we are all forever morphing, the process of self-discovery is never ending. But the most important step on that inward journey is always the first. And I would soon take it.

One weekend, my parents and I were out at their country house in Hampton Bays, sitting on the terrace overlooking Shinnecock Bay. It was good to be back in New York on familiar ground, and I was so pleased to have landed the WCBS-TV job (even if I "reeked of insincerity"). My parents were very proud of me and often brought up my TV job to their friends.

Dad and I were chatting about the flowers he was having planted in the yard when I happened to glance down and what I saw shocked me.

"Dad, your ankles are really swollen," I said, alarmed.

I thought I detected a moment of hesitation. Then, Dad just brushed off my comment and went on about the flowers.

Mom was the communications director in our family, so she was the one who later gently broke the news that Dad had been diagnosed with lung cancer. This whole time period is a blur. Dad didn't want to discuss it more than absolutely necessary and certainly didn't want to take advice from me about what to do about it. I basically went into shock and, taking my cue from him, sort of pretended it wasn't happening, talking only to my mother about it out of Dad's earshot. In his desperation to live and his fear of going through chemotherapy, Dad had briefly brought in some quacks who were trying to convince him that he didn't have cancer but rather, heavy-metal poisoning. These so-called healers were scary. They tried to blame my mother for Dad's illness, holding up the larger metal pots from the kitchen cabinet that they claimed were filled with toxic metals. They scolded my mother for using these to cook. The sad joke is that my mother hardly ever cooked anything and certainly never used the large kitchen pots. Anita was more likely to swim the Atlantic than she was to whip up some big bubbling stew for Dad. But they didn't know that. When I confronted these con artists and warned them that I would call the Better Business Bureau on them, along with every other government agency I could think off, they disappeared. Dad called me in and accused me of chasing off the people who were trying to save his life.

Dad deteriorated quickly. Although I was very shaken by this, I never let on—especially to him. Carrying on the grand alcoholic tradition of gratuitous stoicism, when I'd visit, we'd completely ignore the fact that he was clearly getting sicker day by day.

If I could choose to redo one thing in my life, it would be this. I would have been more compassionate toward my father during his final months. I would have made a point to visit daily, no matter what, which I didn't. I went by only a couple of times a week. I would have talked with him from my heart so that he could have experienced the real me and I could have experienced the real him. Unfortunately, neither of us was very self-aware at the time. Neither of us had any understanding of what true communication is. Neither of knew how to express our feelings. Oh, we'd debate politics with passion, but that was the extent of our comfort zone.

We all know that being honest about things that come up moment to moment can be messy and uncomfortable. And when you want to make up for years of withholding and superficiality in just a short time, it can feel overwhelming and impossible. That's how I felt when faced with my dad's inevitable departure. There was one day toward the end, when he was in a wheelchair and wanted me to take him out to lunch. I had already arranged a lunch with a bunch of friends at a trendy restaurant and really wanted to be with them instead. I remained with my dad, but I think he sensed that I wanted to bolt and it hurt his feelings. I will always feel guilty about that. These are the kinds of things you do when you don't know who you are and look to friends for reassurance and identity.

Part of the reason I didn't know who I was stemmed from my family's belief system, which centered on acting and drama. The closest my parents got to being "real" with each other was during their heated arguments. With their guards down, they had no choice but to stop acting, at least temporarily. As I observed all this, I developed a belief that authenticity was scary and equated it with being out of control. When "real" comes out in short, ferocious bursts, it *is* scary. Their arguments, especially when I was a little kid, terrified and depressed me. The fact that I was an only child, with no sibling to talk to, only made me internalize it more. Those internalized feelings from early childhood were what I tried to suppress with alcohol.

I don't want to single out my parents, however. Many families that came into being in the rigid 1950s—where conformity was prized above almost all else—experienced stilted communication and hid behind phony or pretentious behavior, arguing behind closed doors. The cultural revolution of the 1960s simply hadn't happened yet.

The day my father died, he was in his own bed and had his family around him, including my mother and my half sister, Gloria. However, I was the only one in the room at the final moment of his death, as the others had stepped out for a few minutes. I'd been at work that day, finished off the story I was working on, then headed over to see him, after telling a coworker I thought he was going to "kick the bucket." How I wish I hadn't gone to work that day. How I wish I hadn't said such a callous thing. This "tough shell" was my defense mechanism against the unthinkable. Today, I can cry and let my sadness out for others to see. Today, I can withstand awkward or very emotional moments. But back then, deep in my disease, I had a profound aversion to any situation that was likely to become what I would consider sloppy or maudlin. It was just total fear. I was not trained or equipped to deal with real emotions.

I spoke to Dad for a few moments, coming up with nothing momentous to say. He, in turn, tried to say something loving.

"You were always my favorite," he uttered with a weak smile, which confused me since I was his only child.

Then he went into a death rattle. It was a loud and unnerving gurgling noise from deep within his throat and his body shook intensely. I watched on in silent horror, not wanting to believe what was happening.

"Your father is almost gone," the doctor said.

After a few minutes, a nurse administered a shot to him, of what I don't know. But as she inserted the needle under his skin, my father suddenly came back to life for a brief second to shout, "No!" Then, just as quickly, he was totally still. His breathing stopped. I was beyond stunned. There was a dreamlike quality to everything around me; it was like being wide awake during a nightmare.

I've always wondered how my dad managed to come back from that unnerving death rattle. He hated being sick, because he couldn't stand being dependent upon anyone else—especially not a doctor or a nurse. He was the boss at work and at home, and it humiliated him to take orders. So there, even in the final moment of his life, he was defiant and wanted to do it his way. I think that's what he meant by "No!"

I didn't cry. I didn't have the ability to express any emotions about this seminal event in my life. I was numb and couldn't feel anything. I was a sleepwalker at the funeral. Neither my mother nor I got up to speak, although Dad's friend Blondie bawled as she took the podium. I did little to comfort my mother other than to try to help her on a practical level. But my mom didn't need my help. She is extraordinarily strong and has overcome a lot in her long life. She is what they call a survivor.

What I did notice was that a world without my father was kind of surreal. All of my career efforts were—in the final analysis—an effort to win my father's approval and respect. Without Dad around to try to impress, I began to wonder what I was doing it all for.

Today, I can say that I very much love my father and greatly admire all that he accomplished during his lifetime. Today, I harbor no resentment toward him, and I mostly remember the good times, when he played guitar for me, when he took me swimming in the ocean, and when he taught me how to play tennis and golf. I'm at peace with my dad because I've worked through the issues I had with him in therapy and, later, through the Twelve Steps. I eventually came to realize that he was doing the very best he could given his own life experience. One of the most important things I learned in therapy is to stop judging others and myself so harshly. While you sometimes have to hold people accountable for the things they do and say—and even bring them to justice—it is important to try to understand them and have compassion for them. I have compassion for my dad and I do understand him, now. I have also forgiven myself for my thoughtlessness toward him. But that process took years.

Right after my father died, my drinking took off full throttle. I was drinking every night after work and starting at lunch on weekends, furiously drowning out my grief with alcohol. Had I been sober when Dad died, I probably would have cried a great deal, but booze is the great silencer of true emotion. They say, *in vino veritas*, which means "in wine there is truth." Well, I say, *in vino nada* . . . nothing . . . numbness. The grief, buried deep underground, seeped up as bitterness and cynicism.

One night, I was at a bar owned by my niece Lorca's then-boyfriend. As the evening got late, he looked at me from across the bar and said, "Every time I see you, you're drunk."

The words stung, but he was right. I went to the bar to drink, and I drank to get drunk.

Lorca chimed in. "Why don't you see a therapist?" she suggested. "I've got a great one."

My behavior *was* starting to frighten me. I was also reaching the point that all alcoholics invariably reach when drinking becomes increasingly less fun because of all the anxiety and stress surrounding it. Given that I was on camera in a big market like New York, I was always worried that I'd say or do something inappropriate while tanked up. Everyone who reads the "Page Six" gossip sheet in the *New York Post* knows you don't have to be famous to be good fodder for the tabloids. I had already gotten quite sloppy at a couple of industry parties and going out on the town was starting to feel like an inevitable date with self-destruction.

Despite all that, there was a side of me that relished getting away with it. The classic alcoholic pattern is a vicious cycle with three major turns—binging, and then remorse, and then euphoria, when you realize nothing terrible happened as a result of your insane and self-destructive behavior.

I would go out on the town with a friend, determined to have just a couple of drinks. I would get plastered. I would have a conversation with somebody I hardly knew, or didn't know at all, while sitting on a barstool. I would wake up the next morning with a horrible hangover, trying to remember all the things I'd said. I would have a cup of coffee and call my friend for a "damage assessment meeting." We would laugh about all the silly things that happened the night before, and then we would hang up.

Convinced that I was not going to suffer any negative repercussions as a result of my escapade—the hangover not withstanding—

I would then experience a rush of euphoria. *I wasn't in trouble. I'd gotten away with it! Eureka! Life was good.* A few nights later, I'd repeat the pattern.

There was more than a small part of me that desperately wanted off the merry-go-round. Sometimes, the damage assessment was pretty damaging. I remember arriving at a friend's wedding tipsy and late, giggling and talking way too loud just as they were exchanging their vows. I thought it was hilarious. The bride and groom, not so much. I got even louder as the evening progressed. My date later said people were talking about me. After nights like those, I would have to engage in strenuous self-rationalization to reassure myself that it wasn't so bad after all.

So, when Lorca recommended a psychologist, I decided I could use some professional help. I spent years attending therapy sessions, once or twice a week, while my drinking worsened. Looking back, it's obvious to me that therapy alone will not get an alcoholic sober! Why did it take me so long to figure that out? Clearly, I hadn't yet *hit bottom**.

A true alcoholic—as opposed to somebody who just drinks too much—will almost never give up drinking until they are totally desperate and stuck in a corner with nowhere else to turn. I still had my high-profile job, my co-op on Central Park West, my friends, and my *enablers** who would drink with me and assure me I didn't really have a problem.

I was content to remain in a frame of mind that allowed me to believe I was trying, through therapy, to get better while still having the freedom to drink. The disease of alcoholism is so profoundly overpowering that your mind will align with your physical cravings and proceed to justify just about anything that will allow you to continue drinking.

The enemy was me! The problem was in my head, my body, and my soul.

My first therapist actually asked me, "Why can't you drink moderately, have a glass of wine with dinner and leave it at that?"

While she was wonderful in many other ways, this question reveals a total lack of understanding of how alcoholism works. An alcoholic, by definition, cannot drink moderately. The first sip triggers cravings that completely overwhelm the body and the mind. Alcoholism takes the drinker as a hostage and totally commands their behavior. That is why so many alcoholics will say, "I couldn't believe the person I'd become."

Perhaps, in her mind, my therapist didn't believe I really was an alcoholic. I did have a clever way of putting on that false good-girl persona designed to convince those in authority that I was a well-behaved person. Sometimes that act fooled the very people who needed to see the truth in order to help me. Still, my drinking stories should have convinced her.

After I related one alcoholic escapade, for which I was feeling particularly remorseful, she said, "Give yourself permission to fail."

To me this sounded like an endorsement of my hard-drinking lifestyle. It was one of the most fantastic pieces of advice I'd ever heard! For a long time after that, any time I would go overboard I'd just announce, "I've given myself permission to fail!"

If someone shares that he or she has a drinking problem or a drug problem with a therapist, I believe it is a therapist's responsibility to *immediately* recommend a twelve-step program in no uncertain terms. The therapist can still see that person as a patient, because therapy is often a crucial component of recovery. But the therapist should not try to counsel a client with a drug or alcohol problem without referring him or her to the only proven program for addiction in the history of humankind. To do otherwise is irresponsible, since alcoholism can be a fatal disease.

The Twelve Steps work because they bring struggling and recovering addicts together to share their experiences. Only an addict can understand the overpowering cravings of another addict. Only an addict can understand how we will promise ourselves—with an earnest vow—to just have two drinks, only to wake up the next morning with a throbbing headache after yet another bender. Only an addict can really understand that feeling of complete powerlessness.

A therapist who is not an addict him- or herself can read hundreds of books about addiction and still not have a true understanding of the depths of the cravings and the mindset and soul sickness those urges foster. It's like trying to know what it's like to die . . . without dying.

While it's possible that my therapist mentioned the idea of my going to rehab or a twelve-step program, I don't recall such a conversation. Maybe I blocked it out. I certainly had a vague awareness that such programs existed. But in my imagination, recovery programs were snake pit–like environments where hobos in fedoras and rumpled trench coats gathered to warm their hands over a burning pile of trash. I told myself that I was certainly not the kind person who could be a part of that.

I was ignorant. The mindset I just described is known as *contempt prior to investigation**. I had no concept of what recovery actually looked like. I think the whole issue may have flashed across my mind once or twice but that's it. Sometimes I look back and think, *What a pity. I could have saved so much time.* But those of us in recovery are cautioned not to regret the past or try to rewrite it. The philosophy is that everything happens in its own rhythm and time. Some of the experiences I was bound to endure may end up being useful to someone else when I share them.

I still believe very strongly in therapy. *Everyone* needs therapy—at some point—to work on their traumas, denial, fears, secret fantasies, fetishes, and so on. Until people take the time to look inside themselves, with the help of a guide called a therapist, they're usually flying blind, unaware of their own motives for saying and doing most of what they say and do. I know I was flying blind until I got some therapy under my belt. But please don't make my mistake and fool yourself into thinking you can cure your addiction by going to a therapist.

Psychologists dealing with addicts or alcoholics need to realize that subtle or oblique mentions about getting help are usually not going to pierce the addict's haze and denial. If you're talking to a person who is almost deaf and blind, you need to shout and wave your hands. It takes a lot to get an addict's attention.

The years I spent on the couch were definitely not a waste of time. Therapy allowed me to become mature enough that, when I finally stumbled upon the Twelve-Step message, I was capable of listening with an open mind. Therapy also helped me clear up many other issues that were plaguing me.

One of my issues was my mixed ethnic heritage. Growing up in the 1960s and 1970s in New York—before Jennifer Lopez, Ricky Martin, Jimmy Smits, John Leguizamo, and others made Puerto Ricans "cool"—being half Puerto Rican meant fending off a lot of negative stereotyping and prejudice.

Some of my friends at private school and in the Hamptons would say, "Why don't you just say you're Spanish?"

This really ticked me off.

"I'll say what I want to say and it's none of your business," I would shoot back.

My adman father also didn't feel that my mother and I needed to advertise our Puerto Rican backgrounds, which we both resented. Usually, this was an unspoken message, delivered with a cough or a raised eyebrow. In fact, my mother defied my dad and often weaved into the conversation something about her Puerto Rican heritage. That was admirable up to a point. I certainly didn't want to make my identity *all* about that one thing. We are all a lot more than our skin color and our heritage. Both extremes were irritating to me. In my father's circle, it wasn't just that one ethnic group that was under fire. There were a lot of shame-based people—from all of sorts of backgrounds—where pretense seemed to be paramount. Some people anglicized their names and hid their true religious origins. I would hear other people whispering about them: *Did you know so and so was a such and such?*

Everybody was pretending to be a WASP, except for those who insisted they descended from European royalty or aristocracy, related to this one or that. As I look back on it now, it was a whole crowd of people who must have had very low self-esteem. Why else would they feel the need to validate themselves in that manner? Perhaps it was also because they knew society punished and denigrated those who came from what were considered less prestigious backgrounds. It's called bigotry.

In therapy, I started to recall some of the prejudice that I had endured growing up, experiences that I had completely buried or denied. Perhaps the most traumatic experience occurred in first grade at a public school in the early 1960s. I had been in class with a whole bunch of white kids. Suddenly, in the middle of the school year, I was yanked out of that class and taken to another classroom with all the minority kids.

I remember taking my first look at my new class as the door swung open. There was not one white kid in there. Everyone was African-American, Asian, or Hispanic. Even at my young age, I knew something momentous was happening to me. Welcome to apartheid, right in Midtown Manhattan. Apparently, school officials had figured out that little Janie Mitchell was Puerto Rican. The fact that I spoke some Spanish might have been a tip off.

This was one of the first times I really sensed that I was different . . . and not in a positive way. I felt shame. This happened to a lot of the Puerto Rican kids. As soon as they gave themselves away as Puerto Rican, boom . . . the switcheroo. As for the Latino kids who were even more ethnic looking, they never even got that far.

As often happens, this abrupt transfer—while certainly psychologically debilitating—also turned into a blessing. My parents were outraged, and I was sent to private school. I remained in private schools all the way through college. My mother had pleaded with my father to send me to private school right from the start, but Dad loved the idea that public school was free. He was more invested in appearing well-off than actually doing the things well-off people do.

The "incident" at P.S. 69 definitely hit a little too close to home for my father. Born in 1916, he used to tell me that the Irish were also subject to tremendous prejudice, with storefront signs reading, "Irish Need Not Apply." There's ample documentation of anti-Irish sentiment, particularly against Irish Catholics, in the late nineteenth and early twentieth centuries. In a similar way to how Puerto Ricans were treated in the mid-twentieth century, much earlier the Irish were also steered away from white-collar jobs. So, my being singled out in that way clearly triggered some very old feelings in my dad. It was probably those painful formative experiences, as the son of an Irish immigrant mother with a big family, that led him to overcompensate by creating a patrician persona. When I hear today's immigration debates raging, I want to shout, "Remember whence you came!"

Due to my private schooling and Dad's social climbing, I often hung out with kids who were very wealthy. It didn't take me long to notice that the truest expressions of their wealth were in the tiny details of their daily existence. I'd walk into a bathroom and every aspect of it was perfect and elegant, down to the monogrammed towels, the heavy onyx wastebasket, and even the soap. Dad preferred to let people infer a wealth, which didn't really exist, with flashy displays. It wasn't just the red Lincoln Continental convertible, it was the ascot he wore on the weekends and the pink jackets he donned in the summertime. Naturally, the genuinely rich kids picked up on the phoniness immediately. And again I felt shame for appearing to be trying to pass for something I wasn't, when actually I was just being taken along on my dad's ride.

This was the beginning of my allergy to status seeking. The idea that one is somehow more valuable and worthy—as a human being—because of a certain lineage or net worth is so wildly absurd that it boggles my mind that this thinking has endured into the twenty-first century.

My mother dealt with my dad's friends by keeping her sense of humor.

"Café society? No, it's more like Nescafé Society," my mom would say, rolling her eyes. Their mindset reminds me of those ignorant people who buy a dog from a breeder—and then brag about the parentage of the dog. The mutt in the shelter is just as good a dog and often healthier and smarter. Certainly, a mutt is less likely to be inbred. But some people fervently believe their dog is better because it comes with "papers." (Barack Obama got a big laugh when he called himself a mutt at one of his first news conferences after he was elected. I can relate.)

I was named after my dad's mother, Jane Mitchell. My mother wanted to name me Rima after the heroine of the classic novel *Green Mansions*. Thankfully, Dad ignored her and told the hospital I was to be called Jane Mitchell. I do love the name Jane, but "Jane Mitchell" just didn't quite fit. I was forever explaining my "exotic" heritage.

My discomfort with my name came up in therapy when I explained to my therapist that my feelings of inauthenticity were accentuated by my "vanilla-sounding" name, which didn't reflect who I really was.

"Why don't you change it?" she asked.

I told her that I had thought about doing that back when I first started my career, when my dad and I were first putting together my ad seeking employment. My father vehemently opposed the change, and it never occurred to me to defy him. But now, he was no longer alive to be offended by it.

"My mom goes by the name Anita Velez-Mitchell," I mused aloud to my therapist. Always ahead of her time, my mother had been one of the first hyphenates of the feminist movement. She abhorred the idea that women lost their names and part of their identities when they got married and insisted on keeping her maiden name in addition to her new last name.

Then, I added, "I could do the same thing. . . .and go by Jane Velez-Mitchell."

I liked the sound of that.

Since I was an on-camera news reporter, I had to inform the news director, Steve. He was a fabulous boss who had recently taken over the position. Steve and I hit it off instantly. We immediately recognized that we were like-minded and didn't quite fit in with the CBS corporate culture, which always seemed to favor dry, intellectual, button-down types. Steve had been hired to boost the ratings by jazzing up the graphics and enlivening the presentation. But at tradition-bound CBS, anyone who shook up the status quo would invariably find himself undermined from within by political subterfuge. The news director post became a revolving-door job. In fact, I went through five news directors in my eight years at WCBS. (Once, when yet another new news director was introducing himself, one of the old-time reporters—who'd had enough—shouted, "We'll still be here after you're gone!")

Steve loved the idea that I was going to change my name to reflect my Latina heritage. "Do it!" he encouraged.

In the summer of 1986, I did my first sign-off as Jane Velez-Mitchell. I immediately felt more authentic. It was like a huge weight was lifted off of my shoulders. This is *me*, take me or leave me!

I was not prepared for the backlash. A lot of the people who I worked with assumed it was a cynical and calculating move designed to boost my career in an era when TV news stations were looking to promote minorities. That theory got a boost when Steve promoted me to weekend anchor a short time later.

"What are you going to change next, Jane, your skin color?" one reporter asked me, her voice dripping with hostility.

Because I knew I had changed my name for the right reasons, I didn't overreact to the criticisms, although they hurt. Some of the verbal assaults came from Latinos who didn't think I was really Hispanic and assumed I was a gringa with a good tan trying to muscle into their territory.

"If you were going to do it the right way, you would have changed your name to Jane Mitchell Velez," said one of the station's only other Hispanic reporters.

"It's my name, and I can do what I want with it," was my overall response.

I felt empowered by taking ownership of my name and, in the process, reclaiming my heritage in a positive way. It helped to heal the trauma I experienced as I was growing up when I was told, verbally and nonverbally, that my Puerto Rican background was something I should keep quiet.

I'm aware now that one of the reasons I drank was to stuff my rage about the discomfort I was made to feel for being Puerto Rican. Why should my background be treated as a liability and not as an asset? *Never let anyone else define you! It will be for their convenience, not yours.*

I've never for a moment regretted changing my name. It was a personal breakthrough.

It was all thanks to therapy that I experienced this personal growth, remembering, revisiting, and processing old experiences from childhood so that I could heal and move on. Up until that point, I was really in denial. I actually believed that I had enjoyed a very happy childhood and had never experienced any discrimination or trauma. This is what I had been told. "You were such a happy child," my dad would always say.

I remained brainwashed well into adulthood. This is how children survive. They adapt. As they grow up, they remember only the fairytales they've been told. In therapy, we return to childhood and try to discover the truth, however painful and inconvenient.

I recently was shocked to review some very old papers of mine, only to realize that—even though I dressed like a hippie—I spent my teenage years under the spell of my father's ultraconservative views. The year was 1971. I was sixteen. My dad was involved, in some way, with advertising for President Nixon's upcoming re-election campaign. President Nixon was holding a White House Conference on Children and Youth, reaching out to the youth vote at a time when so many young people had turned against him because of the Vietnam War. I applied and was accepted and went to Estes Park, Colorado, along with a thousand others. I wrote this after returning home: "Ethnic minorities and various vocal groups were over-represented . . . they drastically under-represented the views of the majority of youth in the nation. This phenomenon, coupled with the active slanting of the mass media in the same direction, succeeded in giving the nation and the world a view of America's youth that was ridiculously out of proportion." Today, I am appalled that I wrote that. I was just parroting my father's views. He had apparently also forgotten that he had married a minority and had a child who was considered one. We were all living in denial!

As for my mother's view of her ethnicity, she points out that Hispanic is not a race. It is an ethnic group. There are white, black, Asian, and indigenous Indian Hispanics and all sorts of combinations thereof. She is absolutely right! You can't just check a box that says Hispanic and leave it at that. Latin America was settled by Europeans just as North America was. Along with European immigrants, there were African and Asian influences. Of course, you also have the original Indian population who were often horribly exploited by the Europeans, yet intermarried with them.

I get irritated when I am asked to check off white or Hispanic. Should I completely abandon my Irish ancestry? Of course not. It's part of who I am. But I am also proud to be Hispanic and want to check that off too. I'm convinced that I have Indian influences, as well. I love it when I spend time in the sun and I get a deep tan. I am definitely a person of color. Suffice it to say, four boxes for an entire human race is completely ridiculous in our increasingly multiethnic, multiracial world. But if adults can't figure it out, how can a kid?

Childhood is a strange time. A child has no power. Adults, by contrast, have a lot of power. They physically tower over you. They have all the money, access, and control. Dysfunction develops in the child as she tries to accommodate the parents by adjusting herself and sometimes contorting her personality to meet their needs and desires. This is the beginning of the codependency that often rears its head years later when these old patterns of accommodation are reenacted with lovers and in other key relationships.

Growing up in the midst of my parents' drama, I adjusted myself by trying to stabilize them and keep them on an even keel. My father had rage issues. He would sometimes lose his temper after a few drinks, and it was a scary thing to experience. In the mornings, he would also sometimes be merely irritable, as people with hangovers often are. Alcoholism makes finding the little things—glasses, keys, pipes, gloves—difficult. At the same time, my mother had given up her glamorous showbiz career to find herself—for the first time in her life—merely a wife and mother. Consequently, she was often "blue," which today we know means depressed. Mom's showbiz training also gave her a tendency toward melodramatic behavior. She was brilliant in extracting the tragedy buried in ordinary situations.

I felt it was my job to keep them distracted and entertained. I was a cross between a standup comedian, a political commentator, and a mediator. This is probably where I developed my tendency toward acting out as class clown and planted the seeds of my career as a professional talker.

After my father died, my mother blossomed in many ways and is rarely blue today. Without the constraints and obligations of a 1950s-style marriage she was able to give free rein to all her artistic passions: acting, writing plays, poems, and even an opera. At ninety-three years of age, she still fills her home with the sounds and energy of actors rehearsing.

While I was in therapy in New York, working on my ethnic identity issues and working out my father's death, I also decided to get married. Perhaps it was because just days before he passed away my father mentioned something about my marrying Michael. Perhaps it was because I felt a deep void and thought I could fill it by "settling down." Like many young people, I also thought if I got married something miraculous would occur, and I would suddenly be "normal." Michael and I were married for just a few years before going to a peaceful mediator for an amicable divorce. Today, we remain what we started as: buddies.

While the marriage was not meant to be, we both agree that our wedding was fabulous. It was at a Bridgehampton beach club, the very club my parents were members of when I was a kid. Just for fun, we made it a costume wedding and asked everybody to "dress nautical." This made for some very kooky outfits. Michael wore an Italian naval uniform with gold epaulettes. My therapist was there as one of the guests, no doubt taking notes. It may not have been the most direct route to a valid identity, but it was a great party.

After I got married, my friends jokingly called me Jane Velez-Mitchell Horowicz, the one-woman United Nations! But I didn't actually add Michael's name because my three names were already a mouthful.

There was one huge, buried issue that I managed to avoid both during my marriage and for the first few years of therapy. I never even mentioned this dark secret to my first analyst, even though it was one of the main reasons I drank. Instead, I systematically fought to banish my uncomfortable thoughts. There was no way I was going to admit to myself or anyone else that I desired to be in an intimate relationship with someone of the same sex.

Me, tagging along with Dad in the Hamptons.

4

Sobriety:
I Want to Stop Boozing

L *iquid courage.* That's what they call alcohol. There are two types of brazen behavior that a person exhibits while drunk: Sometimes she will do crazy things, things that she would never, ever, even remotely consider doing while sober. But other times, alcohol can give a person the guts to do something she secretly fantasizes about doing but just doesn't have the courage to do while sober.

"It was the alcohol talking."

That was how I nervously explained to my new boyfriend, Stephen, how an out-of-town work trip had turned into an R-rated, vodka-filled escapade.

Stephen, whom I'd begun dating after Michael and I parted ways, was the son of a prominent Beverly Hills psychiatrist. In fact, Stephen's whole family was in the therapy business. His analyst dad had a high-profile list of clients, his mom was a psychiatric counselor, and his sister was a marriage and family therapist. *Bingo!* I imagined the prospect of round-the-clock analysis. It was very enticing.

Although he was a producer in the TV business, Stephen was also a "shrink," albeit unlicensed. He is a brilliant interviewer and investigative journalist, but I think he really missed his calling. His swift, cut-to-the-chase analysis of people is often more on target than a drawn out diagnosis by a pro. He grew up with the analytical gene and learned the lingo. He loves to joke that, after our first date, a friend asked him what I was like and he replied, "Aside from the fact that she's probably an alcoholic and a lesbian, she's terrific!"

Stephen is very funny, and that's one reason why we were together as a couple for a decade. By this time, it was the 1990s, and I had finished an eight-year stint in New York and headed out to Los Angeles to anchor for a news station in Hollywood. The move was thrilling.

While Stephen and I were dating, one of my assignments sent me to Washington, D.C. After I filed my report, I went with my producer—who also happened to be one of my drinking buddies—to a D.C. nightclub to meet two of his best friends, who were a couple. He assured me they were terrific, which would turn out to be an understatement. Initially, I wasn't impressed. They were extremely late, which annoyed me. My producer and I spent several hours at the bar downing vodka and tonics while we waited for them to show up.

Meanwhile, we had a good view of the action on the dance floor. In what has since become a cliché but was rather cutting edge at the time, the nightclub had several women in cages who were dancing. These G-string-clad women threw their hair extensions around, wiggled their asses, shook their breasts, flipped upside down, and through various other contortions, kept me fixated on them while the strobe lights flashed. Sometimes, in places like this, the obscure lighting is a blessing. But these dancers were high caliber.

It must have been the combination of drinking for several hours while staring at these very underdressed and overendowed sex bombs that brought my dark secret to the surface.

After the couple finally arrived, my producer and his buddy immediately went off to smoke some cigars, leaving the girlfriend and me at the bar.

"How rude. I can't believe they just took off like that," I said to her, somewhat exasperated by the whole evening.

"Men," she responded with an all-knowing look.

I couldn't help but notice that she was beautiful. She had wavy, blond hair, a spectacular body, sparkling eyes, and a perfect smile. She also had a very good sense of humor. Eventually, we ran out of small talk. The guys still hadn't come back.

"I'm so sick of sitting here. Let's go look for them," I suggested.

"No, let's get lost and make them look for us" she laughed.

The place was absolutely packed. As we got up to push through the crowd, I impulsively took her hand and held it. What was I doing? It took me a second to admit to myself that I had crossed a line. To my shock, she didn't pull her hand away. Just holding her hand and leading her to the dance floor made me delirious with anticipation. *What was going to happen next?* I had no idea, but I wanted to find out.

Soon we were on the dance floor being jostled about by the crowd. We were wedged together, face to face. Again, my alcohol-fueled impulses took over and I kissed her on the lips. To my amazement, she kissed me back, and we began to make out.

Eventually, her boyfriend sauntered back. But rather than try to stop us, he just watched with a big grin. I'm forever grateful that they were both so receptive and nobody smacked me. I was definitely cruising for a bruising that night. It would take me years to express my true sexual identity in an appropriate manner: sober and with somebody who wasn't attached.

When I got back, Stephen didn't find the story all that amusing. But it wasn't the same-sex make-out session he was upset about. He was annoyed that that I went out of town and got drunk. He was tired of all my drinking escapades. We'd been together a couple of years by this point and my act was getting old.

"You've got two more," he said to me with a certain nonchalance that made me realize he was deadly earnest. He vowed to walk out on me if I blacked out two more times on his watch.

The night I hit bottom was a night to remember. A dear friend of ours was having a party. Stephen and I were invited and various friends and colleagues were coming. The Hollywood Hills home was chic and a great party house, as we certainly proved that night. My ex-husband Michael was on hand, as well as a few colleagues and old friends. It was kind of like an episode of *This Is Your Life*.

I got the brilliant idea of teaching everybody how to do "snake-bites." That's when you down a jigger of whiskey or tequila and then, as a chaser, suck the juice out of a lemon wedge that a friend is holding in his or her mouth. It's a real icebreaker. This got a lot of laughs. It was silly and fun. However, at a certain point, the snake bit me and I blacked out.

This is the definitive mark of alcoholism, where you are there but then again, you don't know that you're there. The most terrible DUI car accidents are usually committed by a driver in a blackout, who doesn't know, for example, that he's even driving, much less that he's driving the wrong way on a freeway.

My blackout wasn't tragic, but it was pitiful. I am told that I knocked the host down a flight of his stairs after I tried to kiss him. Apparently, I became the kissing bandit when under the influence. The host was a very good sport, but Stephen was not amused. He was actually quite livid.

"Why do we have to go?" I implored him as he carried me out of the party over his shoulder.

"Because you are drunk and out of control!"

"But why do we have to go?" I implored again, like a child, unable to grasp the answer he gave me repeatedly.

The next day I woke up to an empty bed. The sun was streaming through my oceanfront condo. People were playing volleyball right outside. I was assaulted by the brightness and the shouts of the players. My head throbbed. There was that horrible sense of remorse as the night before came back to me in flashes, a PowerPoint presentation of unladylike behavior. Looking around the room, I immediately assumed Stephen had followed through on his threat of leaving me. I felt sick.

But another part of me went *click, click, click*. There was this convergence of factors. I had just destroyed yet another relationship. I felt totally alone, and I hated myself. I was also too tired to do a damage-assessment call or engage in my customary rationalizations.

At the age of thirty-nine, I was getting too old for this. What might have been brushed off by a teenager as a silly escapade felt really ugly as an adult. I felt totally spent. At that moment, I finally admitted that I needed the kind of help that went far beyond talking to a therapist. It was a brief *moment of clarity** where everything changed, and I surrendered.

I felt a rising tide of relief as I walked down the stairs toward the phone. I was an army general waving the white flag at the enemy. Finally, the war was over. I headed straight to my office, picked up the phone, and dialed an old friend from college with whom I had recently reconnected. He had just gotten sober and had been bugging me to join him.

"Abbott, hi. It's me. You win. I had a bad one last night. I'm done. Seriously. I'll do whatever you want me to do."

"Great, I'll pick you up in an hour," he said.

I hung up the phone and walked from my office into the living room. There was Stephen, sleeping on the couch. If I had noticed him on the way into my office, I would never have made the most important phone call of my life.

Abbott had been trying to get me sober ever since he had accidentally stumbled upon a group of sober people in Hollywood while looking for the entrance to a comedy club. By sheer accident he followed these people through another door. He loved what he heard and told me, "This is for you."

Of course, like any good practicing alcoholic, I didn't want to hear it.

"Stop trying to tell me what to do, Abbott. I'm a big girl and I can handle my own life." Thank God he didn't give up on me. I had Abbott to call at the moment that I hit the skids.

That was when I experienced a miracle. On the very first day of my adventure into sobriety, I realized something profound, namely that *I did not have to drink*. With Abbott as my guide, I walked into my very first get-together with other sober people. This happened to be an outdoor gathering at a gorgeous park on a gently sloping hill. The glistening Pacific Ocean was our backdrop. The day was spectacular, sunny and warm. The people all seemed to sparkle in the bright sunlight. They were laughing and clapping and seemed happier than any group of people I'd ever seen assembled anywhere. Everything seemed to be happening in slow motion. I looked around and saw this beautiful senior citizen with long, flowing silver hair walk up to the front of the assembly. She was slim and elegant and looked like she had once been a supermodel. She smiled and started talking. I don't remember exactly what she said. It was more her aura that struck me. She glistened like the ocean! She was vibrant and so alive. I looked at her and said, "Wow, I'd like to be like her when I'm her age." It was a classic Twelve-Step moment. I saw a sober person and *wanted what she had!*

Tears filled my eyes. "I think I can do this," I whispered to myself with a certain amazement. Though embarrassed by my display of emotion, I couldn't stop myself from choking up. I was profoundly moved by these people who looked like they were strolling around in heaven. In short order, the obsession that had plagued me for decades was lifted. For some, it's a very slow process where the cravings remain and staying sober is a grueling *one-day-at-a-time** effort. Others find that a psychic shift occurs in a mere instant, and the world suddenly changes. I'd say 75 percent of my cravings disappeared immediately. The other 25 percent withered away within a year or so.

I don't use the word "miracle" lightly. I used to be someone who couldn't go one single night without a drink, no matter how hard I tried. Before I got sober, the notion of any kind of spiritual conversion would have made me roll my eyes. I was too jaded and too accustomed to failing to believe I could really experience a profound transformation. But then it happened to me! I was—in a manner of speaking—born again, not according to the classic religious definition but definitely in a spiritual sense.

Embarking on my new life, I said goodbye to my cynicism and my desire to be "cool" and embraced a whole new way of living. Everything changed. I cannot exaggerate the euphoria that I experienced upon realizing that I was free of the obsession to drink. I've never served time, but I imagine it's the same kind of ecstasy people experience when they're released from prison after decades behind bars.

They say life begins at forty. Well, in a few months I would turn forty with a whole new life ahead of me. I felt like a teenager. I was to discover a very simple way of living, designed for very complicated people. There are twelve steps to the formula that allowed me to shed my alcoholic skin and metamorphose into the better person that was hidden within me.

At times, it can be a joyous adventure; at other times, it feels like a slow stroll over hot coals. I had to go into my discomfort zone and confront things I wanted desperately to avoid, revealing embarrassing drunken moments to total strangers. I had to take *contrary action**, doing the exact opposite of what my alcoholic tendencies would normally compel me to do, like going to sleep at a decent hour when I wanted to stay up all night.

There's grief involved. As I went through the Twelve Steps, I mourned the death of the old Jane, that addicted personality who had so many flaws but to whom I was still emotionally attached in many ways. It's hard to let go of the ratty old slipper you're used to shuffling around in. As I let her go, I had to find new qualities to replace the old. I'm still finding new qualities. It's really a process of learning who I truly am.

Long before I got sober on April 1, 1995, Stephen and I had made arrangements to go on vacation to Mazatlán, Mexico. Even though I was just a few days sober, we decided to go anyway. I was terrified that I wouldn't make it through the week. Having gone on many vacations at Mexican beach resorts, I knew that drinking was the beginning, middle, and end of almost every activity. For a week, everywhere I turned people were throwing back tequila shooters and swilling margaritas. There were even bars in the pools. It was the ultimate test.

If I can get through this vacation sober, the rest will be a breeze, I told myself.

I did everything I could to distract myself, essentially returning to childhood. They say, when you get sober, you return, emotionally, to the age you were when you began drinking. So, I became a ten-year-old child! I got my hair weaved. I got a henna tattoo. I painted a piece of pottery. Stephen was right there with me, painting his own little statues of dolphins. I'll never forget how he supported and encouraged me during those crucial early days, making me laugh about the whole situation by pretending we were in a mental ward.

Laughter is perhaps the greatest replacement therapy of all. When you're laughing, you're not thinking about drinking because you're naturally intoxicated.

As soon as I returned from the vacation, I asked for the help of a very wise woman who had been sober for many years.

"When you feel like having a drink, or you get depressed, take a hot bath with aromatic salts. The urges and the feelings will pass," is what this sober mentor told me.

Julie (not her real name) had lots of gems that you might call tricks of the sober trade. The basic premise is that you cannot replace "drinking" merely with "not drinking." The recovering alcoholic must reward herself in different ways. For me, the whole process was like learning to walk again.

By this stage of my disease, I associated so much of what I did with alcohol consumption that I had to retool a lot of my daily habits. For example, I associated going out to the beach at sunset and watching the sun disappear behind the ocean with drinking because I always used to bring a glass of wine with me. It wasn't so much that I craved alcohol. It was that I didn't know how to enjoy an experience like that without alcohol. The two were enmeshed.

It took me a while to disentangle alcohol from everyday pleasures and reinvent them. I soon learned to take a hot cup of tea with me to the beach and watch the sun set. There's a reason they call non-drinkers teetotalers. The desire to sip tea or coffee, with its little caffeine punch, becomes a new craving.

"Learn to sit through the feelings. Know that they don't last forever." That was another pearl of wisdom from Julie.

The most frightening aspect of new sobriety? Old feelings I'd been stuffing for years came roaring to the surface. Out of nowhere, the world would go black. An enormous sense of doom would envelop me. Everything seemed toxic and almost evil. I distinctly remember walking with my dog on the beach one day when this occurred. It was a gorgeous day. I was near the ocean in a part of California that the whole world longs to visit, and, yet, it suddenly all seemed tainted and sinister to me. I remembered what Julie told me and kept walking.

"The feelings will pass, the feelings will pass," I kept repeating to myself. I walked about a mile until I reached the jetty and watched as yachts and sailboats came in and out of the marina. My dog began playing with some other dogs. For a few moments, I forgot about myself. After a while, I realized that the darkness had passed and I was okay again. The whole thing had lasted about forty-five minutes. Julie was right. The feelings don't last forever. In any case, there are plenty of other options to deal with those feelings other than having a drink. I called sober friends. I went to the movies. I journaled about my feelings. I exercised. I slept. I ate.

There was also the other extreme, what we call in sobriety the *pink cloud**. Overall, I was so relieved that I was no longer crippled by a craving to get drunk that I actually felt a little tipsy on life. In fact, the dichotomy of sobriety is that it can be intoxicating all by itself. At first, I wondered, *How the heck will I be able to socialize without having a drink in my hand?* But I quickly realized that I was actually more comfortable at parties as a sober person, because I didn't have to worry about doing or saying something wildly inappropriate.

I can't really get into that much trouble when I'm sober, I realized somewhat giddily.

At the point that I got sober, I was so tired of my years of living dangerously that I relished the sense of safety and security that I got from having all my senses and wits about me. It's kind of like regaining your virginity . . . a miracle. Still, I was convinced that when I got sober, "fun" as I had grown to define it was over. Boy was I wrong.

It didn't register completely at the time, but before I'd gotten sober, I'd gotten some clues that sober people can still party until dawn. Back when I was still drinking, I met a woman who—to this day—I call my guru. Debbie is a rollerblading teacher, and I had signed up for some classes with her at a parking lot along Santa Monica Beach. I showed up for my first class, in typical fashion, late and badly hungover.

"I need to get some coffee before we do this," I muttered, as Debbie energetically laced up our blades.

Years later, Debbie chuckled as she told me that she immediately recognized me as an addict. (Just like some people have "gaydar," some people have "drunkdar.")

One evening, a couple of years before I quit drinking, Debbie came to my place for a New Year's Eve party. She showed up in a short bright-red party dress that showed off her taut body. She quickly took center stage. She had a wand full of glitter and went around sprinkling my other guests, who were too tipsy on champagne to put up a fuss. Next, she started dancing and was soon surrounded by astounded gawkers. She moved like a stripper.

"You are lots of fun. We've got to go out barhopping sometime," I slurred.

"Sure," she smiled back. "But I don't drink. I'm thirteen years sober."

I was shocked. *How could anyone be having that much fun and not be wasted?* It was one of those early moments of partial revelation that gave me a flash of what could be. It was as if the clouds opened up for a moment and then moved back in. I wasn't ready to act on what I saw just yet. But as I look back, there were many contributing factors to my ultimately embracing sobriety. Debbie's joyous attitude in sobriety had a definite impact. Now more than twenty-seven years sober, she remains one of those people who is truly high on life. From the moment I met her, I wanted what she had. That's another example of why they say the Twelve Steps are about *attraction not promotion**.

As I got some sobriety under my belt, I also began to enjoy the thrills of sobriety. There are a lot of things that it's more exciting to do sober. Take karaoke. I used to love karaokeing back when I drank. "Desperado" was my signature song, and I could butcher it in a way that was strangely hypnotic. "Summertime" was another favorite.

When I sang "hush little baby . . . " the crowd would scream, "Hush! Hush!" I barely noticed.

I found kareokeing sober to be much more intimidating. Suddenly, up on stage, I actually noticed that I was off-key and tried to adjust. I found myself actually paying attention to the response of the people watching and listening. Like Sally Field, I wanted them to like me. When I managed to deliver a pretty good rendition of the Latin classic "Besame Mucho," and got some applause, I was jazzed. It was much more fun to be *present**, experiencing the moment in all its . . . perspiration.

But the real challenge of sobriety was the spiritual work I was challenged to do. I wouldn't have been able to stay sober without a major spiritual housecleaning. Because of my father's alcoholism and the alcoholism in his extended family, I know that I was genetically predisposed to alcoholism. Then, watching my father's drinking, I was also environmentally exposed to it.

But another component of the disease, which is both a cause and an effect, is a spiritual toxicity. Some call this the alcoholic's *soul sickness**. This rancid attitude manifests itself in an overall cynicism about life, a sense that life is a joke and not worthy of being taken seriously. Perhaps more than anything else, practicing alcoholics abhor earnestness. The alcoholic dichotomy is this: while alcoholics exert tremendous energy pretending to be happy-go-lucky and care-free, alcoholism is really a terrible coping method for an underlying fear and pessimism about life. After all, we drink to escape. So, obviously, alcoholics—in feeling the need to drink a lot—believe there is much from which they need to escape. At the end of a long week, reporting on murders, rapes, and other senseless cruelty, all I could think of was hitting a bar and knocking back the best chardonnay that bartender had to offer. That's why experts call boozing or drugging *self-medicating**. The Twelve Steps helped me break down the wall of cynicism and confront the fears buried beneath.

They are listed in the back of this book so you can refer to them. But here's how they helped me. They gave me a simple system, upon which I could always depend, by which to live a more honorable life. The first few Steps are about change. As I started on them, I had to admit that the old way I was doing things had left my life *unmanageable**. I acknowledged that I really needed to change to survive!

I was a mess when I first got sober: *spiritually bankrupt**. Somehow, I had managed to hang on to my job, my condo, my car, and my 401K. So I guess that made me a *high bottom**, which is sober-speak for not being a Bowery bum. But my bottom didn't feel all that high when I turned myself in. I felt like I skidded in on my ass.

When I finally surrendered, I was forced to accept the obvious truth that I had ignored for years: when it comes to alcohol, my willpower is useless! Addiction pulverizes even the superwillful. It was actually a relief to stop pretending I had any control and accept that I was *powerless** over booze. The Steps then led me to the next logical conclusion. Since I am powerless, obviously some "other" power is needed to overcome my addiction. The Steps call this a *power greater than ourselves**.

This stops some people from moving forward because it brings in the God issue. That's a shame. There are a plenty of sober atheists and agnostics who work the Steps. I was relieved to find out that we all get to choose what our higher power is. It could be your conception of God, or nature, or . . . anything you want to make it . . . Marilyn Monroe, your cat . . . what*ever*! You can also change it whenever you want. Right now, my higher power happens to be everything BUT me. In other words, when I get my ego out of the way and reach out to whatever else is there, that's when I feel in contact with my higher power. God is not me. And I am not God. That, to me, is the crux of the issue for addicts. Here's a good shorthand: *EGO = Edging God Out**.

As an addict, I used my drug of choice—alcohol—to alter my perception of reality. Was it dreary and raining outside and making me feel down? I just fixed a cocktail and adjusted the weather from within. Was I yelled at by my boss? I'd just go to the bar and drink and drink until I was making up dirty jokes about him. You get the idea. Addiction is all about not accepting *life on life's terms**. I wanted to control everything! What a relief to give that up. So, while your higher power can be anything you want it to be, if you hope to plug into it, first unplug your willful, ego-based thinking.

The Steps then asked me to take an honest inventory of my life, admitting the things I'd done wrong, all those terrible secrets that had me walking around with guilt and shame. Like many addicts, I irrationally clung to my worst traits, bragging about my ability to exceed the speed limit, work on little sleep, and, in general, sidestep the rules that seemed to govern everyone else. I was the classic addict in that I considered myself special and different: sometimes above, sometimes below, but never the same as anyone else. They call this "terminally unique" because it's an attitude that often leads to various kinds of termination, from jobs or even from life itself. The Steps forced me to face my character defects unflinchingly and then become willing to let them go.

As part of my shift into a more spiritual, less narcissistic existence, I was told I needed to get on my knees and pray every day to establish an ongoing relationship with my higher power. My first reaction to this suggestion was, "Please tell me you're kidding." As a triple type-A recovering clubhopper, the idea of my getting down on my knees and praying felt stupendously weird. In my mind, it was right up there with speaking in tongues. However, as my wise mentor Julie informed me, it feels embarrassing and stupid, but nobody has to watch and it works. She was right.

I try to get down on my knees and pray every morning. The truth is I don't bat a thousand on this. I have to admit that I am more likely to get on my knees if I have a big day ahead of me or my life has hit a rough patch. When I'm skating, when things are just golden, I mix it up a little bit. On good days I'll just say a quick prayer, sometimes in the bath or in the car.

"I can't. You can. Please do!" is one of my favorite quickies.

I cop to being a lazy spiritualist at times. I want to get more consistent, because when I do pray with gusto, in an unhurried way, it really puts me on a spiritual beam that allows me to meet the day's challenges in an evolved manner.

Working the Steps required me to make amends by apologizing to those people I had hurt, except when contacting them would do more harm. I apologized to several ex-boyfriends. My ex-husband, Michael, was definitely on the list. So were members of my family and some coworkers. I'm sure there are people out there who I still need to apologize to and, if you're reading this and you're one of them, please accept my apology.

A wonderful aspect of this process is that you can also do *living amends**, making up for past harm done by doing something positive, perhaps charity work or a donation to a cause. I regard all the time and energy I spend on animal causes and the donations that I make as a way of exercising compassion, in part, to make up for past insensitivity and self-centeredness.

Finally, the Steps instructed me to carry this message to other people who are still suffering and who could use the guidance. There are a lot of people out there who are like I was, a slave to their substance of choice with no clue how to escape. In my case, it wasn't drugs or pills. Like most people my age, I dabbled, but I wasn't hooked, or even that interested. Alcohol was definitely my first and only true love in the substance department. By telling my story, others may get ideas on how to deal with their own substance of choice, be it alcohol, pills, cigarettes, sex, food, sugar, a person, a behavior, or stuff. It may help inspire them to get the help they need.

Why was I so afraid of getting that help myself? There was, of course, the embarrassment of acknowledging to myself and to the world that I had this problem. But as my wise mentor Julie pointed out, nothing you do sober is ever as embarrassing as what you've already done drunk.

I've used the Twelve Steps in every aspect of my life, which is what is suggested. I no longer waste my time and energy trying to control things that are clearly beyond my control. This is a central theme of recovery. Hence, the *Serenity Prayer**, which says: "Grant me the serenity to accept the things I cannot change, the power to change the things I can, and the wisdom to know the difference."

Control issues stem from ego and fear. When alcoholics are in their disease, their egos are almost invariably out of control. Self-medicating is all about playing God, trying to control everything by altering and adjusting one's perception with booze. It's like that joke, "The more I drink, the more interesting you get." In sobriety, if you're talking to a boring person, there's no way to make that person more interesting. This is why sobriety is described as dealing with life on life's terms. Of course, as I already mentioned, underneath the alcoholic's egotistical, and often manic, desire to control everything is a deep fear and pessimistic belief system that their perception of life needs to be adjusted by mood-altering substances because, in its unvarnished state, life is just awful. The happier a drunk acts, the more depressed he or she actually is.

Back when I drank, ego and fear were the two horsemen of my own personal apocalypse. Thanks to the Steps, I have methods to get my ego and fear out of the way, or at least get a *daily reprieve**. My favorite prayer is to ask my higher power to free me from ego and my fear.

"Free me from ego. Free me from fear. Free me from ego. Free me from fear." I say it over and over again, preferably on my knees, until I feel a sense of humility overtake me, indicating my ego has gone out for a Starbucks, undoubtedly to return, but just not right away. Free of ego, I ask my higher power to make me a conduit for whatever message it needs to send or whatever job it needs me to do.

I say, "Help me get out of my own way, so I can suit up, show up, do the next indicated thing, stay out of the results, be a worker amongst workers, and humbly be of service."

Then, I get up and feel a tremendous sense of freedom. Since it's no longer about me, all my fear is gone. I have *surrendered the results** and am free to merely do *the next indicated thing**. To me, that is such a fabulous discovery: get rid of your ego and you also get rid of your fear.

In the Twelve Steps, there are certain promises made to the alcoholic. The notion is that, by practicing these principles, we alcoholics will experience true freedom, happiness, serenity, and peace. We are told we will lose the sense of being a victim and the self-pity that comes with it. We are promised we will lose the narcissism that became so malignant in our lives. Instead, we will become genuinely interested in helping others. We are also told we will develop coping skills that will help us deal with situations that used to completely devastate or baffle us.

All of these promises are based on elevating our internal state of being so that we value things differently. The Twelve Steps help us develop a criteria for living based on fundamental spiritual tenets like self-forgetting and being of service to others. Once I got sober, I started feeling these powerful inner shifts. Many of the egotistical reasons I desired to get ahead fell by the wayside, in a very natural and unforced way. I can take no credit for it. In the same organic way, I began to harbor a passion to do something meaningful for something or someone beyond myself. I always loved animals but about a year after I got sober, I developed this determination to do something about animal suffering. I began to feel a calling. It sounds a bit dramatic, but that's really the accurate description. The many hours that I once spent trolling bars and nightclubs were now mine to use in a positive way. I jumped into action as an animal-rights activist.

Partying it up a tad too much in West Hollywood on Halloween, 1993—two years before I sobered up.

5

Veganism/Animal Activism: *I Want to Make a Difference*

One day when I was eight, my mom and my dog, Mr. Monday, walked me to school as they often did. I said goodbye to them both and went inside. My mother tells me that, on that particular day, Mr. Monday began howling after I left. With good reason, it turns out. Animals are incredibly intuitive. When my mother picked me up from school that day, I immediately noticed something was amiss.

"Where's Mr. Monday?" I asked.

Mr. Monday was gone. My parents had given him away . . . without telling me they were going to. I was shocked and deeply traumatized. At that age, it was impossible for me to articulate my feelings.

I don't remember if I cried, but I do remember going into a prolonged state of depression. Being the only child in the household, Mr. Monday was my salvation, my best friend, and my brother. I cry today when I think about him. *Where did he go?* I'll never know.

How could they have done such a thing? My mother was opposed to it but my father insisted we get rid of him. We were moving to a fancier apartment and Dad didn't want the dog to mess up the new wall-to-wall carpet. So, they called the man who had originally found Mr. Monday in an alley behind a bar. Cosmo was a pool hustler and an alcoholic, a forever down-on-his-luck friend of my mom's from her showbiz days who seemed to have walked out of a Fellini movie. I had been begging for a dog for as long as I could speak. One day, he walked in with this little brown-and-white dog and I was ecstatic. Mr. Monday wasn't trained and he wasn't neutered, and we never got him trained or fixed. So, naturally, he had accidents in the apartment. Dad wasn't pleased. Did they ever read a book about dog training or seek some help? No. They got rid of the dog, breaking my heart in the process. Some of my fondest memories of childhood are with Mr. Monday, my best buddy and soul mate.

I've since learned that kids usually feel tremendous empathy with the discarded dog. Because kids relate to animals, the child's thinking is along the lines of *could I be next?* The unconditional nature of ideal love is undermined by the possibility that has now entered the equation. One member of the family was tossed out for making mistakes or simply because he had become inconvenient. The betrayal of that animal leaves a lasting scar on the child who concludes that his or her parents are not to be trusted.

We moved into our fancy new digs with the wall-to-wall carpeting and without Mr. Monday. Literally, the first thing I did was knock over a lamp and walk away. The lamp was on and the bulb burned a hole in the new carpeting. My dad was furious. "What were you thinking?" he demanded. I burst into tears. All the pent-up rage and grief I felt over Mr. Monday's abrupt disappearance came spilling out in a torrent of sobs. My parents couldn't figure out what had made me so upset. I didn't say anything about Mr. Monday. How could I? I only made the connection decades later when I had processed the loss of my dog in therapy. As a reminder, the burn hole was still there in the now ancient carpet in my mother's apartment. Dogs are more important than carpets. Children's feelings are more important than carpets.

Mr. Monday was my "Rosebud." He was my first love and the heartache I felt over his abrupt removal from my life changed me forever. Life was no longer idyllic. I got sarcastic and mischievous. But through that tragedy, I also found my passion and my mission . . . to stop animal suffering.

Decades later, I finally got another dog. Baja was adopted from an animal shelter. This amazing dog had a big, distinctive black patch over her left eye. One day, looking at Baja, I suddenly remembered—with a jolt—that I used to call Mr. Monday Black-Eyed Mitchell, which was odd because Mr. Monday didn't have a black eye. Feeling like I'd seen a ghost, I rummaged around and found a painting I did as a kid of Mr. Monday. In that painting, I had also—for unknown reasons—given Mr. Monday a circle of black around his eye. It matched Baja's perfectly. I got the chills. Suddenly, I felt like Mr. Monday was with me again, just in a slightly different form. Perhaps there is a secret dimension that would make sense of this often crazy and cruel world, if only we could tap into it.

Since my mom followed a mostly vegetarian diet, I was raised that same way. She'd told me that when she was a little girl in Puerto Rico, she had experienced her own trauma involving the loss of a pet, which had set her on the road to vegetarianism. She had bonded with a little pig who she'd named and grown to love. One day, arriving home from school, she whiffed the unmistakable smell of pork and, unable to find her pet pig, realized they had killed her friend for dinner. What a betrayal. My mother became hysterical and refused to eat. From that day forward, she refused all meat but fish.

So, thanks to my mother's influence, I ate mostly fish, vegetables, fruits, nuts, and grains growing up. On a few occasions in the summertime, when I was a child, somebody would bring hamburgers over for cookouts. But by the time I turned twelve or thirteen, I had shunned most meat and had become pescatarian, meaning the only flesh I ate was fish.

In high school, I began learning about vivisection and the other horrors that were perpetrated upon animals. Had I not started drinking and partying around that time, I would have had the energy to jump into animal activism back then. Unfortunately, my lifestyle derailed any plans to put my passion to work, and I failed to do anything but talk about saving animals. We did adopt a cat, whom I named Anisette after the liqueur. That was an indicator of how important alcohol was to me as a teenager. I even named my pets after booze. In fact, years later when I adopted a parakeet, I named him Tequila Sunrise. Still, I was aware of the wrongs many animals suffered; I just didn't have the gumption to follow through on my feelings.

When I finally got sober, I found that I could no longer ignore the cruelty toward animals that was all around me—the fur coats; the veal; the unnecessary torture of laboratory animals; the slaughter of horses; and the unspeakable horrors of factory farming, where 10 *billion* pigs, cows, lambs, and chickens are raised and slaughtered for food every year. To me, they were all Mr. Monday.

I did news reports about these issues, and the more I learned, the more distraught I became. I realized that this was America's dirty little secret. While Americans pride themselves on loving animals and castigate other cultures, such as the Koreans for eating dog meat, we are quite possibly the cruelest society on earth because of the sheer numbers of animals we slaughter to eat, wear on our bodies, or torture in our labs.

The first time I saw a video of a factory farm for pigs while doing an investigative report on factory farming, I thought to myself, *This can't be real.* But it was. Orwellian doesn't even begin to describe it. Pigs—which have a higher IQ than dogs—are kept in crates the size of their bodies, unable to turn around or even take a step, stacked by the thousands in dark warehouses where they never see the light of day. The pigs would become psychotic. Watching the videotape, I was emotionally shattered by their screams.

"My god, they can't even scratch themselves," I would tell any-body who would listen. Many people not only didn't care, they thought I was nuts *to* care. How's that for backward thinking? But before I could change anyone else's behavior towards our fellow crea-tures, I had to change my own.

"So, I hear you're a vegetarian?" The question was posed to me by a fierce activist, Marr Nealon. She was working as a publicist for Howard Lyman, the author of the astounding book *Mad Cowboy: Plain Truth from the Cattle Rancher Who Won't Eat Meat.*

I had just interviewed Lyman for my newscast at KCAL-TV/Channel 9 in Los Angeles. Lyman had become a lightning rod for controversy after his explosive appearance on *The Oprah Winfrey Show.* Lyman is a former fourth-generation cattle rancher who, after a life-threatening illness, turned against his industry and decided to expose the grotesque way animals are fed and treated.

"It has just stopped me cold from eating another burger," Oprah declared on her show in 1996 after Lyman laid out his claims that some cattle, which are by nature herbivores, had been fed ground-up cattle parts.

Said Lyman, "We've not only turned them into carnivores, we've turned them into cannibals."

Livid because Oprah's remark sent cattle prices tumbling, Texas cattlemen filed a defamation lawsuit against her. They eventually lost. Lyman became a cause célèbre. His book tour brought him into my studio and my life.

More than a decade later, serious public health issues still abound in the business of raising and slaughtering animals for food in America. If you have any doubts, just look at the footage shot by the many courageous, anonymous, undercover investigators for the Humane Society of the United States (HSUS) and other organizations such as People for the Ethical Treatment of Animals (PETA). These videos are widely available on the Internet.

One Humane Society investigation sparked a national uproar over the treatment of cows. Posing as a worker, the HSUS investigator infiltrated a slaughterhouse in Chino, California, packing a tiny video camera. Broadcast in early 2008, the video shows the Hallmark slaughterhouse workers engaged in horrific, sadistic abuse of downed cows. These are cows too sick to stand. By law, they are supposed to be removed from the food-supply chain as they are considered unfit for human consumption. Downed cows are said to be at higher risk of mad cow disease and other illnesses, since they are likely to wallow in feces and have weakened systems. The workers were caught on tape kicking the sick cows, jabbing them in the eyes, zapping them with painful electrical shocks, torturing them by forcing water down their throats and violently prodding them with forklifts, all so they would move toward the slaughter pen. Because of the atrocities uncovered at the slaughterhouse, which was not only barbaric but which potentially compromised the safety of the food, the USDA issued the largest beef recall in United States history. Sadly, most of the food had already been consumed, with much of it sent to school children. In a sad irony, this slaughterhouse supplied a company that was one of the largest distributors of beef to a USDA program that sends meat to needy families, the elderly, and the National School Lunch Program.[1]

Even those who've snickered in the past at animal activists found themselves horrified by the video showing cows being hit and literally

---

[1]   *http://www.msnbc.msn.com/id/23212514/http://www.hsus.org/farm/news/ournews/ undercover_investigation.html, accessed April 2009.*

run over by farm vehicles. The moaning of those tortured cows is something that would leave only a sociopath unmoved.

"Am I a vegetarian? Yeah, sure." I told Marr. I wasn't really. I still ate shrimp and clams, rationalizing that I needed something to order at a restaurant, but I fancied myself a vegetarian. "So do you eat dairy products?" Marr persisted.

"Ah, yeah," I stammered, thinking about what Howard had just told me about infant male calves being ripped from their dairy cow mothers, moments after birth, to be chained in darkened veal crates.

My mind was doing the math. Meat and dairy: it's all part of the same hideously cruel system. When you buy a quart of milk, you're subsidizing veal.

Marr watched me squirm. "You know what I call dairy?" she asked, not waiting for the answer, "*Liquid meat**." She topped it off with a withering look.

That was the moment I became a *vegan**. Going vegan means eliminating all animal products—without exception—including dairy, eggs, fish/shellfish, and even bee products. As a vegan, I do not eat animals, and I don't wear them! That means no fur, no leather, no wool, and no silk. I also shun cosmetics, personal-grooming products, and household cleaning products that contain animal ingredients or are tested on animals. One person taking these actions saves the lives of many hundreds of animals a year.

I consider this to be a prime example of how sobriety inspires meaningful change. Had I not recently gotten sober, I would have probably drowned Marr's message and the discomfort that came with it at the local bar. Drinkers don't really look for solutions. A drinker's solution is always . . . another drink. But since I was sober at the time I met Marr and Howard, I was able to listen, learn, and proceed accordingly.

Without a doubt, getting sober and going vegan are absolutely the two best decisions I've ever made in my life. They totally transformed me. I used to complain bitterly about this world. I used to wonder why we couldn't achieve peace. Then, I learned something astounding: *"Peace begins on your plate."**

I was having lunch with a woman who does a lot of work for peace. She is a brilliant, accomplished and—in most ways—an extraordinarily compassionate human being. She was telling me about her work to stop violence when I looked down at her plate. She was eating lamb, and it was rare. It was swimming in blood.

"I'm sorry, but I'm having a disconnect over what you're telling me about your work for peace and what's on your plate," I said, trying hard not to be hurtful.

She looked startled. "Now I feel bad about what I ordered."

I explained to her that I wasn't trying to judge her. I was trying to point out that, to truly be peacemakers, we have to try to practice peace in every action that we take throughout the day. Peace isn't out there. It's inside.

I have spent time with lambs at amazing sanctuaries like Farm Sanctuary and Animal Acres. Lambs are like little children. They're gentle and playful, soft and trusting. They jump with excitement and make *baa'ing* sounds that touch the soul. How can we cut their throats and call ourselves civilized? We can't. To my friend's credit, she did not become defensive and kept an open mind, visiting a vegan restaurant on her own and exploring the issue. I always say, *Personal growth is a process, not an event!*

Today, my dual mantra is: *As long as I am sober and as long as I can get through this day without killing or harming another living creature, I am a winner, no matter what else happens.*

By going vegan, the average American consumer can become a hero, sparing the lives of hundreds of animals every year. I was taught to visualize all those pigs, lambs, calves, chickens, rabbits, and other creatures gathered around me, nuzzling me, thanking me for letting them live. As a vegan, I also do not donate to research causes that experiment on animals. And I don't invest in the stocks of companies that use animals in any way. A fascinating side benefit has been that my unusual investment criteria has helped me weather the market well, even in turbulent times. Shunning animal exploitation forced me to invest in some of the most forward-thinking, technologically advanced companies out there. You don't have to be exploitative to make money.

There's a tremendous euphoria that comes from going through life without killing. Just as sobriety cleansed and elevated me, so did going vegan. I would say that both transformations are miracles. The vegan transformation I've experienced goes way beyond diet. It's really allowed me to put my spiritual and moral concepts into action on a daily basis.

Every morsel of food I put into my mouth is an environmental, political, moral, and spiritual choice. Every household product I buy is an environmental, political, moral, and spiritual choice. I always try to think before I choose. Sometimes, when I'm in a quandary, I pray before I choose. When I'm torn or weakened by cravings, I ask my higher power for guidance. I've worked on many animal causes. Some of them involve assisting animals left to fend for themselves in time of war, like the Israeli-Hezbollah conflict in 2006, where hundreds of thousands of citizens evacuated southern Lebanon during the Israeli invasion. Does anybody even think of what happens to animals during times of war? The animals in zoos are left to starve. Farm animals are abandoned and left to die a slow death. During the Lebanon conflict, Best Friends Animal Society, based in Utah, rescued 295 dogs and cats from the war-ravaged streets of Beirut, flying them out of the country and back to their huge animal sanctuary in aptly named Angel Canyon, Utah. I simply donated to that rescue effort.

"Serious" people are prone to shake their heads and ask, "Why not help the people affected by war?"

I do care about the people. It's not a competition. Helping people and helping animals are not mutually exclusive. In fact, such efforts are totally compatible and dovetail in many ways. The day we are incapable of leaving a donkey to starve to death in a time of war is the day we will have evolved as a species beyond war.

How we treat animals is a litmus test for our level of civility and compassion. Animals are the most helpless, most powerless, most voiceless creatures in our world. If we can torture and exploit them, and we do, then we are capable of torturing and exploiting anyone less powerful than ourselves.

Being kind to animals is also good for our health. Studies show the countries with the highest longevity rates have heavily plant-based diets. In fact, my mother, who has followed a mostly vegetarian diet, is ninety-three and in excellent health with all her wits about her. I definitely think her diet is a factor in her longevity.

"My friends used to make fun of me because I would invite them over and serve them vegetarian food," my mother recently told me. "Oh, Anita, they would say, you are so eccentric!" My mom smiled as she savored her punch line: "Well, I had the last laugh. I went to every one of their funerals."

Becoming a vegan allowed me to get rid of most of the toxic elements of my diet, and as a result, I feel more energetic. They lie to us when the ads say that milk is good for our bodies. Actually, the opposite is true. Dairy is one of the most common undiagnosed allergies in America. Lots of people with dripping sinuses, dandruff, acne, and other unpleasant conditions see those problems disappear when they give up dairy. When I gave up dairy, the colds that used to plague me every winter simply went away.

What's more, we are the only species that steals the mother's milk from another species and drinks it for ourselves. Cow's milk is meant to fatten up wobbly little calves, not humans. America's obesity crisis is intertwined with our massive consumption of dairy products. Humans are meant to drink the milk of their human mothers until they are weaned. After that, they do not need milk. There is plenty of calcium in tofu, almonds, cabbage, fresh orange juice, and other fruits and vegetables. Google CALCIUM SOURCES and a host of dairy-free alternatives will pop up.

So many people say, "Oh, but I can't give up cheese."

A couple of months after I went vegan, I ordered a salad and didn't notice they'd put cheese in it. I took one bite and spit it out in disgust.

Cheese, which I used to love, now tasted repulsive to me. It seems my taste buds had returned to their natural state. We are conditioned to crave certain foods to which we might not naturally gravitate. Lots of children do not initially like the taste of meat and spit it out. But under pressure from their misguided parents, who erroneously believe that it's essential for their well-being, these children gradually develop a taste for it and then get hooked. It's just like alcohol. I was conditioned to crave alcohol. Thank God my parents didn't condition me to crave meat.

My nephew Paul also became a vegan. He has a daughter, Nicole, who has never tasted meat or dairy products. When Nicole was little, some of the other parents would look askance, wondering if Paul was doing the right thing by raising his child without any animal products in her diet. Nicole, now twelve, is not only very healthy and beautiful, she is one of the tallest girls in her class and one of the top students. So much for needing to shove meat and dairy down a child's throat for them to thrive. It's all nonsense.

The last thing we should be doing is pushing meat and dairy on our kids. That's what they get when they eat at fast-food restaurants. With new studies showing that almost one in five 4-year olds in America is obese, the obvious conclusion is that there is something seriously wrong with our current meat, dairy, and sugar-laden diet.[2]

Instead, we should be giving our children real food: sandwiches made with thick whole-grain breads and stuffed with veggies;

---

[2] *http://www.google.com/hostednews/ap/article/ALeqM5iWYxFm-xYioKQmzsZjCWRKW fNbiwD97D9NB00, accessed April 2009.*

casseroles and stir-fries made with brown rice, bok choy, and tofu; hot cereals made from organic oats. If they're exposed early, they will grow up enjoying these healthy, real foods. Anybody who is repeatedly exposed to fast food is almost guaranteed to become hooked on it.

The Machiavellian minds that have turned America into a *fast-food nation** realized that, if you pack any food with enough fat (which comes in the form of dairy and meat) plus sugar and salt, people will crave more of it. Nature gave us built-in cravings for fat, sugar, and salt to help us withstand times of famine. Now those natural urges are being exploited, sparking an epidemic of obesity. We are, quite simply, a nation of junk- and fast-food addicts. Within that overall addiction, there is the subset addiction to meat, dairy, sugar, and salt. Like any addictive substance, the *user** can never quite get enough to satisfy the craving. Eating fast food triggers a desire for more of the same. Hence, the long lines at the drive-thru burger joint. Addicts will always seek ways to justify and legitimize their habit. Sadly, in America today, the powers that be are giving fast-food addicts all the ammunition they need to commit slow suicide, equating fast food with everything from patriotism to protein.

"But where do you get your protein?" People always ask me when they find out I'm a vegan. Just as we're sold a bill of goods about milk being good for us, we're also brainwashed to consume far more protein than is necessary or actually good for us. If protein were so good for us, we'd be—by far—the healthiest nation on earth. But we're far from it. Protein is important, but not in the grotesque quantities we're consuming. We've falsely associated protein with strength. A horse eats grass and grain. Yet, it's one of the fastest animals on earth. A horse is plenty muscular and totally vegan. If you want to run like a horse and not look like a house, switch to veggie burgers.

As I got deeper into the animal-rights movement, I began to look for ways to use my reporting skills to help animals. Sometimes my animal activism sparked resentment in the newsroom. In the news business we have "kicker stories," lighthearted segments that run at the end of a newscast designed to leave people laughing. Some of these kickers involved animal exploitation, and I refused to read them as written. They weren't funny to me. Taking frozen turkeys and using them as bowling balls isn't cute. It's obscene and disrespectful. These were once sentient beings who lived horrible lives and were subjected to horrific deaths. To use them as props, as if they were never living, breathing creatures, is callous, not to mention wasteful. Others in the newsroom mocked me for these beliefs. I totally expected to be ridiculed.

There are three stages to a social-justice movement: ridicule, anger, and acceptance. When they made fun of me, it just confirmed my suspicions that I was on the right track. Sometimes people would get angry and adopt a pose of righteous indignation. In their minds, I was some kind of dangerous kook threatening the proper and established order of things. I'm sure this was what dealing with the "flat earth society" was like. But, on the bright side, in the last couple of years, I've seen a big shift in attitudes. Whether it's the Michael Vick dog-fighting case, the Canadian seal hunt, or the scandal over downed cows being tortured at slaughterhouses, animal issues are finally being treated more seriously by the media and the public at large. On my show, *Issues*, on HLN, I've been able to do numerous stories on animal rights, including a one-hour special on animal issues that looked at puppy mills and factory farming. But my first big breakthrough in getting animal stories on the air came thanks to my dear friend and mentor Harvey Levin. An attorney and journalist, Harvey is one of the smartest people I have ever met. In 2002, Harvey started a syndicated TV show called *Celebrity Justice*. It was a precursor to his current mega-hit TV show/Internet site *TMZ*, which stands for *Thirty Mile Zone*. The concept is that everything important in the celebrity/showbiz world happens within a thirty-mile radius of Hollywood. *Celebrity Justice* was the first iteration of this new genre of reporting on celebrities in hot water.

By this time, I was more than seven years sober and had been vegan almost as many years. My reputation as a lush was pretty much behind me. Now, I was more known for my veganism and animal activism. Some people jokingly called me "Granola Jane." It's amazing how easy it is to change your reputation. Most people actually have very short memories. I experienced a genuine transformation and presented my new self to the world. I was delighted to find that most people were extraordinarily accepting of my new identity.

At *Celebrity Justice*, there was a meeting every morning at 7:30. At this meeting, we would each have to present story ideas. All the stories had to involve two things: celebrities and justice. I spent a lot of time chasing celebrities in and out of Los Angeles courthouses. Divorce, drug addiction, drunk-driving accidents, sexual harassment lawsuits, assault cases, murder, and molestation trials: these were my stock-in-trade for the three years the show ran. For public relations people, whose job it is to keep a lid on the private lives of Holly-wood's nutty, addicted, out-of-control celebrities, our show was their worst nightmare come true. We exposed the messy reality behind the glamorous façade in a way that had never been done before: using court documents. Divorce papers almost invariably provided juicy details about celebrities, details not usually seen on television.

But we also had to do some celebrity-friendly stories, if only to keep our studios from being torched by some publicist we'd driven mad. One way to do that was to focus on the favorite charities of movie and TV stars. One of the biggest causes in Hollywood is ani-mal rights. There are more stars passionately involved in animal pro-tection than virtually any other cause. I took this ball and ran with it.

Working in coordination with PETA, the Humane Society, and Farm Sanctuary—three amazing organizations—I profiled numerous stars and the animal issues closest to their hearts. Pamela Anderson has a cruelty-free clothing line and protests against cruel factory farm-ing. Dennis Rodman posed nude for the "I'd rather go naked than wear fur" PETA campaign. Alicia Silverstone has a passion for veganism. Joaquin Phoenix starred in an ad campaign to get us to stop eating turkeys for Thanksgiving. I interviewed *Babe* star James Cromwell, who delivered eloquent arguments that pigs should not be kept in tiny crates. Comedian and political pundit Bill Maher vented his anger to me about the absurd laboratory experiments being conducted on primates to prove that smoking is bad, which we already know.

Here's a typical example of how these animal stories would unfold. While driving to work from the Venice area to Glendale, a trek of about thirty miles, I would scan the radio stations for celebrity gossip, which in Hollywood, comes on almost as often as the traffic and the weather. I would be weaving my Toyota Prius through the traffic on the 405 freeway, which was considerable even at 6:30 AM, desperately scrounging for a story idea.

One morning, I heard a reporter say Robert Redford was going to be showing up for the grand opening of the Natural Resources Defense Council's new "green" building in Santa Monica. My ears perked up: a celebrity! But as Harvey would invariable ask me, "Where's the justice?" Then, I remembered that I had recently received a form letter from Robert Redford asking for help in his battle to protect whales from the military sonar that often disorients and kills them.

When Harvey asked me at the morning meeting, "Whaddya got?" I was ready. "Robert Redford is fighting to protect whales and will be in Santa Monica this morning at the grand opening of the NRDC's new green building."

Harvey gave me a look. I could read his mind: *It's always the same thing with this one . . . animals, animals, animals.* But the man now known as the King of Hollywood for having exposed the bad behavior of so many big celebs, from Mel Gibson on down, is really a very soft touch. He loves animals himself and always rescues older dogs from the pound.

After pausing for a moment, Harvey shot back. "If you can get a one-on-one interview with Robert Redford, you can do the story."

I gulped. That was a tall order. A celebrity of Redford's caliber doesn't just plop down and gab on camera with anyone who strolls by, especially not for a "tabloidy" show like ours. "Don't worry, I'll get him," I said with a certain bravado, and I headed for the door.

It was wall-to-wall media at the NRDC offices. I was quickly informed that Mr. Redford was only giving interviews to the networks with whom his people had made prior arrangements, but I was welcome to attend the rooftop news conference where Redford would appear. I knew that wouldn't cut it. Harvey had specifically said I needed to get a one-on-one interview.

Back on the street, I trained my eyes on some public relations guy who was holding a walkie-talkie.

Giving him my best sad puppy-dog look, I began begging. "Look, I'm on your side. I'm an environmentalist. I drive a Prius. I'm a vegan. I devote my whole life to saving the planet. Please help me out."

The PR guy sighed and grudgingly relented. "He's coming in via the alley in the back."

Racing to the alley, I hid behind a dumpster, clutching my wireless microphone. My photographer was nearby, also out of view. While dozens of media outlets had converged on the building, we were the only ones in the alley. Suddenly, a sparkling-red Thunderbird convertible pulled up and out popped Redford, as handsome as ever.

I dashed out from behind the dumpster with my mike in hand, my cameraman trailing me. "Mr. Redford, I got your letter about the whales!" I cried out.

Startled, he looked at me. "Who is that?" he asked a member of his entourage. Before anyone could answer, Redford disappeared inside the building.

"Well that didn't work," I said to my photographer ruefully.

This was starting to look like a big waste of time. But I wasn't about to give up. We went up to the roof to tape the news conference.

A symphony of clicking cameras greeted Redford as he walked to the podium.

As he passed me, he said, "I do want to answer your question."

I was thrilled! *I'm still in the game*, I thought.

After the news conference, as he was walking out, I blurted, "Mr. Redford, a quick question about the whales?"

But he was surrounded by some of Hollywood's biggest executives and just smiled. My photographer and I went inside, purportedly to photograph the green architecture. But my real purpose was to get Redford. We were lurking outside the room where he was talking to the big three networks when a publicist made it very clear to me that I was wasting my time.

"He is *not* giving any other interviews," I was informed with a stern look.

It's at times like these that my old class-clown, defiant self comes in handy.

"Okay. I hear you," I said demurely.

My photographer went to the bathroom. A couple of minutes later, Redford came out to go to the men's room himself. The publicist glared at me, and I was furious that my photographer wasn't there at that moment. I proceeded anyway. "Mr. Redford, if I could just have a couple of seconds to ask you about the issue of military sonar and how it impacts the whales?"

"That is not going to happen," the publicist intervened, clearly furious.

Then Redford spoke. "It's okay."

At that moment, my cameraman returned. "Roll on *everything* and keep it on a two-shot of me and him the whole time," I whispered urgently.

Robert Redford is not only a gorgeous, charismatic guy, he's a kind person. He's kind to the whales, and he was kind to me. We got several questions in when Redford decided to ask me a question. "What do *you* think about the whales?"

By this point I was in a state of overexcitement, and I responded dramatically, "I'm devastated. I think about them all the time."

Redford gave me a quizzical look and literally began backing away. The interview was over, and I felt idiotic. I had responded like some whale-obsessed stalker. But once outside, I promised not to beat myself up over it and allowed the euphoria I felt to have full rein. "We got it!" I whooped to my cameraman.

My one-on-one interview with Robert Redford was heavily promoted during that night's *Celebrity Justice* broadcast. Score one for me . . . and the whales. Tragically, the U.S. Supreme Court later ruled in favor of the military and, right now, the whales remain at risk of underwater torture due to the military's insistence on using sonar during training exercises.

The list of big names who opened up to me about their love for animals goes on and on. I am proud to say that, because of these reports, *Celebrity Justice* won two Genesis Awards from the Humane Society. This is one of my proudest accomplishments. But with animal rights, you can never pause more than a moment to savor past victories. There is always so much more to do to stop the suffering that's everywhere.

Around the time I worked at *Celebrity Justice*, I teamed up with a vegan cookbook author to create America's first vegan cooking show on television called *VegTV*. Sometimes, we would throw a big party, cook a fabulous vegan meal, and put the whole thing on TV. It was a blast. While I'm no longer associated with the show or the website, I'm proud to have helped showcase delicious vegan recipes and vegan products.

When it comes to vegan products, America has come a long way in a very short time. Today, in Whole Foods, your local health food store, or food cooperative, there are great-tasting alternatives for every animal product—from butter and milk to mayonnaise and cheese.

Many of the *faux meats** and *faux dairy products** are showing up in mainstream supermarkets. Today, it's easy to be vegan. If your arteries are getting clogged from too much meat, just switch to Smart Bacon or veggie bologna. Sick of whipping up that tired turkey recipe every Thanksgiving? Try Tofurky. It comes with gravy, giblets, and even a plastic wishbone. Soy alternatives to ice cream, like Tofutti Cuties, are the rage.

It's no longer a sacrifice to be compassionate. It's an adventure. Going vegan will have you checking out Indian, Thai, and Ethiopian food. Most of the world subsists primarily on fruits, vegetables, and grains. It really is the most natural way to eat. And nobody gets hurt.

Switching to a vegetable-rich diet is also the single most important thing you can do for the environment. According to an in-depth study by the United Nations, published in November 2006, meat production is the single, biggest cause of global warming, far beyond transportation. Google UN REPORT MEAT PRODUCTION GLOBAL WARMING, and read the study for yourself!

As an animal-rights activist, I have found every day to offer a new challenge and a new opportunity to stop animal suffering. The e-mails come in nonstop, wave after wave of urgent messages. "Starving Dog Owner Busted!" "Benji and Gabbi are looking for homes!" "Create Change For Farm Animals" "Free Billy the Elephant!" "Dig In and Take a Stand for the Animals!"

It's not uncommon for me to get several dozen e-mails a day, each imploring me for help. Sometimes I feel overwhelmed, and that's when my Twelve-Step principles kick in and provide me with guidance: *Just do the next indicated thing,* I tell myself. *Stay out of the results,* I add. Those are my rules. I take the appropriate action and don't waste any energy on whether the outcome will be positive.

While I've had experiences where I've fought for animals and lost, I'm also proud to have been a part of some major milestones in the animal-rights movement, including the passage of Proposition 2 in California in November 2008. The historic initiative was passed by an overwhelming majority of California voters and simply said: farm animals must have the room to stretch their limbs, turn around, and lie down.

Can you imagine anyone being against that? Yet, the factory farm industry spent millions of dollars trying to defeat this modest proposal to treat farm animals with basic decency. That says everything you need to know about factory farming. Its cruelty is institutionalized. Its modus operandi is torture.

Every state should have a ban on cruel confinement. But it takes work! The summer before that initiative faced the voters, I would wake up on Sunday mornings and bike over to the Santa Monica Farmers' Market which was packed with a cool crowd of mostly affluent, liberal shoppers. They mulled over organic vegetables while being serenaded by live bands singing Crosby, Stills, and Nash or some equivalent.

"Hi! I'm a volunteer with the Humane Society of the United States, and we need your signature to get this crucial measure on the November ballot to give farm animals the basic right to turn around and stretch their limbs." I would say all this quickly and with a big smile, while holding out a pen and thrusting my petition-laden clipboard toward the shopper.

"Not now," was a frequent response. "Later," was another. I was slightly amused to get a "not now" from one of my yoga teachers, who didn't recognize me as he brushed past rather brusquely. He often spoke of peace, serenity, and harmony with nature while we students were holding a pose, like downward dog. But I'm sure we all have disconnects between our principles and our daily practices.

I was also armed with some photos. Shoppers would take a look, flinch, and gasp, "Oh, that's terrible." The photos revealed row upon row of pigs stuck in their narrow gestation crates, unable to turn around. The photos showed their tortured expressions. I also had a photo of hens crammed into filthy cages, too crowded to spread their wings. Beneath that was a snapshot of a veal calf chained by the neck and unable to fully lie down.

"Can't you see I'm talking to someone right now?" some people would snap.

"I'll sign but I don't want to see the pictures," was another common refrain.

I quickly realized that a lot of people don't want to be confused with the facts when it comes to what they eat. If they took a good look at those photos, it would ruin the omelet or steak-n-eggs they were planning to have for Sunday brunch.

I collected over a thousand signatures. But I was just one of thousands of volunteers. Together we got more than 800,000 signatures, qualifying our initiative to appear on the November ballot. Then we had to campaign for votes and raise money for television ads to show the ugly truth of factory farming.

I was one of several people who threw a party at the Beverly Hills home of film producer Tracy Tormé and his wife, Robin. Tracy is the son of legendary crooner Mel Tormé. He and Robin are always fostering homeless dogs and throwing parties for animal organizations. This party was a huge success. It was so packed that I worried somebody was going to fall into the pool.

"I know it's very crowded here tonight," I yelled out to the more than four hundred people packed into the backyard. "But at least you can turn around, which is more than we can say for factory farm animals."

Americans are decent people. They watched the ads and they got it! California voters said "yes" on 2. It was a huge victory for the animal movement, signaling that American consumers want change. I hope the food industry and the Department of Agriculture are listening.

I have had the privilege of working with some of the pioneers in the animal movement. Gene Baur of Farm Sanctuary, Wayne Pacelle of the Humane Society, Ingrid Newkirk of PETA and Lorri Bauston of Animal Acres are just some of my heroes. Any given day, somewhere along Santa Monica Bay, a selfless activist by the name of Peter Wallerstein

is rescuing seals, sea lions, pelicans, and any other seafaring creatures who find themselves in trouble, usually man-made trouble.

One night I was out on the beach when I saw what seemed to be a
dead pelican. It made me very sad. The next morning I went out to
the beach and the dead pelican was in a different spot. I stared at it,
perplexed. Who moved it, I wondered. Then suddenly, I saw a flash
of white. The pelican had just flapped its giant wing. It was sick but
not dead. Frantic and not knowing what to do, I called Peter. Peter
works for virtually nothing and seeks no recognition. His reward is
getting a fishhook out of a seal's skin or freeing a bird stuck to a plastic bag. Peter was there in minutes. He silently approached the pelican from behind, threw a net over it, and, within seconds, had the
animal in his rescue truck headed to a rehab facility. I was so
impressed with his speed and his skill that I threw a fundraiser for
him that helped him buy a new rescue truck. There are many others
like Peter, who work tirelessly to help voiceless creatures who can
only say thank you with the wag of a tail or a contented sigh.

*This is the first social justice movement that seeks to benefit
another species, not human. It is the final frontier in the journey
toward true civilization.* One day, humans will look back and view the
treatment of animals in the early twenty-first century as barbaric and
the mark of a primitive society. We can evolve and we must.

I can earn only a daily reprieve from the sadness that engulfs me
when I think of the billions of suffering animals on factory farms, in
puppy mills, in laboratories, in fur ranches, and in zoos. I get my
daily reprieve by doing something, every day, to try to stop the suffering. You can do something too.

6

Coming Out as Gay:
I Want to Be in Love

There's a certain kind of love that I used to think only existed in novels like *Jane Eyre* and films like *Casablanca*. The longing and angst captured in those great works seemed incredibly romantic but unreal. Then, it happened to me. I was in my late forties when I fell truly, madly, and deeply in love. In the past, I'd had other significant relationships where I'd felt loving feelings, but *this* was totally different. This was like walking through an invisible door and entering a new dimension. Everything changed.

As far back as high school, I knew something about members of the same sex made me squirmy and uncomfortable. I just couldn't define exactly what. But I knew whatever that mystery element was, it scared the wits out of me. I didn't even want to think about it! However, someone was always reminding me of my subconscious desire.

In my first year of high school, there was this girl who changed her name from something very ordinary to something like Leaf. She struck me as terribly cool. She smoked and made out with boys and used terms like "balling." She was very popular. I can see now that I had a crush on her. Back then, all I knew was that I was very aware of her presence and that I always felt awkward around her, while simultaneously trying to impress her. I would go up and try to bum a cigarette and attempt to engage her in conversation. But right from the start, I couldn't handle my attraction and was terrified of anyone picking up on it.

One day, I totally blew it! I was talking about something in class and for some god-awful reason I experienced a Freudian slip and said, "When I was a little boy . . . " I shocked even myself into silence. Leaf and her entourage of cool girls stared at me and then whispered among themselves, while my face burned with humiliation.

"That explains everything," said one of Leaf's cool friends. I wanted to die.

I immediately created a faux crush on a very handsome French teacher as a smoke screen. Some of the other girls teased me about my crush on this teacher, and I remember thinking, *I'm such a phony*. But somehow, I felt compelled to do that without even thinking it through. I was driven by my subconscious embarrassment over my genuine tendencies. I had no awareness of the importance of being true to myself. That wasn't even a concept that had entered my consciousness.

Given all my unusual proclivities, I certainly couldn't afford to add "gay" to the list. Then again, the word "gay" never crossed my mind. I never let myself even get that far in my own head. No, I was going to be a heterosexual, dammit. And I was determined to date a lot of good-looking boys to prove it.

I had a good friend who decided, right around the time she entered college, that she was gay. Today, I applaud her for her courageousness in stating who she was and for her determination to be true to herself. It was clear to me that her mother was none too thrilled about her sexual orientation. That sent another message to me. Being gay would only create a lot of angst. It didn't seem sexy at the time. It seemed depressing. Also, I certainly didn't mind dating boys.

I think there are different kinds of lesbians. Some really won't have anything to do, romantically, with the opposite sex. I, however, loved guys. I felt more comfortable around them, and I liked getting attention from them. It was just that the relationships I had with them were superficial. The depth of the feeling was not there. In a way, when I was with guys, I acted like one of the boys. That should have told me something. Still, I remained in complete denial.

The fact that I was a practicing alcoholic also enabled me to stay blind to my real nature. When you're a problem drinker, you don't look for ways to get out of a problem. You just look for ways to drown the problem. I was self-medicating in a major way. This allowed me to keep up the pretense of being "normal" and "heterosexual" to others and to myself. But sometimes, I would get a stunning reminder of what I was hiding.

As I got older, into my late twenties and thirties, every so often—out of the blue—I would meet a woman and would experience what

I can only describe as a chemical reaction of intense attraction. It would make me crazy. I hated it.

One day, I was with my boyfriend when I ran into one of these women in a department store. We'd vaguely known each other through other friends, and she paused to say hello to me. My discomfort needle was peaking. I was hoping she couldn't see what I was feeling. Suddenly, a bead of perspiration dripped down the side of my face. I felt completely naked.

"Wow, is it hot in here," I said, flushed. I felt like an idiot. I was sure she could see in my eyes that I was sexually attracted to her. It was a nightmare. Sometimes I acted rude to women I was attracted to. It just seemed easier to say something off-putting that would get them to leave me alone, rather than have to deal with the roiling feelings that I was sure could be detected through my expression, my voice, my overall behavior. (Mind you, over the years, I've undoubtedly been rude to some women to whom I wasn't sexually attracted. So, if I've been rude to you, please don't jump to conclusions.) But seriously, it was no way to live. It certainly was a big reason I drank so much.

In my mid-thirties, I'd *pulled a geographic**. That's how alcoholics describe how we literally run from our problems by switching locales. Sometimes, we try to escape by dashing straight across the country. This is when I made my previously mentioned move from New York to Los Angeles for a new job. It was the roaring nineties. I loved LA and I loved my dream job, anchoring at a Disney-owned news station that was based in a studio on the Paramount Studios lot in Hollywood. But as we recovering alcoholics like to say, *Wherever a drunk goes, their problems follow, because they always take them-*

selves with them. This was the time of my final alcoholic stretch before I hit bottom and was corralled into recovery by my old college classmate and newly sober buddy Abbott with the support of my then-boyfriend Stephen. On the bumpy road to hitting bottom, I was having fun . . . a little too much fun in the nightclubs of West Hollywood. My partying was out of control. Once again, I found myself at the therapist's office in an attempt to stop.

It was with this new therapist, who operated out of an office on fashionable Robertson Boulevard directly across from the Ivy restaurant, that I *finally* got mature enough to really capitulate to my drinking problem and get sober. I've talked about my recovery as a miracle. Perhaps a better description is a series of miracles. After I sobered up, I began changing rapidly and in many different ways. Not only did I become a vegan and get into animal activism as I related in the previous chapter, but I also grew increasingly dissatisfied with my relationship with Stephen. He wasn't doing anything wrong. He was always a sweetheart! It was that I was starting to get more honest about myself. The numbing effect of alcohol was wearing off. Buried issues began rising to the surface. I finally had to confront my sexuality.

I danced around the issue in therapy for a while, until I had one of my episodes. I met a woman in a casual setting and had one of those deeply uncomfortable reactions of intense attraction, the kind that would make me agitated and self-conscious. Making matters worse, the woman happened to be a movie star and was quite charismatic. I began avoiding the place where we would regularly run into each other. It was a breakthrough when I admitted this to my therapist. It turned out to be easier to offer him this concrete example than it was to explain my sexual urges in the abstract. My analyst simply accepted what I had to say, nodding his head in the affirmative, without judgment. He was a man of few words. Consequently, when he did speak, I listened.

"So many people have these same feelings, Jane."

"Really?" I asked hopefully.

He nodded. "Lots of people come in here and tell me about similar experiences."

Hmmm. I was taking it all in—like the GPS voice says when it's trying to find its way, I was "recalculating."

I want to stress that I probably never would have admitted *any* of this if I hadn't gotten sober. Talk about feeling naked. When you're used to hiding behind a bottle of wine—and that's taken away—then it really feels like there's nowhere to run, nowhere to hide. That's when you have to confront reality. I could no longer drink down the scary feelings. The only alternative was to own them.

But considering I was still living with Stephen, there were more than a few hurdles left. Was I really ready to identify myself as *not* being heterosexual? It would have been much easier to say I was bisexual and leave it at that. However, what I realized was, when going to great lengths to get honest, why stop at the halfway mark? One day, while on my way to the therapist, I was running late as usual. LA traffic is madness, and I was not the most prompt person at the time. I decided that, since I'd already missed the start of my session, I would pull over and get my car washed instead.

While that was happening, I called my therapist on a pay phone. "Hey, I'm so sorry. I'm not going to make it. Can we at least talk on the phone until my time is up?"

"Sure, Jane."

Somehow, being on the pay phone felt safer than talking to him in person and I decided, around the time my car's tires were getting shined up with Armor All, to just blurt it out. "I think I could be gay," I said to him, shocked at myself for even saying it.

"That's an important thing you've just said," he replied. "Good for you, Jane." The relief that I experienced just saying that to another person was extraordinary. I drove out of the car wash, high on truth-fulness. But how would I break the news to Stephen with whom I'd spent the last decade?

It turns out that, long before I admitted to my therapist that I was gay, he already suspected. Stephen was a very astute observer of the human condition. He loved taking me out to a very cool little resort in Desert Hot Springs, known for its mud baths and massages. He would always make the spa reservations, and I would always insist upon the same thing: "Make sure you get me a male masseuse!"

One time, when the supposedly male masseuse turned out to be a woman, I reluctantly followed her into the massage area. This was not an attractive woman. In fact, quite the opposite. But my reluc-tance had nothing to do with that. I had an aversion to getting mas-saged by any woman. I got up halfway through the massage, claiming to have a headache, and left.

"You really have to look at what that's all about," Stephen told me when I told him I had abandoned my massage midway.

"No, really, she was awful," I insisted. And, frankly, she was. But there was more to it than that. We both knew it.

"Sexuality, wow!" Stephen loved to exclaim in response to the twists and turns of our private life. Again, these telltale signs were before I had my breakthrough in therapy. This is one of the reasons why therapists say that people who are homophobic are frequently reacting to their own repressed homosexuality. I was not the least bit homophobic, politically or intellectually, but not wanting to be touched by women is a physical manifestation of the same principle. You consciously push away what you subconsciously seek. It's a contrarian indicator.

In the late summer of 2002, Stephen and I attended the Farm Sanctuary gala at the Beverly Hills Hotel. Kim Basinger was the keynote speaker at the star-studded affair. While everyone was in black tie and evening gowns, Basinger showed up in overalls, still looking extraordinarily sexy.

"She's black tar heroin for men," Stephen sighed, staring at the willowy actress.

I laughed. Little did I know that I was seconds away from meeting my own black tar heroin. I was checking out the silent-auction items when someone tapped me on the shoulder. "Hi! I'm Sandra. Mind if I interview you?" She was holding a video camera and was smiling.

Ask me where I first met most of the people I know, and I probably couldn't tell you. But I remember everything about that first encounter with Sandra. Something about her took me by surprise. I stared at her. She was slim and taller than me, with short blond hair, and a very straight yet petite nose. She smiled confidently and was very engaging. We did the interview and chatted about her work shooting and editing videos for animal causes. I felt a little light-headed. Then, Stephen and I went home.

As fate would have it, Farm Sanctuary asked me to work with Sandra on a video project about the abuse of farm animals. The video was to be shown at college campuses. It turns out that we were almost neighbors. Both of us lived at the beach about a mile apart. In short order, I found myself going over to her place to drop off some videotapes. I was driving south on the alley that skirted Santa Monica Bay. She had come downstairs to meet me and was standing by the side of the street. I spotted her when I was still a couple of short blocks away. My pulse quickened. Why was I so excited about dropping off these tapes? I didn't dare to explore the question.

"Hey! Here are my tapes."

"Thanks."

That's when I noticed that she had a rather large "J" tattooed on the inside of her arm.

"What's the J stand for?" I asked.

"Oh, I dated someone whose initial was J."

That's my initial, I couldn't help but notice.

"So, when should we get together and work on this video?" I asked.

We set a date. I continued chatting with her. I realized that I didn't want to say goodbye. Finally, I drove off, looking at her in the rearview mirror. She seemed to be staring at me too. *What is it about her?* I wondered.

We began working together in a small Venice editing studio. I remember when I first walked into her office on Abbot Kinney Boulevard, there were hundreds of videotapes stacked on shelves. "What are all these tapes?"

"Oh, it's hundreds of hours of animal suffering that I've logged and documented to create a database. So, when Farm Sanctuary or some other group needs a shot of a downed cow or a crated veal calf, or a monkey in a lab, they can find it quickly."

Being an investigative reporter myself, I knew how painful it was to view even a minute or two of some of the extreme torture to which animals are subjected. Most people don't have the stomach to handle even five or ten seconds. Yet this woman, sitting there at her editing console, had viewed hundreds of hours of brutality. I was blown away.

The editing process was slow and filled with gruesome imagery of cows too weak to stand being dragged to slaughter. We talked a lot. In a subtle way, she let me know that she was gay. Later, she let me know that she was involved with a British woman. They lived together. Sandra and I took frequent breaks to get coffee. One night, we went to dinner at a small, dimly lit sushi bar down the block from her work place. She was eating vegan as well. Sandra elegantly nibbled at her food, smiling at me. I was listening to her talk when the thought first crossed my mind. *I would love to be with her.* It was quickly followed by another thought. *That will never happen. Don't even think about it.*

But once I actually allowed the thought to enter my mind, it was *all* I could think about. I was quickly in the throes of a wicked crush. I began working out furiously and trying to look as good as possible, just in case a window of opportunity would ever arise.

A couple of months later, I learned that she had broken up with her British girlfriend. She cried on the phone as she told me about how they had parted ways. I was sad for her. But somewhere in the recesses of my psyche, I also felt that this was my moment. I was reaching the point where I felt I had to say something or I would spontaneously combust. It didn't help matters that Sandra told me that she thought a female friend of mine was cute. Like me, my friend was a brunette and a journalist. I was surprised at how jealous I felt.

One evening, coming home from my *Celebrity Justice* gig in the Valley, I found myself stuck on the 405 freeway, which is infamously gridlock-prone. Nothing was moving. I had agreed to shoot a pilot for some kind of exercise show with a friend of a friend, one of those Hollywood-esque projects that we all get sucked into from time to time. I was late and getting agitated.

Stephen was traveling around the country as a producer for one of the biggest shows on TV. My wise mentor in sobriety was touring Cuba. Stuck in traffic, I began having a meltdown. There was nobody to call. My crush was out of control. I had to do something. I sat there with my hand on the cell phone. *If I don't let her know how I feel, I will regret it forever.* I knew this was true. Yet, it was so scary. If she had no interest in me, I might scare her off and lose her as a friend. It felt like a near-death experience as I pressed send and called her.

"Hey Sandra, can I talk to you for a minute? I've got a question to ask you."

"Actually, I'm with a client. Can I call you back?"

"Sure." I hung up. I sighed. I had taken that first step, one little phone call that constituted a giant leap in my personal evolution.

When Sandra called back I hemmed and hawed and finally asked her if she found me attractive at all. She seemed shocked by the question.

"You've got a boyfriend. What are you talking about?"

Gradually, the story of my attraction to her spilled out. "Well, I won't go out with somebody if they are involved with somebody else." Sandra was very clear on this point. I told her that I would talk to Stephen.

Stephen is a very cool guy. He is one of the least judgmental and most accepting people I have ever met. I confessed to him that I had become infatuated with Sandra, whom he'd met. He was very understanding. We'd already discussed some of my therapeutic breakthroughs on the subject and he knew about my occasional little crushes and my make-out session with the woman in the D.C. nightclub.

"Go for it," he said. "If you feel that way, you really do have to check it out."

I'm forever grateful that he gave me the freedom to be me. Today, Stephen and I are still very close friends.

Sandra was still leery. She thought I was one of those women she'd run into many times before: a straight girl who just wanted a little experimentation on the side. She urged me to go on the Internet to meet women. But I had no interest in other women. I kept asking her the same question in a multitude of different ways: "Sandra, are you saying that if I didn't have a boyfriend, you'd consider going out with me?"

Finally, one day, when we were both at a beach party, she offered, "Hey, I'm going out with a couple of girlfriends tonight to this club in Long Beach. You want to come?"

I said yes.

Sandra, another friend of hers, and I were on the dance floor at Executive Suite, a lesbian nightclub. It was packed and the DJ was working the crowd. At some point, the friend disappeared, and Sandra and I were left on the dance floor. Then, the music switched. Kylie Minogue's sexy ballad, "Slow," began playing.

Our eyes met. Sandra gave me a look that said, "Come over and slow dance with me."

I did. It was the moment I'd been waiting for my whole life. All of a sudden everything made sense. There was a full moon out when we left the club. Inside the car we kissed. She put her hand on my heart and pressed down on it. I surrendered to her completely.

As kd lang likes to sing "Love is everything they said it would be." I was in a state of perpetual euphoria for months. My experience has been that in private, people are often the exact opposite of what they appear to be in public. While I may seem like a tough broad when I'm grilling a guest on a crime show, on a personal level I like someone who's stronger than me. While Sandra is a beautiful, feminine woman, she has a natural dominance that is very sexy. However, it must be said that I've been known to turn the tables from time to time.

As our relationship blossomed, my career took a very strange turn. I was assigned to cover the Michael Jackson molestation trial, which was getting underway in central California in a dusty agricultural town called Santa Maria, about one hundred and seventy miles north of Los Angeles. I began driving up there on Sunday nights, covering the trial all week, and then driving back on Friday afternoon to be with Sandra for the weekend. The separation only made me desire her even more intensely. It was a geographical aphrodisiac.

When I finally saw her on Friday nights, I was dizzy from the anticipation of it. When I said goodbye to her on Sunday nights, I would go into "Sandra withdrawal" on the long drive north to Santa Maria.

It was a very intense time in my life because I was also working incredibly hard. I was one of more than two thousand reporters from all around the world who had converged on Santa Maria to cover a trial that quickly became a three-ring circus. Rabid Jackson fans and impersonators chanted and screamed outside the courthouse. Jackson himself pulled many bizarre stunts. He danced on top of his SUV after his arraignment, provoking a stampede of fans and curious locals. He showed up to court late, in his pajamas, seemingly oblivious to the judge's threats to have him arrested for his tardiness. The King of Pop made numerous side trips to area hospitals, setting off chaotic media frenzies each time. One day, the entire Jackson family pulled up in a huge touring bus and stepped out one by one in matching white outfits, turning the trial into a Las Vegas act.

My routine was also a hard act to follow. My morning wake-up call was often a live radio interview at 5:00 or 6:00 AM. I would be fast asleep when I'd hear the phone ring and pick up only to hear, "Joining us live from Santa Maria where she's been in the courtroom covering the trial for *Celebrity Justice* is Jane Velez-Mitchell with the very latest developments . . ." After bringing several morning shock jocks and their sidekicks up to date, I would then go to court, take notes on the proceedings, track my reports, and do my live on-camera segments for *Celebrity Justice*. Then, I'd get ready to go live for an hour at 5:00 PM (PST) for *Nancy Grace*. I was thrilled to be Nancy's reporter on the scene for the length of the trial. I also want to thank Nancy for giving me my big break and thinking enough of me to ask me *my opinion of the case!* That was another breakthrough, both personal and professional. After years of working as an "objective" news reporter, having to stuff down all my personal opinions, I finally got a chance to tell America how *I felt* about the story I was covering. It was a rush! That's one thing about personal growth. It feeds on itself. Once you get honest about one thing, you want to get honest about *everything!* After getting off the air at 6:00 PM, I would often continue to do radio interviews late into the night. I often had other TV hits added on to this schedule as well. It was stressful and I missed Sandra terribly.

I would have enjoyed talking to my colleagues about my "girlfriend." But I wasn't "out" yet so that part of my life remained a secret. I only disclosed it to one fellow reporter who had become a close friend. She, in turn, told me that several people had already shared with her the rumor that I was gay. Still, nobody said anything to me directly. So, I didn't bring it up. This is part of the toll that being "in the closet" takes. While everyone else is gabbing about their spouses and children, showing off photos of the one they love and rattling off their accomplishments, the closeted gay remains silent, thereby feeling different and separate. I hadn't counted myself as gay for very long. But already, I could see the psychological stress of having to live a secret life.

Sandra had wanted to visit me in Santa Maria to get a firsthand look at the trial everyone was talking about. I now regret that I repeatedly put her off. Part of it was that I didn't have time to show someone around given my grueling daily schedule. But in all honesty, another part of it was that I wasn't ready to reveal to the world that I was a lesbian. She resented being told that she wasn't welcome there. That was just one of the many little stressors that ultimately ended up causing problems for us.

Prejudice about homosexuality clearly affects how gays operate in the world. Those constraints definitely have a profound impact on the intimate relationships of gay people. Simply put, gay relationships are under greater stress because of how society views gay people.

When you're in love, you want to express that love whenever you're together. But even in liberal Los Angeles, two women holding hands are going to get second glances. Two women kissing will literally stop traffic. In order to avoid being seen, Sandra and I would often pull each other into an alley to exchange a kiss, pressed up against a brick wall.

One night, we went to see a movie together. What could be more all-American than making out in a movie theater? I'd certainly done it with guys. But without saying a word, Sandra and I both made a beeline for the back row so that nobody was behind us to look at us as we made out. In certain cases, feeling the need to be surreptitious can make a kiss feel even more exciting. All these moves we made to keep our romance a secret only added to the sexual tension between us, even when we were just having a cup of coffee at the local hangout. So, I guess there is a positive side to the stealth nature of many gay relationships.

Once Sandra and I were in the full swing of dating, we found ourselves playing around like teenagers, setting up a tent in her living room, which we called "Make Out Island." We would try to watch a movie. But often, hours would go by and we'd later realize the DVD was still repeating the opening title because we never pressed play. We were oblivious to anything but each other.

Celebrity Justice was cancelled right around the time the Jackson trial ended in a stunning acquittal on all counts. Completely exhausted, I returned to Los Angeles. Sandra and I moved in together. The idyllic nature of our early romance evaporated as we were hit with a series of unpleasant surprises. We undertook an extensive remodeling of our beachside condo. That was stressful enough. Then, we discovered mold in some of the walls, which was complicated and time-consuming to eradicate.

Then, I found out I had early stage breast cancer, which I'll tell you more about in Chapter 12. I had two surgeries and radiation. Sandra was there for me every moment of the process. She was a true life partner for that experience. Then, Baja, my beloved dog of fourteen years—who had lived with a trusted elderly couple during the Jackson trial—got very sick and died. It felt like one thing after another.

The early days of our affair, where nothing seemed to matter but playing truth or dare and lounging in bed, had given way to a full season of life and death issues that kept us scrambling.

We also accomplished a lot while we lived together. I began doing more commentary for various national TV shows on a wide variety of issues from crime to celebrity to politics. Sandra edited a cutting-edge, award-winning documentary about animal rights that has been shown around the world.

With Sandra as my invaluable researcher and proofreader, I wrote my first book, *Secrets Can Be Murder: What America's Most Sensational Crimes Tell Us about Ourselves.* Together, Sandra and I also produced numerous videos that helped raise money for animal causes. We were a good team. Sandra directed, videotaped, and edited. I wrote the copy and often narrated it. The result was usually a video that inspired tears and generosity. Sandra and I both share an unquenchable passion to end animal suffering and that was a strong bond that kept us going through all sorts of turmoil.

One night when I was flipping channels, I happened upon Larry King interviewing the famous financial guru and author Suze Orman. To my amazement, she was discussing the fact that she's gay and in a relationship with a woman. I was really impressed with how matter-of-fact she was. It inspired me. I thought to myself, *I'd like to come out*. All my long-time good friends certainly knew that I had "switched teams," as some liked to put it. None of them seemed terribly shocked or upset.

When you're in the closet, you feel like the sky will fall down if anyone finds out. A lot of the fear is self-generated. While it's certainly good for a day or two of gossip, given all the other cataclysmic events around us, an admission of gayness is usually old news in a week.

I was doing a lot of freelance work during this time, including some radio. One night, in the late summer of 2007, I was on KABC-AM talk radio with a delightful late-night host by the name of Al Rantel. Al is one of those Log Cabin Republicans, which is to say a gay conservative. We were talking about the latest scandal to hit Washington.

Senator Larry Craig had been caught in a men's room stall in the Minneapolis-St. Paul International Airport making what an undercover cop called a foot-tapping signal used by persons wishing to engage in lewd homosexual conduct. While Senator Craig pleaded guilty to disorderly conduct, the Idaho Republican later insisted, "I am not gay."

We were talking—on air—about the hypocrisy of people like

Craig who had a long record of antagonism to gay rights, having voted against gay marriage and having supported banning gays from serving in the Boy Scouts.

Here I was, on the radio, chatting—at length—with an openly gay talk-show host about Senator Larry Craig's hypocrisy, and I hadn't said a word about being gay myself. Meanwhile, Al was regaling his listeners with the story of how he came out. As the conversation wore on, minute after minute, I became increasingly uncomfortable attacking the Senator for dishonesty while I, myself, was lying by omission. I felt like I was trapped in a pressure cooker, and the force applying the pressure was my own conscience. I was torn and had no idea what to do.

Then, during the commercial break, I suddenly remembered Suze Orman. I turned to Al, with whom I felt very comfortable.

"Al, listen, I'm in a relationship with a woman, and I think I want to mention that coming out of the break."

Al grinned. "Really? Well, it's up to you!"

My mind was racing. I only had a couple of seconds to decide. "I think I should call my partner first," I added, quickly dialing Sandra on my cell phone. "Hey, Sandra, turn on the radio. I'm going to come out."

The commercial ended, and we were back, live, on the air.

"Al, considering the subject we're talking about tonight, I want to be honest. I think I should mention that I live with a woman and . . ."

Frankly, I don't remember what the heck I said after that. But I do remember Al joking, "Okay, is there anyone in this place who is not gay?"

It wasn't long before *The Advocate* magazine called and asked for an interview. I said sure. What I've learned about activism is that, whether it's animal rights or gay rights, you have to take advantage of any and all opportunities to spread the word, since you never know when you'll get the next opportunity.

The Advocate reporter came out and spent the afternoon with me. Eventually, I was part of a long article looking at gays in the media.

He wrote, "People like Velez-Mitchell are coming out all the time in the broadcast news business. 'If it does impact my career, well, so be it,' she says. 'Life's short. When you're lying on your deathbed, are you going to remember that you had two more years working in a cubicle, or are you going to remember that you were true to yourself and maybe encouraged some other people to be true to themselves?'"[1]

After that article came out, several people wrote to me and told me that my words had inspired them. I was happy to be of service, in a small way, to people who may still be conflicted about coming out. I also realized that I was part of a chain reaction of honesty. Suze Orman and Al Rantel inspired me to be honest. I inspired someone else who will, in turn, inspire yet another person to live honestly. Perhaps, one day our whole society will get honest about issues surrounding sexuality. *When will we realize that love rarely comes in the package we expect?*

After sputtering for a while, Sandra and I finally ended our intimate relationship, once and for all, after several exciting years

---

[1] *http://www.advocate.com/exclusive_detail_ektid53880.asp?page=2, accessed April 2009.*

together. We remain good friends. We continue to work on projects together to help animals and people. She will always have a special place in my heart. She was my first true love. But hopefully, she will not be my last.

Sandra and me. She was black tar heroin for me.

Baja, my longest relationship.

7

Workaholism:
I Want to Stop Being a Slave

"RRRRAAAAAIIIIIIISSSSSSAAAA." The word came out of my mouth like a cannonball and shot across the vast marble hall, echoing for what seemed like minutes. This was the late 1980s in Midtown Manhattan. Raisa Gorbachev turned and looked at me, clearly startled. She had entered the gigantic space from the worst possible vantage point for me. She was all the way on the other side. It seemed like she was a football field away from where I was being contained by velvet ropes and security personnel. Still, I was determined to get an interview with her no matter what. I locked eyes with her and then, like an overeager Little League coach, began motioning her to approach me.

"Raisa, Raisa, Raisa, come here. I have to ask you a question."

She seemed transfixed. Who was this impudent young woman who had screeched the first name of the first lady of the Soviet Union at the top of her lungs? Apparently, she felt the need to find out. Brushing aside her handlers, she approached me. When she got close enough, I asked her a couple of questions about world peace, and God only knows what else, and she went on her way. I was thrilled. My assignment had been to get a one-on-one interview with the wife of the leader of the Soviet Union, and I'd accomplished it . . . against all odds. It was an exclusive! Little did I know I was about to become the laughingstock of the New York press corps.

I was watching the *CBS Evening News* that night when the story about Raisa Gorbachev's visit to New York City began. I wasn't paying all that much attention until the piercing sound of my own voice erupted from the TV set with a force that seemed likely to destroy the speakers.

"RRRAAAAAIIISSSSSAAAAA" I heard myself scream. I hadn't realized how rude I sounded until I heard myself played back. *Boy, was I loud*. The national news correspondent doing the report regarded my scream as an assault on Mrs. Gorbachev and international diplomacy. His narration went something like, "Mrs. Gorbachev had a wonderful day in New York until her visit was marred by the notoriously obnoxious New York press corps." Apparently, he was referring to me! The next day, when I went into work, everyone was snickering. "Raaiissaaa," they would cry out when they saw me. It was not one of my finer moments.

It would take me years to learn that I was suffering from *over-*

functioning*, which is a symptom of workaholism. As a recovering workaholic, I now recognize when I start to overfunction and put on the brakes. Overfunctioning is a *problem of perception** that is incredibly stressful and can be debilitating. I felt that I was never prepared enough . . . no matter how much I prepared. I felt that I had never done quite enough work . . . no matter how much work I had done. I felt compelled to go to work . . . even when I was too sick and should've stayed home. I felt that, when I was given an assignment, it *had* to be accomplished, even when it was virtually impossible to do so. Hence, I lacked the kind of boundaries that would signal to me that I was crossing a line and doing something inappropriate. Therefore, I screamed at Mrs. Gorbachev. Yes, I got the interview but—in the end—it would have been more appropriate for me to have simply returned to the newsroom and explained to my bosses that I couldn't get close enough to her to accomplish the assignment they'd given me.

There were other examples. In August 1989, I was assigned to cover the twentieth anniversary of the Woodstock music festival. A cameraman and I traveled up to the original concert site at a dairy farm in upstate New York, where they were holding the anniversary concert. It appeared to be mostly a gathering of very stoned and very tie-dyed Deadheads lost in a time warp and, therefore, kind of depressing.

"God's house has many mansions, and those mansions have many rooms," one Deadhead explained to me when I asked him why he was attending.

What*ever*!

Experiences like this are one of the reasons I try to resist nostalgia. You can't go back. If you can, you probably never left. But there were other reasons why this assignment, which at first seemed like it would be so much fun, was anything but a party.

This was in the time before everybody had a cell phone. We were so far from New York City that we'd lost the signal on our two-way radio in the news van. I had to phone the assignment desk to read a supervisor the copy I'd written in order to get approval before I put my words on tape and sent them back. Approval was part of the procedure. The executive producer, back in the newsroom, didn't like it when you sent your voice tracks back without first getting their OK. There wasn't a pay phone anywhere to be found in the rolling countryside. I was running out of time and didn't want to miss my "slot," the time when the story was scheduled to run. I spotted a farmhouse and told the cameraman/driver to pull up. The door was open. I called out "Hello! Anyone home?" No answer. I walked into the kitchen, spotted a phone on the wall, and began dialing.

I was almost at the end of my script when a very large, very angry farmer came barreling into the kitchen and began shouting.

"What the hell? Who are you and what are you doing in my kitchen?"

"Ahh, I'm so sorry. I can explain. Just give me a second, Sir, I'm just about done," I responded and continued reading my script, racing to get in the last few words.

"If you don't git the hell out of my kitchen this minute, I'm going to get my rifle and git you out!" the farmer yelled.

He stormed out of the kitchen, and I assumed he was going to get his rifle. I hightailed it out the door and into the news van.

"Let's get outta here now . . . before Farmer John comes back!" I yelped at my photographer, who was behind the wheel.

I had always regretted being too young to attend the original Woodstock festival. Now, I also regretted being assigned to cover the anniversary of it. Perhaps if I hadn't been so overfunctioning, I could have stopped doing interviews earlier in the day, to give myself enough time to drive to the local town and make a leisurely phone call. We might have even found time for a cup of coffee or a bite to eat. In all the decades I worked in the news business, I can only remember sitting down for a leisurely lunch a handful of times. That's sick!

One of my nicknames was "One More Bite." That's because I was always begging my photographer to let me get one more sound-bite— that is, one more interview for my story.

Like any addiction, workaholism is based on a need to escape and a desire to control. I dove into my work to escape having to look at myself. As a breaking-news reporter, for many years, I was constantly scrambling. One minute I was reporting from the scene of a murder. The next minute I was in a news van racing to the scene of a fire. My other nicknames included "Rocket Socks" and "Roadrunner." There were a few other names that I wouldn't want to repeat in polite company. One producer loved calling me "Exxon Valdez" after the rogue shipping vessel that crashed, creating one of the worst man-made environmental catastrophes in history. Apparently Velez and Valdez were close enough. Being an environmentalist, I wasn't thrilled with that moniker. When they started calling me Exxon, for short, I said, "Okay, enough, guys."

Racing around like a fiend, I had little time to contemplate my repressed homosexuality or other issues that I needed to work on. Getting a story done every day, sometimes several stories a day, allowed me to feel in control of my life. With breaking news, there is no delayed gratification. You do the story, and it airs almost immediately. Quite often it airs "live." As a reporter, I always saw the outcome of my labors and that helped me feel in control and productive. I could say to myself, *Here's what I accomplished today. I'm a productive, upstanding citizen. Everything's okay.*

Workaholism is a sick form of self-reassurance. The cosmos is a scary place, and we try to find anchors that give us security and therefore make it feel less scary. Work is a very strong anchor that provided me with an identity, a sense of my place in the world, and a sense of accomplishment. That's certainly not all bad. It's just a question of balance. If that's the *only* way I define myself, then there's something unhealthy going on.

Workaholism is certainly not just my sickness. It's a societal sickness. Many people in the news business pride themselves on saying, "I have no life." I have heard those exact words come out of the mouths of producers, reporters, anchors, and others, many, many times. It's a badge of honor in our workaholic culture to be so consumed with work that there's no time for anything else. To have leisure time is to be a loafer. To be a person without a career is to be someone who doesn't really count. We pass judgment on those who are simply living their lives for the sake of what they experience as human beings. I'd be lying if I didn't admit that I still look askance at those people I meet who have no discernable source of income or detectable career. In America, the first thing we ask people when we meet them is, "What do you do?"

I asked somebody that recently, who was from India, and he responded, "I don't wish to define myself in those terms."

I loved his answer. But certainly, in the United States, most people do define themselves by what they do. I was no exception.

One of the reasons workaholism is hard to kick is that, in our society, it tends to be rewarded. If you are the first person at the office and the last to leave it often makes you appear indispensible. In the case of my line of work, reporting, if you are always ready to roll and never say no, you are likely to be called first when the big story hits.

New Year's Eve 1986: I had spent the entire day and night grappling with the rowdy crowds that had converged on Times Square to watch the ball drop. I had done several live reports in the frigid cold, standing on the roof of a live news van. It was late at night and I was ready to do my final live shot for the late newscast when someone spoke into the device that was plugged into my ear.

"Jane, there's a huge fire in a hotel in Puerto Rico. We've got you booked on a flight to San Juan leaving in just over an hour. Start heading toward Eighth Avenue and a crew will meet you and take you to the airport."

Let it be noted, this was not a request; it was a directive, as most communications from the *assignment* desk usually are. I felt a combination of excitement and dread, especially when I began hearing that there could be a massive death toll.

That turned out to be a weeklong saga as I did a series of reports on the infamous Dupont Plaza Hotel arson fire that left ninety-seven people dead in San Juan.

December 1988: I was called into the boss's office and told that I would be hitching a ride the next day on a cargo jet laden with relief supplies, headed to Soviet Armenia. There had been a massive earthquake there, killing tens of thousands of Armenians. Aid was pouring in from around the world, and I would be riding in with some of it. Did we have visas? No. Did we have any contact information? No. Were we headed into a region under martial law? Yes. How much time would we have in Armenia to get our reports done? We had exactly as long as it would take to unload all the cargo and refuel for the return flight, or about twelve hours on the ground. Was this a tricky assignment? Yes. I was starting to think that they gave me these kinds of assignments because I would always come back with something, no matter what. It was a backhanded compliment, which sometimes left me feeling like I'd been smacked upside the head.

We landed in the middle of a snowstorm. The airport seemed like a movie set depicting another century. A long line of old men in black coats and bowler hats greeted us solemnly. My producer allegedly spoke Armenian, but I got the impression that she couldn't say much more than, "Do you have a cigarette?" and "I love you." However, the two of us did our best to charm the men in the bowler hats. In her broken Armenian, my producer pleaded with the officials to let us go, with our photographer, to the areas hit by the quake. We were assigned a handler, who was a KGB officer and told we were being taken to a hotel called Armenia One. We would be held there until the cargo plane was ready to take off and then transported back to the airport. We would be given absolutely no access to the quake victims.

We weren't in a position to argue. With our new KGB friend, we got into a military jeep and took off into the night. We were rolling video as we hit roadblock after roadblock.

"Wow, this is what martial law looks like!" I marveled as we encountered soldiers in tanks. Everything seemed designed to reduce the mobility of the population. I would jump out and try to engage the soldiers, some of whom spoke broken English. The more I smiled and laughed, the more they smiled and laughed. We were getting every bit of tape we could, but so far nothing on the quake, which was our assignment.

Once ensconced in Hotel Armenia One, we were directed to the bar designated for tourists. There was another bar for the locals, which we weren't allowed to enter. I was taken aback by the rigidity of everything and everyone. We couldn't even *talk* to anyone from Armenia . . . except for Mr. KGB. I decided that, since this assignment was a total bust, we would have to start drinking vodka. This was long before I got sober, and I loved buying rounds. It turns out our KGB fellow loved drinking them. After half a dozen shots, this thirty-something Armenian began telling me, in his very deep voice and halting English, his heartfelt dreams of escaping to the United States and how he desperately wanted to get his hands on Kurt Vonnegut novels.

"If I give you my address will you send me *Slaughterhouse-Five* and *Breakfast of Champions* from America?" he asked, his words slurring slightly. He seemed like a nice guy trapped in a terrible job in an awful country. I took him upstairs to my hotel room. No, we didn't fool around. I had packed my suitcase with Twizzlers, Jujubes, and other American candies. Somebody told me that it was useful to grease the wheels. I was pulling everything out of my suitcase to see what interested him. It was touching because he was fascinated with anything that was American . . . even candy. It made me realize how much I took my own freedom for granted. This weird visit felt like a tour of a giant prison. I couldn't wait to get out. It was the same reaction I'd experienced visiting East Berlin a few years earlier, long before the wall came down. My growing distaste for Armenia was exacerbated by their refusal to let me do my story.

"Look, I'm going to get in big trouble if you don't help me," I said breathlessly to Mr. KGB. This wasn't exactly true, but I felt frustrated enough to use the line in this situation. "You have to take me to the quake zone! They sent me halfway around the world to get this story and I have nothing!" I spoke with urgency, grabbing his shoulders and looking into his eyes. "Help me."

He looked back at me. It was decision time. "I will violate the curfew," he said to me ominously, sounding like Lurch from *The Addams Family*. "Come with me."

Mr. KGB, my producer, my photographer, and I took off in the predawn hours and headed for God-only-knows-where. We drove a considerable distance. A couple of times we stopped and our handler spoke to the men at the checkpoints. We were let through the barricades. Finally, we pulled up to a pitch-black, ancient brick building. We went in and stumbled around. Someone approached. Lights went on. It was a hospital. More discussion in Armenian. We were led to a room. We flipped on the lights and woke up about two dozen earthquake victims.

I was kind of horrified because I knew this was very intrusive. It doesn't excuse it, but luckily, the patients didn't seem to mind. In fact, they were eager to tell their stories of being trapped in the rubble and how they were dragged out. They showed me their broken arms and their cuts and bruises. Several complained bitterly about the shoddy Soviet construction that had collapsed on them. They seemed happy that someone was listening to their grievances. The KGB man translated what they were saying, speaking English into the microphone. Mission accomplished. We returned home and put together a series of interesting reports, although I would have preferred less drama in the process.

Looking back, I wish I could have accomplished all my assignments with serenity and calm. Many stories seemed to demand a "take it to the limit" approach, but that doesn't mean we have permission to run roughshod over anyone who comes into our path during a work assignment.

In the fall of 1989, a tropical storm was brewing in the Caribbean, and it was headed straight for Puerto Rico. I was sent down just before the flights were cancelled. We were at an oceanfront hotel in San Juan when Hurricane Hugo hit. While the Katrina debacle has since overshadowed all other hurricanes, Hugo—at the time—was a destructive monster that got a lot of attention.

I did one of those on-camera hurricane stand-ups that have now become so de rigueur they're a joke. Holding on to a pole, I let the Category 5 hurricane winds blow me around as I dodged flying coconuts and shouted above the howling storm. Hugging that pole with all my might, I fought the winds trying to wrestle me away into the abyss. I was so determined to get a dramatic, windblown stand-up that I never gave a second thought to my own safety. That's not courage, that's workaholic weirdness. Today, I might do the same stand-up, but at least I'd have the good sense to be terrified.

At a certain point the winds seemed to subside. We jumped in our car and headed for our feed point, the location where we'd put our tape into a deck, and it would be fed back to New York via satellite. It turned out the hurricane had just taken a brief intermission. As we drove, the storm sprang back into action with a wallop. Streets signs and pieces of wood began flying into our windshield. It was like nothing I'd ever experienced.

"Where the hell are we, Tracy? I can't tell one palm tree from another."

"Don't worry. I was a pathfinder in Vietnam," my photographer assured me.

We arrived at the feed point only to be told that the satellite equipment had been badly damaged during the hurricane and there was absolutely no way for us to get our reports back to New York. We couldn't even do a phone report because all the phone lines from Puerto Rico to the States were down due to the hurricane. That was terrible news because my station had spent quite a bit of money sending us down to Puerto Rico and expected a payoff. It was a big story. There were a couple of other stateside reporters milling around and fuming as well.

Standing there drenched from head to toe, I just couldn't accept the idea that Tracy and I had done all of this work and nobody would see or hear it. I walked around the satellite center and headed down a hall. I heard a man talking in Spanish to someone. I walked into this supervisor's office. He was on the phone. I was confused.

"How come I can't make a phone call to New York, but you're able to talk to somebody on the phone?" I asked him with some irritation, as he hung up.

"I was talking to one of the other islands, not to the United States," he huffed.

I got an idea. "Call that island back and ask them if *they* can call New York?"

The hurricane wasn't hitting every island with the same ferocity at once. "If so, we can patch a call through that island and then I can reach New York."

"We'll try," the supervisor sighed. I closed the door to his office so none of the other reporters could see what we were doing. Sure enough, we patched through the other island to New York, and I began doing phone reports for my news station. They used network footage of the hurricane to wallpaper my voice. It was a genuine "exclusive" and a "first" because nobody else, not even the networks, could get anything out of Puerto Rico at that moment. Eventually, after a couple of lengthy reports, I told the other reporters my secret and they all started doing it.

If necessity is the mother of invention, then workaholism is the mother of ingenuity. My addictive work habits made me a very loyal employee. I rarely thought of my own safety as, over the years, I confronted not only hurricanes but dangerous drug pushers, angry protestors, and even out-of-control, drunken sports fans. Often, it paid off. But as I look back, a lot of the energy I was expending on a daily basis was unnecessary and over the top. I noticed some of the other reporters seemed more nonchalant about their assignments. Some reporters erred in the opposite direction and seemed too laid-back, almost to the point of being lazy. Finding the right balance, somewhere in the middle, is perhaps the hardest thing for an addictive personality. The gray areas are very complicated for us and involve all sorts of intricate judgment calls. Now, when I'm overfunctioning, I tell myself: *I do enough, I am enough, I have enough**. I also pray, on a daily basis, to be freed from overfunctioning and *reverse pride**.

Reverse pride is the kind of guilt that is ego-based and therefore grandiose and self-destructive. Put another way, I experience two kinds of guilt. I feel appropriate, necessary guilt when I've done something wrong, and I usually attempt to assuage my guilt by admitting I was wrong and rectifying the problem I created. But sometimes, I experience inappropriate, neurotic, and unnecessary guilt that simply drains my energy and messes with my head. This bad guilt is based on my ego-driven needs to be perfect or to be perceived of as special or superior in terms of my abilities. Reverse pride occurs when my ego gets wounded because I failed to be that "special" person I so want to be. I now realize that's *stinking thinking** and have learned how to identify and squelch that toxic thought process. There's a silly sober saying that works as a good note to self: "My ego is not my amigo."

Today, when I am unable to accomplish an assignment that is simply not feasible, I do my best to avoid feeling irrational guilt. I know I am only in control of so much and tell myself it's illogical to feel guilty over that which I have no control. In fact, it's a form of playing God because I'm responding to a situation that's out of my power as if it were somehow in my power. In Twelve-Step lingo, the healthy work attitude is described this way: *Suit up, show up, do the next indicated thing, be a worker amongst workers, humbly be of service, and let go of the results.*

Now, for all my friends who are likely to roll their eyes and say, "Oh, please, you're still a total workaholic," I can only say, "I'm not claiming to be cured!"

That would be a big fat lie. I struggle with it on a daily and sometimes on an hourly basis, and, at most, I earn a daily or hourly reprieve from the disease of overwork. But I've got the tools to keep a healthy attitude when I remember to use them.

By the time Sandra and I got together, I thought I had become pretty healthy psychologically. I was certainly very involved in maintaining my sobriety. But she diagnosed me as a workaholic and told me it was hurting our relationship. She had a point. Living with a practicing workaholic is like living alone because the compulsive worker isn't ever really *present*. The compulsive worker is always somewhere else mentally, focusing on a task or project instead of on her lover or her family.

The worst example of my workaholism, which I will forever regret, was insisting that Sandra and I bring a video camera with us on vacation to the Tahitian islands so we could shoot videos of all the world-class chefs we'd encounter while they whipped up our special vegan meals. On paper, it seemed like a good idea.

We were visiting some of the most idyllic, exotic locales on the planet. What better way to show people that one can have a fabulous vacation and still eat healthy? I thought we could edit it together and pitch it as a healthy eating travel show. If that didn't fly, we could share it on the Internet to spread the word.

Unfortunately, the constant videotaping robbed our vacation of romance. Sandra was the videographer, and I was always telling her to shoot this or that, and she got mighty sick of being on assignment and bossed around. Finally, at this particularly gorgeous resort in Bora Bora, she refused to keep shooting.

"I've had it with this nonsense!" she fumed, as she put down the camera, grabbed a canoe, and aimed for the watery horizon.

So, I took the camera and planted it at the edge of the swimming pool. The pool boys stared at me with intense curiosity as I hit the record button and gave a running commentary on healthy vacationing while swimming in front of the camera. Now that's *not* healthy.

I was supposed to be on a sexy vacation in Bora Bora. Instead, I was Bora Boring as I continued to work!

Workaholism can also be described as the Superman Complex. This is when we feel that everything is our responsibility, that we are holding the weight of the world on our shoulders. No wonder I was a follower of Ayn Rand when I was a teenager. Her philosophy can be summed up this way: a tiny percentage of heroic individuals, who rely solely on reason to divine the objective truth, operate in their own true self-interest, achieving most of society's accomplishments, while the majority of lazy-minded people use faith as a crutch and leach off the productivity of this miniscule elite. Her philosophy has been derided as both simplistic and fascistic, which it is. But it's a very seductive notion for someone with addictive thinking who needs to either do it all . . . or do nothing at all. While I quickly outgrew Ayn Rand's questionable beliefs, I was still carrying the weight of the world on my shoulders.

When you feel responsible for everything, you have a tendency to micromanage. I irritated some photographers because I always wanted them to get shots of things I saw and I would tell them what to videotape. Finally, when the technology arrived, I began shooting some of my own stories with a semi-professional Sony digital video camera. This was a lot of fun for me. I got a kick out of seeing videotape that I shot myself on television. It was also uniquely appropriate to *Celebrity Justice*, the show I was working on at the time. Working alone with a small camera, I could sneak around and get shots before anyone noticed, in places where a cameraman with a larger professional camera would immediately be stopped. Most important, as a workaholic I could now work even more!

In January of 2004, while working at *Celebrity Justice*, I was told to book a room at the Beverly Hills Hotel. My mission? To infiltrate the now infamous summit of Michael Jackson advisors that was convening in an undisclosed hotel room there. Jackson's lawyers and financial advisers were gathering to map out a battle plan to resolve the King of Pop's escalating personal and financial troubles. It was the story everybody was talking about. Not only was Michael Jackson hemorrhaging money at a mind-boggling rate, he was in the throes of a legal and public relations nightmare. He was facing child molestation charges after appearing on a documentary holding hands with an underage male cancer victim and talking about having sleepovers with boys.

The hotel would certainly not allow a photographer and me to roam the halls searching for the summit. Hence, I packed my small video camera into my luggage and checked in to the posh, world-famous hotel. I began my reconnaissance early in the morning, tucking the camera in my beach bag. I checked out the conference rooms and the pool area, and searched every inch of the hotel. Nothing.

Disappointed, I returned to my room—only to discover that, in a wild coincidence, the summit was being held in the room directly opposite mine! Right outside my door now stood a guard from the Nation of Islam, complete with signature bowtie and suit. *Bingo!*

By technically staying within my hotel room and simply leaving my door open, I had a fabulous and safe vantage point from which to videotape the comings and goings of this bizarre collection of businessmen, Louis Farrakhan disciples, and waiters with trays of food. I was the only reporter on the scene. . . at least at first. It turned out that a producer from *ABC News* had booked a room two doors down. She was also armed with a mini-camera. We aimed our cameras at each other and just laughed.

Meanwhile, a small army of professional photographers and journalists had converged in the hotel lobby furiously trying to get access to the summit. But they were not allowed in. As tends to occur whenever the words "Michael" and "Jackson" are involved, the day got progressively more insane and chaotic. A couple of wily journalists figured out ways to slip inside the hotel and were lingering in front of my room, peppering the Nation of Islam guard with questions and poking their heads in the summit room whenever the door opened. Finally, hotel management appeared and imperiously told them all to get out. Only those of us who had booked and paid for hotel rooms were allowed to stay.

The legendary Associated Press crime reporter Linda Deutsch turned to me and asked, "Can I come into your room?" The other reporters standing behind her were also looking at me hopefully. Perhaps I could throw a party in my room, one suggested, and invite all of them. I thought about it for a millisecond. I could keep my advantage and say no. But I would alienate all these journalists whom I'd have to face in the field down the road. Also, I was a huge admirer of Linda Deutsch's work and loved the idea of being able to help this seasoned professional. I decided I would make all of this part of my story.

"Come on in," I invited them. Linda Deutsch immediately picked up the phone to file a report on the wild events of the day. I video-taped her as she dramatically recounted the bizarre developments, talking a perfectly worded story into the phone off the top of her head, barely glancing at her notes. She was amazing. The chaos of it all made my report even more exciting. I was pleased to have been able to help out these other reporters and got a better story out of it as a result. Letting them all into my room was a welcome departure from the strict workaholic ethos of "win at all costs." Life doesn't have to be a zero-sum game. We can all win.

When it comes to many aspects of my life, including work, I need to examine my intentions. I have asked myself the following questions and continue to ask them on a regular basis. *What is my intention in my work? Am I simply out for money, power, and prestige?* If so, I need a major attitude adjustment and possibly a new career.

What is my work accomplishing to make this world a better place in some way, shape, or form? If the answer is nothing, then I must change what I'm doing and how I'm doing it.

We Americans need to completely rethink our definition of success. It can no longer be just about the paycheck, the title, the perks, and the bonuses. We're destroying the rest of the world with our rapacious greed and our ego-based definitions of success. Ironically, it's not making us any happier. My best days at work have always been when I was able to do something to make someone else's life better.

Often, my contribution was simply to expose an injustice and shame somebody into doing the right thing. In 1983, after the horrific bombing of a U.S. Marine Corps barracks in Beirut, my assignment desk in New York got a call from a woman whose husband, a marine, was badly injured in the attack. He'd been transported to a military hospital in Germany. She was desperate to visit him but didn't have the money for plane fare. To her complete amazement and disgust, she learned the military wouldn't pay her way. We did a story profiling her plight and found that, in short order (surprise, surprise), she was transported to Germany to be with her severely wounded husband.

At *Celebrity Justice*, I profiled a woman whose fairytale Hollywood marriage had disintegrated into a vicious divorce battle. Her husband was very well known in the film industry and was playing hardball with his soon-to-be ex. She was frozen out of funds.

"I'm homeless. I live out of my car," she explained when I met her on a street corner in Los Angeles. She told me that she was forced to use public restrooms to wash off. Meanwhile, her estranged husband was living in luxury in Malibu. The day after the story ran, she called and thanked me profusely. Many of her old Hollywood friends had seen the piece and were stunned to learn of her homelessness. She was being inundated with offers of help. Her husband was also, apparently, quite embarrassed by the story and, in its wake, was more willing to play ball with a decent settlement. That made me feel good.

Freeing myself from workaholism has been a constant struggle because work is not something I can abandon completely. With alcohol, I can just say no . . . period. But with work, I have to make judgment calls on a daily, hourly, and even minute-to-minute basis as to what is appropriate and healthy and what is sick, addictive behavior. It's all about *managing the gray areas**. When I use the Twelve Steps in my work, I find that I can stay on a spiritual beam and make the right choices based, not on my ego and my neurotic compulsions to control, but on what my conscience tells me is the morally correct thing to do. That's called emotional sobriety. I simply try to do what I have to do, humbly, to be of service in some way to a higher cause than just myself. I feel gratified when I see that my actions have helped some other human or creature in some manner.

On Friday, October 17, 2008, I woke up unusually early. I was living alone at this point and wondering what would happen next in my life, personally and professionally. I was what they call "between projects," also known as "on the beach." Conveniently for me, I lived on the beach. Yes, I was on national television almost daily, giving my opinion, and I was doing a steady stream of fill-in hosting at truTV and elsewhere, but I didn't have a full-time gig. I wasn't anxiety ridden about that. I was finally in a place where I could let the river take me where it wanted to go. It was 6:30 AM, and I was drinking coffee and staring at a palm tree outside my window when I got a text from New York: *Expect a call at any moment!*

The next thing you know, I was on the phone with a very charming CNN executive who told me a slot had opened up and asked me if I'd be willing to start hosting a new show on the HLN network for the foreseeable future. It would be called *Issues with Jane Velez-Mitchell*!

"Sounds wonderful," I replied, "especially since I've got a lot of them."

Could I host from LA that very day and then get on a plane to New York to start from there Monday? *Does Pinocchio have a wooden nose?*

"Absolutely!" I was off to the races.

What an adventure! My two little Chihuahua mixes and I boarded a jet for Nueva York and headed straight to my mom's apartment in Midtown. Soon, I was living back in the very room I grew up in. Mom was about to turn ninety-three, and it was great timing to be there with her. It was especially fun because it was all so spontaneous and unplanned. Once again, I'd come full circle back to the city where I was born. The last time I had held a full-time job in New York was nineteen years earlier. Back then, I had been grappling with alcoholism and authenticity issues. This time, I was more than a dozen years sober and I finally knew who I was. I wasn't going to be a workaholic. I was just going to be me.

8

Addiction Hopping:
I Want to Stop
Eating Compulsively

I was thirty-nine years old when I finally got sober, and it was around that time that I also gave up smoking for good. My father had died of lung cancer about a decade earlier. That really brought home how utterly suicidal smoking is. After my father passed away, I would get nauseated whenever I lit up. After that, I almost never bought a pack of cigarettes. But addictions often travel in pairs and *booze/smoking* is perhaps the most common pair of bad habits that feed on each other. I no longer craved cigarettes—in fact, they repulsed me—*except* when I was drinking. With a glass of wine in one hand, I would suddenly get a yen to light up and impulsively ask somebody for a cigarette. For years, I was an occasional smoker who simply bummed cigarettes. When I finally gave up drinking, the last vestiges of my smoking habit simply fell away. Without booze, cigarettes had zero appeal to me. Now, when I get a whiff of cigarette smoke, I instantly feel sick. Now, when I see people standing outside an office and furtively smoking, I want to walk up to them and yell, "STUPID! YOU'RE GOING TO DIE!" But how would I have felt if somebody did that to me back when I was smoking? Once you figure something out it becomes obvious . . . to you!

Ditto for pills. I was never hooked on them but had, on a few occasions, popped a Valium recreationally with a glass of wine. Bad idea . . . although so commonplace that the joke was, if someone at a stadium in LA asked if anyone had a Valium, everyone in the stands could immediately produce one. But just because a lot of people were doing it, doesn't make it right. Again, as soon as I gave up drinking, the desire for Valium completely disappeared. I never really even thought about it after that. Self-medicating with legal prescription drugs is a rampant crisis in America and one that desperately needs to be more openly discussed . . . but we can revisit that another time.

So, fortunately, as I entered my forties, alcohol, tobacco, and pills were all a part of my past. Good riddance! However, when deprived of our old drugs, addicts are positively ingenious at creating new ones, and I'm no exception.

My new rules were no mood-altering substances, period, except when required by a doctor for medical reasons. And that's when sugar strutted into my life and gave me a come-hither look. Sugar . . . the tasty dominatrix who gave orders that I felt strangely compelled to obey. Back when I drank, the notion of buying a pack of sugary cookies and gobbling a few down would have seemed absurd and ridiculous. It would have never even occurred to me. Then, I stopped drinking and *my body* immediately began craving sugar. I say my body because it was literally a physical craving. The very first day I went without a drink I felt compelled to distract myself with candy. Instead of cocktails and a smoke, I was quickly chug-a-lugging coffee and chomping on Twizzlers. By the way, this is completely predictable since it's a classic early recovery behavior.

Back when I drank, a certain amount of the alcohol turned into sugar in my system. So, I had been getting my sugar fix inside my booze. It's a drug within a drug. Remove the booze and the sugar craving remains. The other aspect of sugar addiction is psychological. Here I was, still living with Stephen, trying to figure out why I had these *feelings* toward certain women and still processing other unpleasant old feelings from my past. Newly sober, everything that I had been suppressing for years suddenly began rushing to the surface. My normal defense mechanism—drinking—wasn't there.

So, where to turn? I did dive into my sobriety with all the fervor of a new recruit, getting actively involved, sharing my struggles with others in recovery on a twice-weekly basis. I raised my hand and revealed things to strangers that I never thought I could share even with my best friends. What a liberation that was . . . and continues to be. I also found my very wise and patient mentor who gave me terrific advice about how to deal with my unpleasant feelings and my self-destructive cravings for sugar and food, plus the occasional throwback craving for a drink.

I was advised to run a hot bath with aromatherapy or get a long massage or journal about what I was feeling or call a sober friend and share. But on many occasions, it was so much easier to just grab that package of cookies sitting on the kitchen counter. Somehow, munching on that sugary, crunchy, yet creamy morsel would distract me from my uncomfortable feelings—if only for a moment. Then, I'd eat another one. This is what's called *emotional eating**.

I quickly figured out that processed sugar gave me the closest thing to a rush that I could get without getting high. It was a legal high. Suddenly, I became obsessed with sweets. Thank God I was already a vegan because that eliminated most of the junk food that I would otherwise have been driven to devour. Since I consumed no milk, butter, or eggs, that knocked a lot of cakes, pies, and frozen desserts off my menu.

However, like any good addict, I soon determined which candies and sweets were vegan and went after them with a vengeance. Some major brands of cookies are vegan. So are many dark-chocolate candies. It didn't take me long to start packing on the pounds.

An appropriate weight is one of the biggest components to self-esteem. The extra weight I'd gained as a result of my emotional eating made me feel unattractive and uncomfortable, instead of confident and sexy. I don't care how many groups are formed to celebrate big-sized women. While I have compassion for their situations, especially being a recovering alcoholic, I don't believe in encouraging people to overeat any more than I believe in encouraging people to get drunk. Overconsumption of anything is a signal that something is out of balance.

My weight gain in sobriety horrified me because one of the selling points of getting sober is that you get healthier and become more fit. The average glass of wine contains just under a hundred calories. So, if you drink four glasses of wine, that's equivalent to eating a large slice of cake. Mixed drinks like margaritas are really fattening. I was thrilled to have eliminated booze calories from my life. So, imagine my chagrin when I was faced with this new high-calorie monster.

"Why can't you just have a couple of bites?" Stephen would ask me when he saw me diving into a pint of sorbet, which, though dairy-free, was loaded with sugar.

It reminded me of when my first therapist asked me, "Why can't you just have a glass of wine with dinner and leave it at that?"

People who are not addicts have *no idea* of how it feels to be one. They can research it for years, just as a man can research for years what it's like to be a woman and never fully comprehend it. You have to be inside our skin to know what it's like.

Lots of recovering addicts and alcoholics get fat. That's because addictions jump! You give up one thing and something else pops up to take its place. The reason for this is obvious. Addicts will use whatever substance is available to escape and self-medicate. In my case, I couldn't afford to get fat. I'm on television.

Some might wonder why I would still even have all these unpleasant feelings and issues, given that, by this stage of my life, I'd been in therapy for years and was now clean and sober to boot! Well, some issues are easier to resolve than others. As my therapist would say of some of my most intransigent private issues, "It's in the hard drive, Jane. We might be able to modify it, but we can't completely delete it."

It was only after years of sobriety that I really got a sense that I could work through *everything* and—through a *spiritual* program—become truly at peace with myself. As for addiction? The work of staying sober never ends. All I can hope for is a daily reprieve from this disease of cravings. There is no *cure* for addiction. There is no *once and for all* conquering of addiction. You can't return to a pre-addictive status any more than you can regain your virginity! As a clever person once said, "Once a pickle never again a cucumber." So, the struggle just keeps morphing into new manifestations. Like Bach, the same theme keeps reemerging in new variations.

The alarm went off. I felt awful. "Uggghhh! Why do I keep waking up with a headache?" It took me quite a few mornings of waking up with a fuzzy head to realize I was getting hangovers again. But instead of waking up with debilitating hangovers from alcohol, I was now waking up with a shaky, fuzzy, headachy sugar hangover. I absolutely hated the feeling. I had come all this way, fighting for my sobriety, and I just detested feeling like I'd been sent back to the same old place.

"When will it stop?" I asked myself as I crawled out of bed.

Once again, I was experiencing the debilitating demoralization that plagues every addict. But the magic of sobriety is that you can always turn to another recovering addict who is further along in the process for help.

I called my guru Debbie, the rollerblading teacher who had shown me that you can have more fun sober. The woman appeared to have given up everything! As a sober, raw vegan, Debbie ate absolutely no processed sugar and didn't seem to miss it. Why should she? She was in her fifties and had the body of a sixteen-year-old.

"Debbie, I can't stop eating all this sugary crap. I have no control. It's embarrassing. " Debbie paused for a moment. "Meet me at Whole Foods in an hour," she replied.

Debbie is a true friend. Without passing judgment on me, she simply guided me through the store and pointed out all the healthy, unrefined sweets—healthy *sugar substitutes**—that would satisfy my cravings without giving me the refined sugar blues.

"Try the dried mango slices. They're incredibly sweet and a lot better for you than cookies," Debbie advised.

I took one out of the bin. After looking both ways, I took a little unauthorized nibble. I was delightfully surprised and shocked at how delicious it was. I scooped up a bunch for my cart. "Papaya's great too," Debbie advised. "You can make a very sweet bowl of fruit with papaya, mango, strawberries, and bananas, then sprinkle coconut flakes over it and, voilà, you have a non-ice-cream sundae!"

The thought delighted me.

"Now, when you want to add something sweet to your tea or cereal, try agave nectar," Debbie said, pointing to a bottle of amber liquid. It looked like it could be maple syrup, which, by the way, is another very sweet alternative during the transition away from processed sugar. After all, it comes out of a tree.

Debbie breezed down another aisle. "Here's something you should carry around with you wherever you go."

She pointed to a box that looked like artificial sweetener, but on closer examination, the label read "Stevia." She explained, "Stevia powder is a natural sweetener that can be used in place of artificial sweeteners. It comes in the same little packets, but unlike chemical sweeteners, stevia is completely harmless."

I was thrilled to find a healthy alternative to those dreadful artificial sweeteners. When I used the artificial stuff, I often found that I consumed twice the calories I would normally consume. That's because I'd eat the artificially-sweet thing, and later, still feeling the sugar craving, I would cave in to my desire for a "real" dessert.

In just a few moments, Debbie had shown me an alternative to all that unnecessary angst. She had pointed out healthy, naturally sweet alternatives that, it turned out, were right there for the picking.

These natural sweets do satisfy the craving for sugar because they *are* sugar—sugar in its unprocessed, natural state. Therefore, it metabolizes more slowly in the body and doesn't create the sugar rush and crash you experience with processed sugar.

Unfortunately, products like stevia and agave nectar aren't available in most regular supermarkets.

"You usually have to go to Whole Foods or another health food store or a food cooperative," Debbie warned me flatly and added, "If you want to be healthy, you have to go all the way. Half measures avail us nothing!"

When I got home, I sampled all of the incredibly delicious healthy, natural sweets Debbie had turned me on to. As happy as I was to have found a way out of my processed-sugar nightmare, I was furious that I had to go hunting with a trained guide for products that millions of Americans so desperately need.

"What is wrong with this country?!" I shouted.

My dog, Baja, turned toward me and must have been wondering, *What's she upset about this time?*

"We have these fantastic, totally natural sweeteners, and you can't get them in most supermarkets!" I told my pooch. "Why is it that anything healthy seems to be kept in some kind of food ghetto as far away from the American public as possible?"

I applaud the major supermarkets that are beginning to carry more natural foods and vegetarian alternatives. However, I notice that these products are often hidden in some little corner that's easy to overlook, while the artery-clogging products are front and center.

"Excuse me, sir, but where can I find the veggie hot dogs?"

"Ahhhh," the supermarket manager will invariably reply, "I think they're in the back of aisle twelve." And off I will go to inspect this remote area of the store.

At a supermarket in Midtown Manhattan, I had a running dispute with store employees who kept moving the organic, macrobiotic, vegan food section to different locations inside the store. It seemed like these products were getting harder and harder to find.

Finally, fuming, I went up to the manager. "Why do you keep switching the location of the health food products?"

He looked at me with loathing. "Ugh, I would get rid of all of this," he said sweeping his hand toward the tiny area allocated to healthy food. He had total distain for the notion of food that's actually good for you. I looked at him. He was overweight and didn't seem very healthy. I experienced a jolt of frustration. Here was somebody who could benefit from this food but was fighting it.

"Listen, sir, a lot of people love these products. The only reason I come into your store is to buy them. So, please don't keep messing with them."

A couple of weeks later, I went back to the supermarket. Once again, the health products had been moved despite my pleas. This time, they were stuck between boxes of processed deli meats and sugary cakes.

I lost it. Looking around and seeing that there were no store employees nearby, I began my stealth operation. First, I cleared out a refrigerated shelf in a much more prominent spot. Then, I simply carted all of the health-food products to that location and arranged them. I placed my hands on my hips and admired my work, suddenly feeling very empowered. I didn't take anything *out* of the store. I just moved it around *within* the store. So I wasn't actually breaking the law. Now, the macrobiotic, vegan, organic veggie lunch had a prominent spot in the store, and ditto for the vegan sun-dried tomato tofu salad. The brown rice and the soba noodles also took center stage.

"This is how it should be," I said to myself with a certain pride. "Now, maybe people who would benefit by eating these products can find them!"

When I saw the manager heading my way, I took off. FYI, I still go to that store every week and the dialogues over the location of the health-food section continue. However, I was pleasantly shocked to notice, just recently, that the deli counter at that very store has begun serving sesame tofu and sweet-and-spicy tofu! Now that's progress!

Like you, I have watched the obesity crisis grow, which is now about to surpass cigarette smoking as the nation's *number-one killer!*

Like you, I glumly note the ever-present statistic that two-thirds of Americans are overweight or obese. Our nation's healthcare costs are skyrocketing because of it. I don't need the CDC to tell me there's a problem. All I need to do is walk out my front door or look to either side of me when I end up in the middle seat of a commercial airplane. This is why I just *lose* it when people respond to calls to eat responsibly with comments like this one, which are plastered all over the Internet. "I HATE being moralized . . . or treated like a child by someone who doesn't approve of choices that are none of their business . . . my instinctive reaction—the urge to flip that middle finger and go have a six-pound cheeseburger, fries, soda, and a pack of cigarettes."

When I hear people rationalize that being obese is simply a "personal choice," I hear myself, years ago, justifying my out-of-control drinking as simply "a personal choice," and "nobody else's business." Thank goodness I didn't kill myself or someone else while driving intoxicated! It wasn't just a personal choice. I was lying to myself. I also hated when people confronted me about it. That's the defiance of the addict! Food addiction creates the same kind of rage-filled defiance. In fact, food is such a primal issue that it fosters a uniquely ferocious defense mechanism: "DON'T MESS WITH MY FOOD!"

There's a classic Twelve-Step story about the insanity of addiction. It's the parable of the man who loves to jaywalk and keeps getting hit by cars. He's barely healed from one accident when he takes to dodging cars again. Predictably, he gets hit again. People look at him and think, *This guy is absolutely out of his mind.* How is that different from me eating myself into obesity through nonstop gluttony and winding up with high blood pressure, high cholesterol, type 2 diabetes, coronary heart disease, stroke, gallbladder disease, respiratory problems, or some form of cancer? *Overdoing it* is the very essence of addiction! Every morning in my prayers, I always ask God to free me from gluttony, because I have just as much capacity for overdoing it in the food department as anyone else!

As a taxpayer and a voter, I wonder why the U.S. government is subsidizing junk food by pumping billions of dollars into the coffers of enormous factory farms? At a health-food conference I moderated in 2008, Howard Lyman, the author of *Mad Cowboy*, explained to the audience that the average hamburger would cost at least twelve dollars if not for all the U.S. government agricultural subsidies! Our government seems to be sabotaging America's health, even as its mouthpieces talk about responsible eating.

As I flip through the nation's most widely circulated newspapers and magazines, it aggravates me that all of this barely registers with the world's most prominent journalists. They write detailed articles about Medicare financing but don't seem to know or care that the U.S. government is helping millions of Americans ruin their health by subsidizing the most fattening, least nutritionally sound food choices! If you're going to subsidize food, why not subsidize what will make us healthier—namely organic, locally produced fruits and vegetables? I was beyond thrilled that First Lady Michelle Obama planted a vegetable garden at the White House. Now let's back up that profound symbolic gesture with some real change!

Because eating is so primal, everyone is conditioned to leave people's food choices alone. Even though the United Nations has cited meat production as the single biggest cause of global warming (causing more damage than cars and trucks on the road), this in-depth study is never mentioned by mainstream journalists. That, to me, is an indication that the media has a blind spot.

One of my favorite exceptions is author Michael Pollan, a critic of America's food culture and agricultural policies. He cut through the bureaucratic BS in a *New York Times* article in 2003 pointing out, "Absurdly, while one hand of the federal government is campaigning against the epidemic of obesity, the other hand is actually subsidizing it, by writing farmers a check for every bushel of corn they can grow . . . undermining our public-health goals by loosing a tide of cheap calories. . . . "[1]

It irks me that in the six years since Pollan wrote his article, little has changed, other than the fact that the average weight of Americans continues to rise.

I'm sure I'm not the only one who is outraged that powerful agricultural lobbies continue to hold sway over our elected officials, keeping their subsidies in place even in the face of the mounting obesity epidemic. This isn't a sexy story, but if mainstream media doesn't start covering it, there won't be any "sexy" people left in the United States. As American consumers, you and I have to do something. We can't wait for someone else to take action, especially not government officials. The U.S. Department of Agriculture shills for the very business interests it is supposed to regulate. That's why it's easier for me to buy corn-sweetened syrup than it is to buy real maple syrup.

---

[1] *http://www.michaelpollan.com/article.php?id=52, par. 11, accessed April 2009.*

As an addict in the throes of a craving, it's hard to make rational, moral choices. I know. As much as I wanted to eat only the natural sweets that Debbie had recommended, my addictive nature kept drawing me back to the bad white sugars. Refined sugar has such a kick that it's very hard for natural sugars to compete. After years of consuming processed sugar, my taste buds had become deadened. While mangos and agave nectar are super sweet, I couldn't appreciate some of the other more subtle sweets, like the nuanced semi-sweet tartness of a strawberry. The sweetness in most fruits simply can't compete with overpowering sugary sweetness of name-brand candies and desserts. It's like telling a heroin addict to switch to pot. Sure, he can enjoy pot, but it's not going to alleviate his craving for heroin. It took me a several years to gradually sensitize my palate to the subtle tastes found in fruits.

My struggles with sugar are not over. While sugar and alcohol are both very addictive substances, they require different battle plans. I am thrilled and grateful that my obsession to use alcohol has disappeared, and I work on a daily basis to stay in the kind of emotional and spiritual shape that will keep that liquid demon at bay. Alcohol is black and white; you can simply avoid it completely. But sugar is woven into so many foods and beverages—in so many different forms—that it's much harder to just say no to all sugars.

After unsuccessfully trying to give up *all* sugars and slipping repeatedly, I came up with a compromised set of rules: I only eat sweets that contain *evaporated cane juice, brown rice syrup, tapioca syrup, agave syrup, molasses, beet syrup, barley malt syrup, date sugar, or maple syrup*. These unprocessed sweeteners, which actually contain nutrients, metabolize more slowly in the body than refined sugar. With this naturally sweet compromise, I can still have a frozen dessert, like organic soy ice cream or a piece of cake from one of the many fabulous vegan restaurants in New York, Los Angeles, and other parts of the country. I shun products that list sugar, corn syrup, or high-fructose corn syrup in the ingredients. These three are the most often used sweeteners in the mainstream products you'll find on grocery-store shelves.

As my addiction hopped from substance to substance, I also developed an obsession with diet soda. Since I was now determined to avoid both alcohol and sugar, diet soda seemed like the obvious alternative. When I first gave up drinking, I felt like I had lost part of my right arm. *What am I going to do at cocktail parties when everyone else is clutching a glass of wine or a gin and tonic?* I decided to invent my own cocktail that looked like "a drink." It was diet soda, with slices of lime and maraschino cherries. But addict that I am, I quickly became addicted to this drink. I later came to find out that drinking diet soda addictively is a very common problem for recovering alcoholics.

Diet soda addiction seems to be developing into a national problem, afflicting many Americans who are not in recovery. I don't have formal research to throw at you. But just Google DIET SODA ADDICTION, and you will get more than one hundred thousand hits, which will include stories of people who say they drink seven or even a dozen cans of diet soda every day. Some of these people report getting migraine headaches and mood swings when they try to stop.

Aside from the fact that many diet sodas contain caffeine (which is addictive), most popular diet sodas are sweetened with aspartame, an artificial substance that has been the subject of a raging health controversy for many years. While aspartame is FDA-approved, consumers have reported numerous adverse reactions ranging from dizziness to headaches to seizures.

As I learned more about unhealthy versus healthy food choices, it became clear to me that, as a vegan with an interest in organic, unprocessed foods, it would be more appropriate for me to be drinking something natural. In fact, others in the vegan movement had already pointed out my hypocrisy to my face:

"How can you call yourself a health-food advocate and drink that stuff?" a vegan lawyer asked me, with a look of disdain, when he caught me swilling diet soda after a run on the beach.

I could have smacked him. "I'm an alcoholic in recovery and my first priority is not drinking. This helps me not drink alcohol so that's why I drink it," I shot back.

But I knew he was right. Couldn't I just drink water?

That, of course, was easier said than done. Just as happened while I was trying to avoid processed sugar, I found myself repeatedly slipping back into my diet-soda habit. It took me a couple of years to wean myself off the stuff. Eventually, I came up with a new cocktail to hold at social gatherings where people were drinking: sparkling water with a slice of lime. If fresh juice is available, I add a splash. It's quite delicious and satisfying.

That's not to say that I'll never slip up. One day, I might be caught with a diet soda in one hand and a sweet snack in the other, but that won't mean I've given up my way of life! When it comes to processed sweets and sodas, I do my best to avoid them, but there are times when I've been weak and will perhaps be weak again when faced with those tantalizing treats. (As for veganism, it is simply against my nature to eat animal products. Slipping up there is not an issue.)

There is one area in my life where I simply cannot slip up ever, and that, as you probably know, is alcohol. If I slip there, I fear I might never make it back to sobriety. It's truly a life-and-death matter for me. My sobriety must be my number one priority. It comes before everything else, because without it, I have nothing. Therefore, as a safety net of sorts, I am slightly less strict with myself when it comes to sugar and soda. I do my very best and, when I fail, I try to make it a very brief departure from my ideals. I am an extraordinarily addictive type of personality and have found that giving myself a little leniency and self-forgiveness in these two areas helps me stay sober. Coffee is the one thing that I haven't even considered giving up. It's all that I have left . . . at least in terms of addictive substances that I can physically consume. There are, of course, the cravings that *consume me* . . . like sex and love. No, I'm not a sex addict by any stretch of the imagination. But I do apply my addictive nature to the field of romance and that can make me . . . codependent!

My healthy vegan kitchen has seen a lot of fun parties in sobriety.

9

Codependency:
I Want to Be Enough

Codependency. Ah, how to define it? This drug has no taste and no odor. It has no calories. It hardly ever results in your getting pulled over by the cops and thrown in the back of a squad car. You don't end up with an embarrassing mug shot. But just because it doesn't make you fall down a flight of stairs or get pulled over for a DUI doesn't mean it's harmless. Codependency is insidious! Like any addiction, it can make you neurotic, dysfunctional, and even dangerous! And it can make the people around you nuts!

Codependency is a type of addictive behavior that usually manifests itself in the form of unhealthy relationships. Often the co-dependent *enables** the behavior of a partner who is a substance abuser. The classic case would be the long-suffering wife who allows, or enables, her husband to keep on drinking by covering for him and picking up the slack for him, even as she may privately express frustration over his boozing. She may be unhappily married to a drunk. However, she's also very happily married to her martyrdom! Codependents are often described as "nice." In fact, they are so "nice" that they give other people leeway to be "not so nice." So, in the end, they may be "nice" but not *good*.

By my early forties, I'd been sober for several years. Still, serenity hadn't exactly kicked in on my personal life. I was forever phoning my sober friends to vent about all kinds of personal relationship problems. I found it incredibly difficult to say *no* to anybody. I was phobic about confronting anyone over a personal issue. One friend finally suggested that I was suffering from codependency and that I needed to get help. Codependency work *is* considered the Ph.D. program of the Twelve Steps because it forces you to get brutally honest about your behavior and what's *really* behind it! But the last thing I felt I needed was another "issue" to add to my long list.

"As long as I stay sober, I think I'm okay," I'd say. "If I need any more help, then I'll go back to a therapist for a tune-up."

This was my glib response at the time.

"*You* are going to have to start dealing with the consequences of *not* being liked!"

The words stung. They came from Stephen's father, who, as you may recall, was a very well-respected psychiatrist.

That particular day was a beautiful beach day. The sun was streaming into our oceanfront condo near Venice, California, and a group of us were sitting in a circle chatting. I felt that one woman in the circle was being coy and passive-aggressive toward me, repeatedly talking past me to my boyfriend and locking eyes with him, as if I didn't exist. Apparently, Stephen's father picked up the same vibe and wondered why I didn't react to the hostility.

When we had a moment alone he looked at me and said, in a firm voice, *"YOU are going to have to start dealing with the consequences of NOT being liked!"*

The words echoed in my mind as I tried to figure out what he was really trying to tell me. Apparently, he knew me better than I knew myself at the time. The good doctor had been observing me for a while and had finally reached his diagnosis: I was too scared to confront anyone for fear of not being liked by them. It took me years of work to arrive at the same conclusion, namely that I am a classic "people pleaser." If I had any hope of growing into an emotionally mature adult, I would have to start standing up for myself and dealing with the consequences of not being liked!

A lot of people who have known me for years or who have watched me on TV would probably say, "That's nonsense. Jane's a very aggressive reporter and interviewer who has no trouble confronting people and even dressing them down when they deserve it."

But that's only something I'm capable of when I've been assigned to do it by a news organization as part of my job. In those cases, my people-pleasing mechanism is directed toward my bosses, and I become aggressive in my desire to please them by fulfilling the assignment, even if it means confronting somebody. However, in my personal life it's excruciatingly difficult for me to confront anyone, stand up for myself, and set boundaries. I do have an unhealthy desire to be liked by everyone. That desire persists even though, intellectually, I realize that it's impossible for any one individual to be everyone's cup of tea.

This is just one facet of this complex behavioral addiction called codependency. Codependency has been defined in different ways by different people. Here's how I see it. You are codependent if you have a psychologically and/or emotionally unhealthy dependence on another person or persons. Basically your drug of choice becomes that other individual or other individuals. It's hard to tell when you're hooked on a person because codependency comes in many gorgeous disguises: kindness, loyalty, friendship, and even romantic love. A related disease is called love addiction.

Where does love end and codependency begin? That's the gazillion-dollar question. The answer lies in the intention behind one's actions toward the loved object. If I do something to enable their self-destructive/addictive or otherwise unhealthy behavior, that's codependent. It's also codependent when I do something I don't really want to do in the hopes of a payback. Codependents love being regarded as that true and loyal friend, lover, or family member who is always there when it counts. We present ourselves as the opposite of the fair-weather friend. Codependents spring to life when drama and trouble sets in. But the codependent is also, either consciously or unconsciously, keeping score and hoping to get something in return. Often that something is attention and admiration. When the codependent doesn't get that payback, we become resentful. We also try harder than ever to win the elusive admiration we're so desperate to get.

About a decade after that comment from Stephen's father, I had totally rearranged my life, come out as gay, and was living with Sandra, when something happened that made me hit bottom on my codependency and forced me to get help. It was 2008. I had just returned to LA after a business trip and had barely walked in the door when I sensed something was amiss. Sandra was friendly enough but distant.

As I prepared to unpack my suitcase, Sandra took me by the shoulders and said ominously, "There's something I have to talk to you about." I felt a chill go through my entire being. Instinctively, I knew I was about to get some very bad news.

She sat me down at the dining room table.

"I'm moving out," she began. "I've signed a lease on an apartment. You can be very persuasive so please don't try to talk me out of this. I'm not staying here tonight. I'll be back in a few days when the movers come. I'm so sorry. I've tried to make it work but it's just not working for me. This is something I have to do. "

I don't think I've ever felt as empty and defeated as I did at that moment. Although we'd broken up in the past, I could feel in my bones that this time it was really over for good. With that, she walked toward the front door and left. I didn't say anything. I was too stunned. I shouldn't have been.

When I told Sandra a few days later that I felt blindsided by her seemingly abrupt decision to leave, she replied, "You weren't blindsided. You were blind." She was right.

They say there are five stages of grief: denial, bargaining, anger, depression, and acceptance. As I look back, I had already been engaged in the first two stages—denial and bargaining—for over a year. Sandra had broken up with me a couple of times before. But I'd always managed to get her back. As she pointed out, I *can* be very persuasive. I did whatever it took. I even wrote her poems begging her to give me another chance. It usually worked, for a while. Then the old incompatibilities—complaints about my workaholism, certain habits of mine that irritated her—would resurface. I didn't feel the discomfort, but she did.

When the curtain fell on the final act, I still wasn't ready to let go. But this time was different. Sandra had moved out and was moving on. I, on the other hand, was moving into depression. I couldn't stop crying. Virtually anything would set me off—a sad song or a chance memory. I felt like I was in a living nightmare. Everything in the condo and the surrounding neighborhood reminded me of her. I'd walk around the beach in a daze, totally lost. Once again, my life had become unmanageable. I knew I had to do something.

And, once again, the Twelve Steps came to my rescue. The very first Step held the biggest key. It reminded me that, just as I am powerless over alcohol, I am also powerless over this "drug" named Sandra. This was a tremendous comfort because I didn't have to think of the end of our affair as a personal failure for which I was responsible. I could stop replaying the relationship over and over again in my mind and second-guessing myself at every juncture. *If I'd only done this . . . If I'd only gone there . . . If I'd only said that.* That *shoulda-coulda-woulda* thinking is terribly alcoholic as well as codependent. The truth is I was powerless over her decisions. I had no control. It was not my fault. It was nobody's fault. It just was.

Step Two was also a crucial guidepost in my recovery from the emotional toll of the death of our intimate relationship. It says, "We came to believe that a power greater than ourselves could restore us to sanity." It took me a long time to understand that this means my codependency is not a relationship problem, but rather a spiritual problem with a spiritual solution.

In pain, there can be spiritual growth. This heart-wrenching turning point in my life was, first and foremost, an opportunity for me to focus on my spiritual development. If I could move from self-will (wanting Sandra at all costs) into acceptance (letting her continue on her journey) then I could move past my codependent behavior and further mature emotionally and psychologically. This appeared to me to be the lesson I was meant to learn through this breakup.

As I mentioned earlier, alcoholics, at the time they get sober, are at the same emotional and maturity level as when they first started drinking. The reason for this is that emotional development freezes at the start of alcoholic drinking. When I was drinking, I didn't allow myself to experience my emotions. Instead, I stuffed them, pushing them down with booze. Because I wasn't actually engaging my feelings, I turned everything into a joke. Through my teens and early adulthood, I never developed ways to handle emotionally intense situations. My strategy could be summed up in three words: minimizing, joking, and ignoring. You know those immature people who giggle through a funeral? That was me. I had started drinking seriously when I was about sixteen. In 2008, I was thirteen years sober. So, that made me—emotionally—twenty-nine years old, when my chronological age was actually fifty-three.

What did all these lofty goals about maturing emotionally mean in real-life terms? The rest of the Steps were clues. Step Three asks us to turn our will over to our higher power. Every morning I would pray and in the process, turn my relationship with Sandra over to my higher power. As I got healthier, I began turning my "friendship" with Sandra over to my higher power. Again, this step is about giving up any pretense of control, which allowed me to move into the final stage of my grieving process: acceptance. But before I could achieve complete acceptance, I had to do the really hard part: Step Four. That is the inventory step, which I could also describe as a *relationship autopsy**.

A truly honest inventory/autopsy of our relationship proved to be an eye-opener. *What was my part in the dissolution?* This is not self-blame, but rather self-honesty. If I had any hope of avoiding unhealthy patterns in future relationships, I would have to be honest with myself about what I did wrong in my relationship with Sandra. By forcing myself to admit my part in the breakup, through a *relationship inventory**, I was also taking myself out of the role of victim, thereby shutting down my round-the-clock "pity party."

After fighting the conclusion for months, I finally had to admit to myself that I was manipulative in the relationship. I was like the bird lover who captures a free bird and then keeps it in a tiny gilded cage, although I don't know how gilded our cage actually was. The point is that I did things to manipulate her into staying with me. I was trying to control her. It took me a long time to admit that I can be very controlling because, more than anything, I want to appear helpful, generous, and easygoing. That's how I'd like to see myself. But any time you give with the intent of getting in return, then it's not really a gift, it's a trade.

Recently, there was a news story about a man who had donated his kidney to his wife. Later, they became embroiled in an ugly divorce, and he demanded his kidney back. The angry, estranged husband accused his wife of repaying his generosity by having an affair.

"We were in a million-dollar home, I was a full-time surgeon, full-time father and a dedicated husband . . . and I saved her life!"

He also admitted he donated his kidney, in part, to save his marriage, which had been in trouble. You don't give somebody a kidney to save your marriage. You don't give anyone a kidney for any other reason but to save his or her life. And you never ask for it back. Despite his seemingly heroic gesture, his motives were suspect and it ended badly.

This is why Eastern philosophies focus so much on "intention." Having the right intention for one's action is the key. In Buddhism, the concept of "karma" relates not just to the consequences of one's actions but even more significantly to the consequences of one's *intentions* when taking an action. (I talk a little bit more about this later.)

How did I manipulate Sandra? I pressured her into moving into a condo that I had bought for us to live in. Then, I pressured her into helping me renovate it. Then, I pressured her into putting her office there. All the while, I played the role of the generous lover who really wanted to make a nice home for us and make life easier for her. But underneath, there was another motivation. I wanted to lock her in, to make it harder for her to walk away. Wouldn't it be harder for her to leave now that she had this home/office where she could live and work and wouldn't have to commute or pay for office space?

Why would I need to manipulate Sandra into staying with me? Could it be that I didn't feel I was enough just on my own? Self-esteem issues play a huge role in codependency. If you don't feel you're enough, just as you are, then you assume you need "value added" to keep the relationship going. Sometimes we would sit around and talk or lie in bed and watch TV, all the while a part of me was saying, "I need to do more. I'm boring her."

It turns out those times in the relationship, where I did nothing and felt like I was uninteresting, were some of her favorite times. Insecurity feeds codependent behavior, and codependent behavior usually backfires.

While I'm secure as a journalist and reporter, being secure as a romantic partner is a challenge for me. Where did all this personal insecurity come from? It almost always comes from the same place: childhood. My father's alcoholism was a giant boulder that sent ripples through the lake of my existence well into middle age. My mother and I walked on eggshells, never knowing exactly when he would suddenly get angry. I also felt that he was somewhat ambivalent toward being a family man. He didn't carry a photo of me or Mom in his wallet nor did he have a framed picture of me or my mother on the desk of his fancy corner office on Madison Avenue. He didn't attend my high school graduation. When I decided not to attend my own college graduation ceremony, he didn't object. And, when he died, he didn't even leave me a golf ball. Clearly, he was detached, and I no longer take it personally. Dad loved me. But as a high-functioning alcoholic, constantly wrestling to control his alcoholic urges, he didn't have that much emotional energy left over to offer me, Mom, or anyone else. The alcoholic's primary love affair and number one focus is always the drink: when to have it, how many to have, what kind of drink to have, did I drink too much, can I have another, what did I say, who saw me drinking, and so on. In my dad's case, his career got the rest of his attention.

After years of therapy and sobriety, I thought I had worked out all the issues I had with my dad. But when confronted with my own codependent behavior in my relationship with Sandra, I had to admit I still had a lot of work to do. The onion was still not totally peeled.

So, with almost fourteen years of sobriety, I found myself jumping into a program that focuses on codependence. There I was able to address the impact of my father's alcoholic rages and admit that the arbitrary and capricious nature of his decisions (which he alone made) in the home, were—at times—emotionally abusive. He gave Mom a paltry allowance, with which she was expected to compete in the wardrobe department with Park Avenue women. (My mother always managed to pull off a fabulous look, but it was her ingenuity and showbiz background that enabled her to do this.) Dad believed that because he made the money, it was *his* money and his sole right to decide how it was spent and how it would be doled out to my mother and me. I see now that it was a very toxic stance, putting my mother and me in the position of supplicants.

My dad's tightfisted, dictatorial ways made my mother neurotic and emotionally needy. Since the alcoholic is simply not there emotionally for his partner, that partner turns to the child for emotional support and this is what my mother did. But a child is not developmentally capable of playing confidant to an adult. I was stuck in the middle of a man whose behavior was either out of control or totally controlling and a woman who was often weepy and blue as a result of being stuck with an alcoholic. With no siblings to talk to about all this, I found myself a lone soldier on a never-ending peacekeeping mission. I felt it was my responsibility to monitor my parents' emotional states in an effort to head off confrontations. This is how I learned to be a caretaker and became codependent.

When I reached my teens, I became bitter and sarcastic. When they would start to argue, I would break the mood by ridiculing them: "Oh, that's a really important issue to fight about! Your tie and whether you got it back from the cleaners. The future of the world really hangs on that one."

While to all outward appearances a confident and successful advertising executive, my father was also very defensive and thin-skinned, as most alcoholics are. The few times I challenged him on a personal level, his outrage was so disproportionate that I sensed it was a cover-up for his emotional fragility, as if to say, *If my own daughter isn't buying my act, is anyone?* That explains my reluctance to confront people or set boundaries. It stems from an irrational fear that any demands on my part will cause them to shatter, just as my father seemed ready to shatter when I made a rare demand or issued a challenge.

Almost everyone who grows up with an alcoholic parent goes through some variation on this theme. This is why there's a support group specifically for *adult children of alcoholics** (ACA). There is also a support group specifically for anyone who is living with an alcoholic or addict. It's called *Al-Anon**. If you need Al-Anon or ACA, just Google them. There are meetings all over the world.

It pains me to reveal all of this because my father also had many wonderful qualities and was often charming and fun to be around. Dad played guitar and sang. He would come home from work, fix a martini, and strum a few tunes on the guitar and belt out a few bluesy notes while waiting for my mother to get dressed for a party or a dinner engagement.

Although he was a conservative Republican, he read the *New York Times* cover to cover every day. He also did the Sunday *New York Times* crossword puzzle . . . in ink. He taught me about politics and economics, and we would discuss the news of the day. Our fiery living room debates about these issues, including his support of the Vietnam War, helped prepare me for a career in journalism. Dad also taught me how to play golf and tennis, and I had a lot of fun with him. Clearly, he was doing his best to raise me properly. I am only revealing some of his character defects because they impacted me so deeply, and I can't tell an honest story without explaining how these forces shaped me.

The personal insecurities I developed in childhood haunted me in my relationship with Sandra. The really important love relationship in one's life brings a lot of childhood ghosts out of the walls. I gave away all my power to Sandra, laying few boundaries and making few demands. Ironically, my flexibility only served to annoy her.

This was a typical conversation; "Where do you want to go to dinner?" Sandra would ask.

"Oh, I don't care. You pick. Wherever you want to go," I would reply.

A shade of irritation would creep across her face. "Listen, I want you to express your preferences. I don't want to choose all the time. I like you to be assertive sometimes."

"Okay," I'd say, still vaguely fearful that I might make the wrong choice, picking a restaurant she might not like or one that was too far a drive.

I was simply repeating the pattern I'd learned as a child: leave the decision up to someone else. Sandra felt like I was acting like a door-mat. My insecurities turned out to be a self-fulfilling prophecy. Insecure people are certainly not as attractive and alluring as secure and confident people, especially when you're talking romance.

Since I had pursued Sandra and coaxed her into a relationship with me, I was always worried that I cared for her more than she cared for me. Also, I knew, when it came to women, Sandra was obviously far more experienced than I was. This made me feel even more insecure.

During one of our breakups, I forced myself to go on a few dates. While the women I met were wonderful people, I couldn't connect emotionally. I was still stuck on Sandra. Ironically, the fact that I felt numb toward them actually made me more confident since I wasn't concerned with the outcome; I didn't care. That, in turn, seemed to make me more alluring to them.

With Sandra, I cared a lot. I was afraid to lose her. Now, I'm coming to understand that a relationship cannot succeed when one partner is fearful of losing the other.

In her excellent book, *Facing Codependence*, Pia Mellody explains how children who have had emotionally turbulent childhoods often suffer from low self-esteem and boundary issues. If a child grows up without respect for her boundaries, she develops what Mellody calls "a damaged boundary system." Imagine a border with a lot of holes to sneak through in either direction. This manifests itself in an inability to say "no" or "stop" or "that's a deal breaker." Even after years of working on this issue, I still have difficulty saying no.

Mellody points out that, "People with damaged boundaries have only partial awareness that others have boundaries. With certain individuals or in certain circumstances they become offenders, stepping into someone else's life and trying to control it or manipulate it."

This gets back to my relationship with Sandra and the ways I tried to control her. When my being "helpful" stopped working and Sandra made it clear that she was sick of living with me, I became angry. During one of our breakups, I tried to control her with anger. I felt the rage inside me well up and explode in an orgy of righteous indignation. *How dare she reject me?* Sound familiar? It was the very same kind of rage my dad used to have, except I was sober, whereas he was drunk. I was experiencing the dry-drunk mentality, where a technically sober person is just as out of control as a drunk. It was a low point for me. Being an advocate for peace, it was shocking to have my own capacity for anger revealed to me in a brief but disturbing outburst. (Incidentally, this is why I am an advocate for gun control. Similar outbursts happen in homes across America every day. When you add guns and alcohol, sometimes the results are deadly.)

There's another aspect of codependence—and growing up with unresolved boundary issues—that affects my personal relationships. I have a tendency to build walls, using certain kind of behavior to keep people at a distance in an effort to protect myself. Mellody points to four basic walls: anger, fear, silence, and words. I use words to build my walls. The problem with these walls is that it's scary to come out from behind them. That's called being vulnerable and experiencing intimacy.

For me, silence can be very frightening. This was one of the issues that damaged my relationship with Sandra. Sometimes, Sandra just wanted to "be" with me. She wanted to just lie in bed and be silent and intimate. I'm not talking about sex. I'm talking about intimacy. Looking into her eyes and being totally silent was frightening. I could feel my protective walls crumbling. With Sandra, for whom I had such intense feelings already, I could only sustain being this vulnerable for a short period of time. I would feel compelled to fill the silence with words, usually with something entirely unrelated to our shared moment, which made her feel cheated and abandoned, something which triggered her own childhood issues.

Again, my relationship inventory has allowed me to look at this problem, which is the first step in overcoming it. All of this is coming out in sobriety because alcoholism is such a flamboyant disease that it often masks other dysfunction. Once I got sober, I was tested in sobriety with real-life problems and, in the process, other hangups surfaced. The dichotomy is that when a personal issue finally rises to the surface and you recognize it, that's when you're closer than you've ever been to overcoming it.

In facing my codependence, I am not taking the position of *look how sick I still am.* Rather, I am taking the position of *look how I continue to grow.* By the same token, those reading this might conclude, *Boy, has she got problems.* Or they could notice, *Gee, she really works on herself.* This is an important distinction. In this society, which prizes appearances above almost all else, we need to be counterintuitive if we are to grow and evolve. As they say in the Twelve Steps, you can save your face or you can save your ass. I've chosen to save my ass.

Stephen helped me get sober
while he taught me how to ski
and analyze everything.

Michael, my first and only husband.
We're still buddies.

Mom and Dad loved to stop traffic on the dance floor.

10

Overconsumption: *I Want to Stop Buying*

F or some addicts, the substance of choice is alcohol. For others, it's drugs. For still others, it's food. But there's one addiction that virtually all of us share. You and I and nearly all Americans are hooked on *things*.

We've been conditioned to identify ourselves as consumers. We are constantly being indoctrinated to buy, buy, buy. And we're all "drinking the Kool-Aid"! It's a cult I'm fighting to escape. But it's hard. There are guards at the exits. And they have instructions from the powers that be: *Don't let anybody out!*

This is where I found myself on my journey, staring at the gates of our consumer culture from the inside and not seeing a way out. I'd given up booze, drugs, cigarettes, meat, fish, dairy, eggs, processed sugar, and diet soda. But—to my dismay—I realized I still had a long way to go on my journey to living a conscious and compassionate life. Now, I had to tackle one of the toughest addictions of all: STUFF. I liked my stuff.

Even within the area of *consumption addiction**, there are many subcategories. Just as drug addicts can be pot heads, coke heads, crack heads, or heroin junkies, in the arena of consumption, people can fall into certain subaddictions. Some "love" their jewelry, others their fast cars. Some are clothes hounds. Others are always buying furniture.

Me, I had gadget lust.

I had to have the latest thing, which made me what they call an "early adopter." I bought into technologies before the kinks were worked out and the prices dropped: flat screens, sound systems, video cameras, walkie-talkies, not to mention all the portable listening devices that have hit the market over the last decade. The guys at my local electronics franchise knew me by name and would swarm toward me with big grins on their faces when I walked in the store, the dollar signs popping up in their eyes. When they nicknamed me "Gadget Girl," I realized they thought I was an easy mark. *I was an easy mark.*

My lust for gadgets extended beyond technology. I had skis and ski boots, golf clubs, bikes, tennis rackets, and rollerblades . . . and I still do. They're all in my garage, gathering dust. Sure, I used them all. In some cases—I needed them. You can't go skiing without skis. If you ski enough, it's cheaper to buy skis than to rent them. However, just as the food addict has to distinguish between food she needs to eat because she's genuinely hungry and food she's eating to stuff unpleasant feelings, I had to learn to distinguish between stuff I was buying for legitimate reasons and stuff I was consuming addictively.

Often, I was "using" the purchase as a drug to escape inconvenient feelings. With "retail therapy," escape often comes in the form of a fantasy. I want to be in perfect shape. I see a racing bike. I imagine myself on it, decked out in one of those tight-fitting outfits and a sleek, colorful helmet, gracefully peeling around a turn as I approach a straightaway. I'm moving so fast I can hear the wind rippling. Wow, I'm impressive.

That's the fantasy I had when I bought a top-of-the-line professional racing bike. I made a vow to start biking everywhere and promised myself I would use it. I even bought one of those ridiculous racing outfits, which looked totally absurd on me when I finally put it on. Here's the problem with this kind of escapist consumption: the fantasy is an *event in your mind*. Riding a bike is a long and sweaty *physical process*. Fantasy requires no exertion. When I finally got on the bike, sans the outfit, it didn't feel anything like the fantasy. My butt hurt from the saddle, and I hated going uphill. Sure, it was fun to ride the bike, but it wasn't what I had envisioned. It never is. To make matters worse, this particular brand was so cool and coveted, the bike store owner wouldn't sell me a lock, saying this is not the kind of bike you can leave locked up for even a second because it'll be stolen.

Just as there were red flags when I began drinking alcoholically, there were warning bells that indicated I was consuming addictively. You could call it a shopping hangover. I would often feel guilty, remorseful, and anxiety ridden after making a purchase. The "high of the buy" wore off within an hour or so when I began to sober up to the reality of an unnecessary and self-indulgent purchase. *Remorse is a key indicator of addictive behavior.* Often the item quickly lost its glitter and glamour as soon as I got it home. It's kind of like when you're dancing at a nightclub and you think your partner is hot until the lights go on and you realize he . . . or she . . . is not.

Why would something seem fabulous in the store and then, at home, not so much? Part of the answer is packaging. Packaging comes in different forms: plastic and emotional. Let's start with the plastic kind. Manufacturers and distributors use a concept called "perceived value." The more "perceived value" something has, the more money you can charge for it. It's a mental trick. My subconscious mind naturally assumes that something that comes in a lot of plastic packaging has to be more valuable than something that is not packaged. Otherwise, why would that item need to be protected with so much plastic, cardboard, and foam? Overpackaging works with almost any product. For example, a memory card for your camera is smaller than a stick of gum, yet it's housed in a five-by-seven-inch-thick plastic wrapping that has to be cut with heavy-duty scissors to be removed.

Almost one-third of all waste generated in the United States is . . . you guessed it . . . packaging. We are destroying the environment with millions of tons of totally unnecessary packaging, much of which is not biodegradable. It's filling up our landfills and our oceans and polluting our skies, and 90 percent of it is completely unnecessary. All to play a head game. What a concept!

Next, there's *emotional packaging**. The advertising industry is in the business of subliminally linking products with primal human desires like sex, love, attractiveness, popularity, status, family, community, and even patriotism. I used to buy into the emotional packaging. For instance, in addition to shopping at luxury department stores and going to the "in" restaurants, I used to drive a luxury German car. Certainly there's nothing wrong with that, if the selection is made for the right reason. For some, the mechanics and the design fit their needs.

The problem with *my* choice was that I had selected this expensive foreign vehicle because I believed this status symbol fulfilled a couple of my primal human desires, especially community acceptance. I was in Hollywood, working at Paramount Studios, and my news station broadcast out of a sprawling studio on the lot. Because I was one of the anchors, I had a primo parking spot that could only be accessed by driving through the historic front gates of this fabled studio.

For twelve years, I pulled up Monday through Friday at the Melrose Avenue gate and a uniformed guard would wave me through. It felt good to be a part of Hollywood, although I was really just a bystander. Even though our news station was—at one point—owned by Disney, I was still not a part of the Hollywood scene. To be a "player," you had to be entrenched in the movie business or well up the ladder on a big nationally syndicated or network television show, several of which taped at the Paramount lot. Most of the people coming through that particular gate were part of Hollywood and they were driving luxury cars. Those were the hood ornaments glittering in the Hollywood sunlight. In LA they say, *You are what you drive*. I figured I needed to have a luxury car too.

Where would I have gotten the idea that a luxury car would help me fit in and open doors? Just look at any luxury car ad. Invariably, they promise a lot more than a smooth ride, insinuating that being behind the wheel of their brand will magically open doors and bestow upon the driver astounding powers and authority, making the impossible suddenly possible. Yikes! Can you say emotional packaging?

It took me a long time to finally realize something rather profound. *The desire to own status symbols actually reveals low self-esteem!* Status symbols are contrarian indicators, and the reasoning is obvious to me now. Why would I feel the *need* to display a status symbol? Obviously, to prove that I am at a certain level of status. But why would I need to prove my status to others if I was secure within myself about my status? I wouldn't. Often, the richest people who come from generations of wealth don't display it overtly. They don't feel the need to because they are completely secure with their status, knowing exactly where they stand on the social ladder: at the top.

Not everyone who buys a luxury item does so to show it off. However, a good percentage do. The test is: What is my intention in buying this luxury item? If it's because it fits my needs and/or I admire it aesthetically, then it can be a justifiable purchase. But many buy for the wrong reasons. Those of us who don't exactly know where we stand on the totem pole feel a palpable insecurity about that. One way to reassure ourselves and feel safe is by wearing a status symbol. Sometimes, a Rolex isn't a watch as much as it's a talisman worn to protect ourselves against an attack on our legitimacy. People actually flash their Rolexes. I've seen them do it. It's as if to say: You can't touch me. I'm wearing something that will ward off your questions and make me feel safe in society. The subconscious reasoning is: people will have to respect me now. This is why "bling" is so prevalent among the nouveau riche and the newly famous. Despite all their money and fame, they're insecure about their social status. Therefore, they compensate for their low self-esteem by piling on the jewelry.

To improve my standing on the totem pole I, like others, have jockeyed for position. One way to do that is by engaging in *competitive consumption**. Just as food addicts become "foodies," bragging about how fussy they are when it comes to restaurants, menus, and recipes, consumption addicts often feel a sense of pride in the selection of expensive items, which—ironically—they often can't afford. *I have only the best skis!* It's a race to see who can outspend whom. It's all so I can say to myself and others: *See, I have impeccable taste!* But compared to whom? A fabulous sober saying is: *All comparison leads to sorrow.* And what exactly was I comparing? Another brilliant sober line: *Never compare your insides with somebody else's outsides.*

The fascinating thing is that once I really understood the concept that status symbols reveal the opposite of what they're intended to show, I became "allergic" to them. *Bye bye, luxury car. Hello, Prius.* I began to see the overconsumption issue through a different set of lenses: Twelve-Step lenses. It gave me x-ray vision to see the insecurity underneath the glitter. That did it for the luxury goods, but how would I kick my gadget lust?

The answer, as strange as it may seem to you, is by coming to know myself more fully, including my acknowledgment that I'm gay. After I came out to myself and others, I was astounded to notice that my desire to buy tech toys waned. It seems I was "using" the gadgets to deal with many emotional issues. First off, I felt like I needed to reward myself with stuff because I was, unconsciously, depriving myself so severely by not acknowledging my true romantic desires. Second, I was using "stuff" to *stuff* my sexual feelings, buying something when I got the urge for *something else*. Third, I was using the gadgets as props to bolster a persona that I had created as a more socially safe substitute for the gay woman lurking beneath. Ironically, collecting walkie-talkies and sports and video equipment is not exactly the preferred hobby of straight girls. I might have been giving myself away by subconsciously telegraphing to others (as well as to myself) that I was not all that I appeared.

Using the Twelve Steps, I put my shopping through a filter of self-honesty, which in turn helped me make better choices. This process completely adjusted my attitude toward stuff. My first step was to *surrender* to the fact that *no material product would ever fundamentally alter my inner emotional state*. That is the big truth that we need to embrace if we're to resist the allure and power of America's over-consumption engine. The second big truth is that we have no "relationship" with the products we buy. They are inanimate objects, not friends! We are encouraged to exhibit "brand loyalty," as if staying true to a product is the same as staying true to a friend. It's not! Putting my consumption through the Twelve-Step process, I finally "got it." While I need to scrutinize what I buy to make sure I'm not subsidizing something cruel or wasteful, I can't express my individuality through product choices! What's unique about me lies within me, not on my shelf, in my cupboard, or in my driveway.

Through the Twelve Steps, I grew more honest about my real motives for buying luxury goods. I'm happy to say that I haven't been in a Needless Markup (i.e., a luxury department store) for more than a decade. I chopped up all my luxury-department-store credit cards long ago.

Even though I was no longer purchasing as many luxury goods, I was still buying too much stuff in general. Following the Steps, I decided to do a *consumption inventory**. I vowed to write down everything I bought—and I mean everything, including food and drink. This inventory was a true revelation . . . and an embarrassment.

I couldn't believe the sheer number of times I had to reach for my little notebook to jot down something I was buying! It became overwhelming and irritating. It also took the fun out of buying the items and showed me that many of my purchases were self-indulgent and unnecessary. For example, my written inventory showed me the obscene number of times I purchased a cup of coffee at a coffeehouse in one week. Then, there were the little items—from chewing gum to cough drops—along with the necessary food and the unnecessary snacks, plus the miscellaneous must-haves from the pharmacy, like contact-lens solution, shampoo, conditioner, and toothpaste, not to mention other essentials like toilet paper. I needed vitamins and a new hairbrush. My dogs needed biscuits and tennis balls. There were always things that needed replacing at home—a broken light or an old vacuum cleaner. We don't fix things anymore. We buy new ones. I realized that I wouldn't even know where to go to fix a vacuum cleaner these days. And, fixing it would probably cost more than buying a new one. We've devolved into a totally disposable society.

Then, I had to look at my impulse purchases, the little things I'd pick up off a shelf while waiting on the checkout line, like the miniature flashlight I "needed." Just like an alcoholic goes out to dinner vowing to have just one drink and ends up downing a bottle of wine, I would go out to buy one item and come home with ten. Given that I am a journalist, I didn't feel so bad about all the newspapers I bought, but I did feel guilty about all the little accessories, like the sunglasses I found myself buying after carelessly losing the previous pair.

Just three days of cataloging was all I needed to prove to myself that I was a Category 5 hurricane of consumption! Maybe you're thinking this is nothing new. After all, we all have to buy toothpaste occasionally. Technically, you're correct, but when I reviewed my personal consumption on paper and pondered all the packaging that went into all those products, it was a mind-blowing wakeup call! Try it yourself. You'll see exactly what I'm talking about.

Next, I began mulling over all of the personal repercussions of my excessive consumption. I was working hard and scrambling to pay for it all. I felt like an engineer on a fast-moving train named "Consumption," shoveling coal into the engine as fast as I could. I was getting exhausted. Where was this train taking me anyway? How long could I keep this up? Was there another way? How about a streetcar named "Desire Less"?

When I also began observing the consumption of my neighbors, friends, and colleagues, it dawned on me that I was actually on the lower end of the consumption scale. Incredible! I was a four or five on a scale of one to ten. I didn't have children to feed, clothe, and house. I didn't commute to work. I lived in a condo, not a big house with a yard to mow. I didn't own a second home that I had to stock and decorate. I didn't have a boat or a second car. *Yikes! If I'm freaked out about my own consumption inventory, what would theirs be like?*

Some of my friends were deeply in debt. Others weren't in debt, but they didn't have any savings in case of an emergency. Still others could afford everything they bought, but their splurges on a giant flat screen or a new pool table or a motor boat didn't seem to make them any happier. And the boxes, foam, and plastic that these big ticket items arrive in only exacerbate the wastefulness of these purchases. Some of my friends were replacing things that weren't even broken, just to get something "nicer." It's called trading up!

After thinking about what I could do to bring about a much-needed change, I decided to hold a group session during which some of my friends and I could share our feelings about overconsumption in a safe place. We gathered at my home one evening. At first, I felt ridiculous holding such a meeting in my home, since it was relatively cushy in terms of furnishings. We weren't exactly going to be sitting on beanbags. Would they all accuse me of hypocrisy and walk out?

I reminded myself this had nothing to do with income or debt. There's already a program for debtors who need help. It's called Debtors Anonymous. No, this was a sharing session about the *feelings* associated with overconsumption, which has little to do with poverty, wealth, or income.

I began the sharing session by talking about how I've struggled with my own overconsumption. "I feel like I just accumulate so much garbage on a daily basis. Everything I want seems to come packaged in all this cardboard and plastic. It just freaks me out when I think of where all this stuff is going and also where it came from. How many forest creatures were killed during the clear-cutting of trees that end up being the cardboard box that I'm going to touch for a second and then toss in the trash? And then I think about all the people making this stuff around the world. Some of them are children living in filthy conditions. I get so depressed, I can't enjoy what I bought because of the guilt I'm feeling."

Then, it was someone else's turn. I'll call him Bob to preserve his privacy.

Bob said, "I shop for this item, and it comes in a plastic package. I know the plastic is destroying the planet, but I can rip open the plastic package. So, I like it better than something that is not packaged in plastic. Why do I like it better? What does that plastic mean to me?" He shrugged and continued, "I drive a mile to the gym and then I step on the treadmill and I walk for a mile. That's madness and yet I do it. I'm addicted to places like IKEA. I have way more books and furniture than I need. I can't fit stuff into my apartment, but I go there and I see it's displayed in these ways that are like, wow, it's color-coordinated and it does something to my eye and like, that's neat. But then I buy it and I put it in my own place and it's like, I don't know . . . it's just okay."

To say that I identified with what Bob shared would be an understatement. It was almost as if I were the one talking.

Another powerful share came from a woman I will call Kate: "How many pairs of shoes does a woman need? I think about this. These shoes are manufactured in China. I was just reading about how the manufacturing fallout is poisoning all the water. But you know something, every time I see a pair of shoes, especially if they are black high-heeled stilettos, I think I need them and often I buy them. I probably have ninety-five pairs of shoes. And I still buy shoes. I have tennis shoes in multiple colors. I have fifteen pairs of black pumps. And it's almost frightening to me to wonder what I've done to other people's lives because of those shoes. What child was involved in putting the sole on my shoe in China? Why am I doing this? What I think I'm becoming aware of is that I make choices that don't really get me the end result I want. What I want is a full, fulfilling life where I don't feel like I am struggling."

This round-robin talking session was powerful and liberating. Everyone said they got something profound out of it. It turns out so many of us are grappling with similar feelings of shame because we know we're using more than our fair share of what the earth has to offer.

Analyzing my own life, and theirs, I began to conclude that having too many physical possessions is akin to obesity. Too much stuff weighs me down, makes me feel less mobile, less spontaneous, less free. It clutters my surroundings and my mind. I end up feeling bloated and empty at the same time. I also feel guilty over all the environmental harm I'm doing.

One purchase often leads to another. If I buy a big-ticket item, I have to get all the accessories that come with it or it won't work right. Some people have so many possessions they have to get a bigger house. It's progressive, just like any addiction . . . until you hit bottom.

I certainly didn't want to live like a hobo with all my possessions wrapped in a bandana on a stick. But I did want to find some balance and moderation. Even moderate spending, in our consumer society, would be wild extravagance across most of the world.

I had an opportunity to live relatively simply when I covered the Michael Jackson trial in Santa Maria, California, from late 2004 through the spring of 2005. Since I was commuting back and forth from Los Angeles, I had to check out of my ground floor motel room every Friday morning and check back in every Sunday night. My schedule was so intense that I had only minutes to pack up on Friday mornings before heading over to the courthouse to work and then driving back to LA after court ended.

For these practical reasons I had to live sparsely, bringing only the essentials into my hotel room. It was through the process of elimination that I realized how few things I really needed to feel comfortable. At the top of my list were a plug-in pot so I could boil water for coffee in the morning, my own soft blanket, my special pillow, candles to create a mood that would offset the Formica and the harsh lighting, my iPod with my favorite tunes, plus some scented oil to put on my body to make me feel relaxed after a long day dealing with crazy Michael Jackson fans and a bunch of stressed-out fellow journalists. Of course, I also needed my work equipment: computer, portable printer, cell phone, charger, and notebooks. And I needed my work clothes. That was about it. There was something liberating about putting all those special belongings in my Prius and knowing I could happily survive on them wherever I went. This really was all I needed.

But I also know that for me, and most Americans, there is hardly any distinction between *want* and *need* anymore. If I *want* something, I will find a way to convince myself I *need* it. This is a bad habit we've grown into in the decades since credit first became fast and easy. In the old days, before credit cards, if someone wanted something, they couldn't just get it. They'd have to save up for it or put it on layaway. But with ubiquitous credit, we can get virtually anything we want at any time!

If there's a silver lining to the current economic crisis, it's that Americans are finally being forced to distinguish between what we merely lust after and what we genuinely need.

I promised myself that I'd cut up all of my credit cards, except for the ones that require I pay in full each month. When I don't use that type of credit, I use a debit card. This way, there is no interest on credit-card debt to pay. I've found that living within my means is actually a spiritual exercise.

Like many others, I went through that phase where I pretended to myself that I could be lavish, wasteful, and self-indulgent and still be spiritual. It was only by taking my consumption through the Twelve Steps that I was forced to acknowledge that *spirituality and excessive materialism are fundamentally incompatible.* Why? It's obvious when you think about it. By its very definition, spirituality is that which is *not* confined to the physical and material world. Consumption, on the other hand, centers on that which *is* confined to the material world. Materialism is the lowest form of what the Buddhists call "attachment." The bliss of nirvana is defined as a state of nonattachment, the deep understanding that I can't take it with me.

When I overconsume, it's always a symptom of toxic self-centeredness. I know that I am taking for myself what I don't need, while so many others can't get what they desperately do need.

Ultimately, like most greed, my overconsumption is rooted in fear and insecurity. If I keep taking, it's because I don't feel *I have enough*. But when I am able to let go of my hunger for more, I can relax and say to myself, *I have enough*. From there, it's easy to deduce, I do enough. Ultimately, that leads me to the realization, *I am enough*. It's a wonderful mantra that has helped me when I start feeling cravings for stuff I don't need: *I have enough, I do enough, I am enough . . .* just as I am right now.

Newly sober Jane trying to learn healthy new habits.

11

Environmentalism:
I Want to Save
My World

O
n my long, steep climb toward a simpler, more honest life, I have reached a somewhat higher altitude, where each consumer decision must be as carefully weighed as a climber's next step on a sheer mountain. I have come to the realization that each consumer choice I make, throughout the course of the day, is far from just a personal choice. It's primarily an environmental and political choice, which therefore makes it a moral choice. To quote Goethe, "Choose well, your choice is brief, and yet endless."

I still lose my footing and fall off the mountain way too often, but the difference today is that I am *conscious* of when I've done something hypocritical and/or morally reprehensible while shopping. Before I became more self-aware, I would tell myself that I was a responsible person. I would tell others that I cared about the environment and nature. But then, I finally forced myself to look at the truth—namely that *my actions were precisely part of what was destroying the environment and nature.* I had always *known* it. I just didn't want to *own* it.

Long before I arrived at this more honest place, I was in Palm Springs when I suddenly got it into my head to go to one of those gigantic warehouse superstores where they sell everything from couches to air conditioners to potato chips. I'd only been in such a store a couple of times in my life. The most apparent thing about these superstores—aside from the cavernous ambience—is how unbelievably cheap the prices are. *Whenever something looks too good to be true, I know that I need to ask why.* But as I perused the shelves of merchandise, I pushed this thought out of my mind, and for some reason on this particular occasion, my greed took over. I snapped up some summer dishware that appealed to me because it had a vegetable theme, featuring colorful peppers, and being a vegan, how could I resist? Did I really need summer dishware? No. But they caught my eye and brought out the voracious shopper in me.

Armed with a supersized shopping cart, I trolled the aisles with a rapacious zeal. I was experiencing a buyer's rush, that breathless high that comes with the sense that one is getting what is called a "steal." I was particularly taken with a set of salt-and-pepper shakers done up in the form of corncobs. This appealed to me in a profound way, per-haps triggering fond childhood memories of cookouts where corn on the cob was always served. I picked up one of the corncob salt shak-ers and turned it over: Made in China.

For a brief instant, faceless people sweating in a rundown factory flashed through my mind, and I thought for a moment about the intense pollution from all the Chinese factories that pump out these kinds of cheaply made, flashy housewares for American consumption.

I bought six sets.

Sated from my shopping orgy, I waddled out of the superstore with my stash, thrilled with all the stuff I'd gotten for a trifling sum. Then, backing out of my parking spot, I slammed the rear of my car into a pole. I might as well have hit a Bodhi tree, because it came with a moment of enlightenment. My gluttonous retail spree was instantly ruined by the realization that I would be getting a car repair bill that would easily surpass a thousand dollars. Was there a connection between the two events? I suspected so.

A few months later, I was frazzled and running late to visit my friends Jim and Sue (not their real names), who had just moved into a new home, when I realized I had forgotten to buy them a house-warming gift. I quickly scanned my possessions to see what I could possibly extract that would appear to be a thoughtful gift bought just for them. Suddenly, I remembered my secret stash of corncob salt-and-pepper shakers. *Perfect*, I thought. But wait, these friends were stylish environmentalists. Would they abhor and ridicule this salt-and-pepper set? Since I didn't have time on my side, I decided to take my chances.

The evening with them got off to a rocky start. I sensed that they had been arguing before I'd arrived. They accepted the corncobs, muttering a word or two of thanks. The small dinner party was uneventful and mildly pleasant. A couple of hours later, as I was leaving, Jim caught me alone. He was holding the corncob salt shaker in his hand.

"Who made these? Some slave laborers in China?" he asked contemptuously.

I was taken off guard and basically ignored his comment. But, in the car home, I was flummoxed. He totally pissed me off. But I also knew he was right.

The moral of the story behind those damn corncobs has never left me. I still keep a set on my kitchen table. They serve as a daily reminder of a profound truth: *If it's that cheap, expect a karma kickback.*

Similar fiascos helped me reach a turning point on the issue of self-accountability. After all, nobody watched me shop. I could usually assume my lazy, unethical decisions were going unnoticed by others, especially since the vast majority of Americans were making precisely the same choices. However, I do believe that the universe has a funny way of letting us know that such transgressions do not completely escape notice.

One of the major problems with our consumer culture is that it's designed to make morally and environmentally correct choices extremely inconvenient. The choices that are the most readily available to us are the choices that are self-destructive and hurt the earth.

It's very easy to find the products that say: WARNING! AVOID EYE CONTACT! KEEP OUT OF REACH OF CHILDREN! These are the products that tell me to watch out for more than a dozen side effects that are worse than the ailment I'm trying to cure. These "goods" are chemical-filled, nonbiodegradable, unrecycled, unrecyclable, and horribly destructive to our environment. These are the products with long lists of obscure and often harsh ingredients, which ultimately end up in our rivers and oceans and get absorbed into the ground.

Ultimately, I've come to the realization that *what is harmful to the environment and exploitative of third-world laborers is not going to serve me well either.* If it's toxic to the earth, it's probably not something I want to eat, pour on my body, or use to clean or improve my home. I have realized that *ethical shopping is in my self-interest.* But to be a truly ethical shopper, I first had to become an informed shopper. I was stunned and profoundly saddened when I became aware of the extreme cruelty that goes into the production of so many consumer items. As an investigative journalist, I've viewed many videos of product testing on animals. It is one of the most gut-wrenching experiences I've ever had as a reporter. Even one glance at animal testing for products will convince anyone with a heart and a functioning moral compass that this should not be as prevalent as it is in the twenty-first century, when we have modern methods that work on the molecular level to achieve the same results.

During a particular eye- and skin-irritation test, rabbits are immobilized in full-body restraints while a substance is dripped or smeared into their eyes or onto their shaved skin. The level of pain inflicted on these animals defies description. Sometimes they snap their necks in a desperate bid to free themselves from the immovable restraints. Rodents and sometimes dogs and primates are immobilized as harsh chemicals are dripped into their eyes and poured into their stomachs. All this even though drugs and toxins often have a radically different impact on humans than they do on animals. Dogs aren't even supposed to eat chocolate.

Using the Twelve Steps, I created a very simple *kindness inventory** that allowed me to put my shopping choices through an ethical filter. If a product fails the test, I won't buy it. It's a very simple test. *Has the product been tested on animals?* If it has, I won't buy it. (For a complete list of compassionate companies, just go to www.caring consumer.com.) This simple test has allowed me to eliminate the vast majority of harsh, toxic chemicals from my home, from my life, and at least in a small part, from the environment.

Like everything in life, it's hard to be completely black-and-white. There are products such as airplane engines that are animal-tested. Traditionally, bird carcasses are shot into the engines to determine if the machinery can still function; suitable density substitutions are used as well. Does that mean I'm never going to fly in a plane? No. Will people who have no ethical considerations whatsoever use this outlandish example to put people like me on the defensive? Probably. To those people I say, "I'd rather be a hypocrite one percent of the time than be a heartless individual 99 percent of the time."

I have found this simple criterion—was it tested on animals?—to be an ideal prism through which to view my choices. It is simply about my having respect for all living, sentient beings. I am an animal. So are they. I have eyes, ears, and a heart. So do they. I feel pain. So do they. I feel loneliness and sorrow. So do they. I dream. So do they. Why would I not respect, cherish, and protect my fellow creatures?

The added advantage of making humane choices is that this decision may very well protect my health and prolong my life. Products that are not tested on animals usually contain more natural ingredients and far fewer ingredients overall than mainstream brands.

There are natural and compassionate alternatives are out there, and they are becoming easier to find as more and more consumers demand them. In 1990, Revlon became one of the first major cosmetics corporations to swear off animal testing and, in doing so, proved that it's possible to produce fabulous, successful products that are deemed safe by using alternative testing methods such as testing on skin cultures. Many other companies are now following suit.

When it comes to groceries, I mostly shop in health food stores or cooperatives because I can get organic, vegan alternatives there. And while I'm picking up my groceries, I can also get my household cleaners, detergents, shampoos, conditioners, toothpastes, and other items that have not been tested on animals and are made with biodegradable ingredients that will not adversely affect the environment. BIODEGRADABLE and NOT TESTED ON ANIMALS are the labels that I look for. A product will proudly state that on the label because it's a selling point. I don't take a salesperson's word for it. If the item doesn't specifically say it, I put it back and then do some research.

Of course, a lot of consumers complain that cruelty-free, biodegradable products are more expensive than the ones that they can find at the corner market. Often, that is the case. It's the law of supply and demand. However, you can help change that! As more consumers demand these kinds of products, corporations will find a way to mass-produce them in greater quantities, thereby allowing the economies of scale to kick in and lowering the price per unit. But they will not do it until we, the consumers, start insisting that's what we want. In the meantime, spending a few dollars more at the checkout counter is a small price to pay for feeling good about what you're using.

Careful label-checking—not price—guides all my shopping decisions now. In fact, it's how I first selected most of the products I use today. I'd wander down the shopping aisles, comparing claims and ingredients for each item I regularly purchased. For instance, I finally settled on a deodorant brand with a label that read: *vegan, cruelty-free, no animal testing of raw materials or final product, no alcohol, artificial detergents, color, or synthetic perfumes.* Now that was a product I could feel morally comfortable using. And, it works great! Nobody has ever accused me of having bad body odor. Meanwhile, I don't have to worry about the growing controversy over the possible health impact of regular deodorants with aluminum.

Likewise, the label of the shampoo and conditioner I decided on said: *No lauryl/laureth sulfates, certified organic, biodegradable, no animal byproducts, no animal testing, no parabens.* Parabens are chemicals used as preservatives in cosmetics and pharmaceutical products, over which there is growing controversy. Laureth sulfates are foaming agents that are also the subject of mounting concern, which is why my natural product brags—on its label—that it has no such chemicals.

The toothpaste I chose contains: *no saccharine, artificial sweeteners, preservatives or animal ingredients* and does no animal testing. You get the idea.

Some health products explain, right on the box, the purpose and the source of each ingredient. I like it when the manufacturer of a product respects my intelligence by giving me definitions and context. Otherwise, all those weird, long names on the back of packages are mere gobbledygook. By using truly natural products, I don't have to feel guilty that I'm harming myself, other creatures, or the environment. These are feel-good products!

Plus, all of the natural products I just described—and use regularly—are made in the United States! Given the scandals over tainted dog food, candies, and other products from China, it's a relief to be able to find healthy products that are made in America. Not only is the purchase of American-made products patriotic, it supports our economy!

Beware: certain brands out there have tried to co-opt the movement toward nontoxic products by labeling their products "natural" without really making them natural. That word "natural" can be twisted to mean almost anything. *Natural* cyanide is still cyanide. That's why I always turn the bottle around and check the ingredients and the other information on the back of the container. I don't want to get bamboozled!

Again, caringconsumer.com is a great resource to find a wide variety of nontoxic, cruelty-free products. Despite my heightened awareness and determination, keeping toxic substances out of my home has been a struggle. Why? One is reason is that other people are always trying to bring toxic substances in! A perfect example occurred just the other day.

While my bathtub was being cleaned, some caulking came loose. I knew it had to be replaced to keep water from leaking into the walls. When I asked the maintenance crew to get some caulk, I didn't know what I was getting into.

They showed up with the caulk. Yikes!

The front of the tube said: "**WARNING**: CONTAINS 2,2,4-TRIMETHYL-1,3-PENTANEDIOL, MONOISOBUTYRATE, VINYL

ACETATE AND ACETALDEHYDE. MAY CAUSE EYE, SKIN & RES-
PIRATORY IRRITATION HARMFUL IF SWALLOWED OR ABSORBED THROUGH
THE SKIN. USE ONLY WITH ADEQUATE VENTILATION. ENSURE FRESH AIR
ENTRY. AVOID CONTACT WITH EYES, SKIN & CLOTHING. WEAR GLOVES &
SAFETY GLASSES. SEE MSDS FOR ADDITIONAL SAFETY INFORMATION.
FOR AN MSDS CONTACT YOUR SUPPLIER. **WARNING**: THIS PRODUCT
CONTAINS CHEMICALS KNOWN TO THE STATE OF CALIFORNIA TO CAUSE
CANCER. **FIRST AID**: SKIN: WASH THOROUGHLY. EYE: IMMEDIATELY
FLOOD WITH LARGE QUANTITIES OF WATER FOR **AT LEAST** 15 MINUTES.
GET MEDICAL ATTENTION IMMEDIATELY. **INHALATION**: REMOVE TO
FRESH AIR. GET MEDICAL ATTENTION IMMEDIATELY IF DIFFICULTY IS
EXPERIENCED. **INGESTION**: DO NOT INDUCE VOMITING. GET
MEDICAL ATTENTION IMMEDIATELY. MEDICAL EMERGENCY?/
EMERGENCIA MEDICA? CALL 800 XXX-XXXX. **KEEP OUT
OF REACH OF CHILDREN, DO NOT TAKE INTERNALLY**."

Somehow, after all that, caulking my tub didn't seem all that
urgent. What did seem urgent was getting this stuff back to the store
and getting a refund! I certainly did not want to financially support
that kind of intensely toxic product. Just holding the sealed tube was
making me itch. Why does caulking have to be that poisonous? The
answer is . . . it doesn't.

A quick search on the Internet gave me a lead on a nontoxic,
water-based caulking material. One website proudly proclaimed, "We
have a full **selection** of **non-toxic building products** for you to
order." The site added, "The Public must demand **healthy homes**
and **living environments**: we have the **non-toxic materials**."

Damn right. But why do I have to go on the Internet, fill out an order, and wait for a shipment in order to caulk my tub? Why aren't these products readily available at the local hardware store? It won't happen until you and I start demanding these nontoxic products! We need to vote with our consumer dollars.

Fortunately, some environmental changes are relatively easy to make, comparatively speaking. For example, I made a couple of simple decisions that radically reduced my consumption of unnecessary, environmentally disastrous plastic. One day, when Sandra and I were still living together, we stopped at the supermarket. She ran in while I waited in the car. The parking lot was packed. It was a busy shopping day. Just for fun, I decided to count how many people came out of the supermarket with reusable bags. I watched and waited. And waited. Plastic, plastic, and more plastic. In the forty-five minutes it took Sandra to shop, I did not see one person leave the supermarket with a reusable bag. And this was in Santa Monica, California, allegedly one of the most environmentally conscious cities in America. *What a bunch of lazy bums,* I thought. *They can't remember to bring their own bags even though it's common knowledge—repeated ad nauseam on newscasts and websites—that the plastic bags they use for the ten minutes it takes them to get home last up to a THOUSAND years.* Then, I looked in the rearview mirror. Sandra was approaching, laden with goods in . . . plastic bags.

Then, I angled the rearview mirror at myself. *What about me? How often do I use reusable bags?* My honest answer was sometimes. I had bought two very sturdy, hip, sky-blue, reusable bags at the Museum of Modern Art store, and they had lasted for years. Every time I walked into a supermarket with them, somebody commented on how cool they were. But when I ran into a store on the fly, I often didn't have those big, hard-shelled reusable bags with me. That's when I accepted a plastic bag. This kind of unplanned shopping happened more often than I cared to admit. So, I was a hypocrite, albeit a conscious one.

Then, I began reading about the environmental catastrophe that plastic bags are creating in our oceans. They are called "little white bags of death" because they spell a slow, agonizing death for the sea turtles and whales that ingest them. They also get wrapped around the necks of seals and sea lions and can slowly choke them. On the Internet, I saw a photo of a little bird trapped in a plastic bag. Just her little beak was poking out. She looked bewildered. She has undoubtedly since died a slow painful death. The only thing required for evil to triumph is for good people to be complacent!

I began wondering if any of the plastic bags I bought ended up choking a turtle or strangling a seal. We always assume that it's somebody *else's* plastic bag doing the damage, not ours. It's a false assumption. Only a tiny fraction of all the hundreds of billions of plastic bags discarded every year is ever recycled. There's a good chance one of my plastic bags flew out of a landfill and into the water and killed a living creature. The photos of this avoidable torture of sea life are all over the Internet. Plastic bags are also threatening living coral reefs because they wrap around the coral and quickly kill it.

I resolved to change my part in the plastic-bag carnage. I did what I often do when I want to make a change. I made a game out of it. I bought some thin nylon bags at Whole Foods, which wrap up into little bundles, and I keep them in my purse. Now, when I forget to bring my purse, I either return home to get the reusable bags or awkwardly carry the purchases out of the store in my arms without a bag. Do that a couple of times and you'll find yourself remembering to bring the reusable bag. It's that simple.

Today, I can honestly say that I have reduced my plastic bag consumption by 95 percent. I will not accept a plastic bag, not for my Chinese takeout, not for my restaurant leftovers . . . never! One bad habit down, thousands more to go.

As for my little spats with those shoppers who regard plastic bags as an inalienable right? I try to explain that plastic bags only came into existence in the 1960s. How the hell did everybody survive shopping before that?

"Mind your own business," one said to me.

I replied, "It *is* my business. It's your world *and* my world you're destroying."

One of the addictions I haven't tried to give up is caffeine, although I've grappled with the environmental and political aspects of coffee. Frankly, caffeine is all I have left, and, right now, I'm hanging on for dear life. Alcoholics often become teetotalers because sipping tea with a little kick of caffeine is a relatively effective substitute for booze. As far as the health-related dangers of coffee, it certainly can't compare to the dangers of getting tanked up and slamming into a tree. The national deliberation over coffee appears to be leaning toward a hung jury. Some say it's awful for you. Others say a cup or two a day can have benefits because coffee beans contain antioxidants. I prefer freshly ground coffee grains, inhaling the steam as I pour the boiling water over the ground beans. It's a fabulous aroma.

Being an addict, I have often gone overboard on coffee (remember, I kept a list), and I really have to watch myself. In moderation, I think coffee is one of life's less pernicious comforts.

The business of growing and collecting coffee can either be terribly exploitative of our fellow humans and the environment or it can actually nurture them. The key is to get coffee that is organic, fair-trade, and *shade-grown.*

"What the heck is shade-grown?" I asked myself the first time I saw that label on a bin of coffee beans at the Santa Monica Cooperative.

One Google search answered my question. Shade-grown is the time honored method of planting coffee shrubs in the shade of tall trees. That practice has long made coffee plantations excellent places for birds and small animals to live. However, to get more bang for the buck, the modern coffee plantation is sun-grown and uses chemicals and pesticides, depriving birds of their homes while simultaneously poisoning their environment. That's why the number of birds migrating to Latin America is plummeting, according to the Smithsonian Migratory Bird Center.

To get shade-grown coffee, you generally have to go to a health food store. Even there, I often find either organic shade-grown or organic fair-trade, not both. Recently, surfing the Internet, I came upon a coffee company that does it all. Grounds for Change is a certified organic coffee roaster specializing in 100 percent fair-trade, organic coffee, grown in shaded conditions. Additionally, the company helps support independent coffeehouses, a great movement in itself. "Every single bean we roast is certified Fair Trade Organic coffee," it boasts on its website.

So, I've been asked, "Is that the *only* kind of coffee you drink now?" The answer is no. There are many times when I'm running around at the office or out and about that I'll drink the coffee that's available (with the reusable cup that I now carry around).

When it comes to environmentalism, as with most things, perfectionism is self-defeating. If I say to myself, *Now, I can ONLY drink coffee that is shade-grown and fair-trade,* I will become overwhelmed by the enormity of my task and probably give up and completely revert back to my old bad habits. Ditto for avoiding paper towels and, yes, even plastic bags. But if I acknowledge that I will not be able to practice this perfectly, I'm already incorporating the inevitable mistakes into my plan. Therefore, when I fail, it's easier to pick up and continue on my path to less mindless consumption. *This whole environmental effort is a process not an event!* As we say in Twelve Steps, there is no one among us who is going to practice these steps perfectly. What we seek is *progress not perfection!* The very same concept holds true for reducing your consumption. Progress not perfection!

As I admitted earlier, I used to be a coffee-house junkie. Gourmet coffees and chai teas tasted great to me. But then I started looking at the number of coffee cups and plastic caps I was using, and I began feeling guilty about it. One day, when I was jonesing for a really good, hot cup of java, I decided to bring in one of my reusable metal coffee mugs to Starbucks and see how they treated me when I handed it to the barista.

The cup was clean, but I still felt weird. Ridiculous thoughts cluttered my mind as I waited for my turn, watching customer after customer order and walk out with their paper cups. *Will they think I'm a nut or homeless?* Finally, my turn came to order. I was actually nervous. I said, "I'll have a grande soy cappuccino wet." Then, I thrust my cup at her and said. "Can you put it in this?" She took the cup, looked at it for a second, looked at me, and said nothing, but simply added up my order and gave me the total. The soy cappuccino was made and handed to me and that was it. I wasn't a freak. Nobody said anything. I was thrilled to have my coffee without destroying all that paper. Now, wherever I go, I carry my trusty reusable mug.

Despite all the changes I'd made, there were still plenty of evil habits to kick. Plastic bottles, for example. Yes, I drank out of them, until I started reading about the environmental devastation they are causing around the globe. Americans throw away *two and a half million plastic bottles every hour!* According to the Clean Air Council. Only a small fraction are recycled. Like most Americans, my role in this catastrophe was played out when I was outside of my home, where opportunities for recycling are scarce.

"Jane, they want to see you on camera. You've got about six minutes until your hit."

This was the warning I got from a production assistant in Los Angeles as I prepared to make a TV appearance. I was just finishing up my makeup and had to move fast.

"Want some water?" the assistant asked helpfully.

Of course I did. I drink a lot of water when I'm on television because my mouth becomes dry from all the talking. Some people perspire. I get thirsty. I took the plastic water bottle. I did this over and over again. I did a lot of appearances on a variety of shows and, because I was always rushing to get on camera at the very moment that water became a necessity, I would always accept a water bottle. But with each passing appearance, I was feeling increasingly hypocritical about taking the plastic water bottle.

One day, the lightbulb went off. *Why the heck don't I just get a metal water bottle and carry it with me?* I saw one, in Starbucks, and have been using it ever since. It's perfect because the metal keeps the water cool. No chemicals leach into the water the way they do when plastic water bottles are left in the heat or sun. In the long run, I've saved tons of money because I no longer buy plastic water bottles. I do buy fresh squeezed juice in plastic bottles. But since that's consumed in my home, I know that plastic is going to go into my building's recycling bin.

All of these changes have helped me feel better about my daily romp through this life. I still have a long way to go. My consumption of other kinds of plastic, for takeout salad and other foods, is still unacceptable. But I'm working on it.

I just bought a Rubbermaid container that is the perfect size for salads and have been taking it to the buffet salad counter at work. Again, I thought people would look at me funny, but nobody even noticed.

What really irks me is that the technology exists to make biodegradable plastic bags and plastic bottles. An acquaintance of mine even started a company that markets a corn-based biodegradable plastic water bottle. On the company's website there's a video that demonstrates how this bottle decomposes and disappears within eighty days! But good luck finding one at the supermarket.

American industry could make the switch to biodegradable products made from renewable resources, like corn. Why don't they? *Because we're still buying the non-biodegradable plastic!* So, what's the incentive for them to switch? There is none. That's why my decisions as a consumer are so crucial. If I buy a product that harms the earth, I am an accessory to that assault. In the final analysis, I'm even more than that. When it comes to killing the environment, I—as the consumer—am the instigator who orders the hit. The companies just carry out the order. As I struggle to change the world I have realized that, first and foremost, I must change myself.

It's always been about the journey.

12

Into Action:
I Want You to Join Me

The journey I found myself on was a dichotomy. The higher I climbed, the less I found myself craving. The liberation from *things* is really the liberation from the *desire for things*. Just like any addiction, it's not about my having the willpower to say no. It's much more about my evolving to the point where I just don't want *it*—whatever *it* is—anymore.

There are a few people I have met who really epitomize for me the spirit of nondesiring and nonviolence. One is Julia Butterfly Hill. This beautiful young woman is famous for her unique and courageous act of civil disobedience. She sat in a six-hundred-year-old California redwood tree for 738 days in order to stop it from being cut down by loggers who had set their sights on that tree and others. For more than two years, Julia remained on a six-by-eight-foot platform made of reused scrap wood with only a tarp over her head. She endured storms and frosts, the hostility of loggers, and the astounded eyes of the world. She is living proof that one person, when sufficiently determined, can make a difference. Her peaceful defiance saved the tree and energized the global movement to save old forests.

I got the opportunity to interview Julia Butterfly Hill at an event called WorldFest, which takes place every year or so in the Los Angeles area. It's an outdoor rock festival that celebrates nonviolence to other humans, the environment, and animals. As the music roars, thousands of people—from the curious to true believers—descend on a massive vegan food court and investigate the many booths that pitch everything from hemp clothing to electric vehicles. Many people bring their dogs. Others adopt homeless dogs or cats while they're there.

For several years, I served as the mistress of ceremonies of WorldFest, bringing my own dog on stage with me as I introduced activists like Julia, who spoke in between band performances. I would also grab on-camera interviews with the celebrities after they walked off stage.

When I approached Julia, I really had very little information about her. She was the famous tree sitter. That's all I knew. Beautiful and slim, Julia wore a small backpack and exuded an energy that is almost indescribable. She just seemed on a higher plane than everyone else. I could see it in her bearing, her speech, and her eyes. She seemed oblivious to the ordinary, even as she urged people to pay close attention to their ordinary decisions.

When I asked Julia what people could do to stop destroying the environment, she pulled off her backpack and showed me its contents. Inside were a simple metal plate, a metal fork, knife, and spoon, a mug, a travel water canister, a napkin made of cloth or hemp, and a few other essentials.

"I carry these with me everywhere I go. I use them. Then I wipe them off. That way, I'm not participating in the destruction of trees and forests. It's very simple, really, and it's easy."

I was profoundly impacted by Julia and the simplicity of her approach. I knew I was meeting a very rare individual. She appeared to have moved spiritually beyond the base cravings that seem to dominate most of our lives. Her most profound message was just . . . her. They say recovery is a program of attraction, not promotion. I was deeply attracted to her simple philosophy and her way of being. Ironically, I craved what she seemed to possess . . . the lack of craving.

She also seemed to have evolved to a place where she was sensitive to all living things: humans, animals, and trees. Julia relates to trees as individuals and families. On her website, Circle of Life Foundation, she writes, "Did you know that redwood trees live in families? They have very shallow roots, but redwood trees are connected to each other through their root system. When you see a group of redwood trees, often they are all part of the same roots, and they feed one another that way."

Years after interviewing Julia, I bought a dining room table made of fine wood. I was possessed with a craving for this item and never considered the family of trees from which the tree, which was killed to make my table, might have been pulled. As I now pause to recall Julia Butterfly Hill and her philosophy, I'm regretful that I wasn't thinking of her message the day I went shopping for that table. This was a major shopping decision that I failed to put through a kindness inventory. After buying a few shoddy things that didn't last very long, I told myself I wanted a good-quality table that would last a long time. But now I realize that I could have purchased an antique table, made of trees that had died long ago. Antiques are, by definition, recycled.

I don't have what it takes to sit in a tree for two years, but I am committing to do a living amends for the tree or family of trees that I killed. I will further reduce my level of paper consumption. As of this writing, I am making a vow to forsake paper towels, even recycled ones, opting instead for cloth napkins and towels. I will also attempt to use only recycled paper when it's within my power to control what sort of paper is used. I spoke to my editor about the paper this book is being printed on. She explained, "The paper we use is from 'sustainable' forest mills. The trees are fast-growing soft pine. To stay in business, the mills actually plant the trees they eventually cut down for paper production and then replace them." This notwithstanding, I feel that getting the story of my personal struggle out to others, who might identify and learn something, could ultimately save more trees than this book destroys. At least that is my hope.

Julia's story is a tale of action not words. With incredible grace, combined with fierce determination, she took an individual action that continues to have reverberations around the world. She is an inspiration for those of us who want to move into action to change the world.

Before she embarked on a mission to save one tree and, metaphorically, save the world, Julia had been a bartender in Fayetteville, Arkansas, with no more than a passing interest in the environment. What happened to change her from an ordinary American into an extraordinary one? A nearly fatal car accident that, Julia tells the BBC, "shoved a steering wheel into my skull and changed the course of my life forever. Almost a year later I was able to walk and talk and be normal again. At that time I decided everything I had taken for granted had been almost taken away from me, and I had to start focusing my attention and my life on the real and important things."[1]

On a far less dramatic level, I had a similar experience. In the spring of 2005, *Celebrity Justice* was cancelled—and, with it, my job. The cancellation occurred at nearly the same time Michael Jackson was found not guilty on all counts in the child molestation trial I'd been covering from Santa Maria for months. I went back to LA permanently, and, for the first time in my then twenty-seven-year career, I had no job.

"I better go get all my medical checkups before my insurance runs out," I told Sandra, who had recently moved in with me.

Like a lot of workaholics, I almost never went to the doctor. Now, I suddenly had a free calendar. I made an appointment for a mammogram and, in short order, found out I had breast cancer.

You never know what's good news and what's bad news: "If you have to have breast cancer, this is the way to do it," my doctor told me. "You had the good fortune to spot it at the very earliest possible

---

[1] *http://www.bbc.co.uk/dna/h2g2/A413786, accessed April 2009.*

stage. If you hadn't gotten that mammogram when you did, the cancer would have probably spread and become a much more life-threatening situation for you. You're quite lucky."

The cancellation of *Celebrity Justice*, which was at first a disappointment, may very well have saved my life. Still, much like Julia Butterfly Hill, the realization that death could be a real possibility, as opposed to a hypothetical one, altered my perception of life. In one instant, when I got the diagnosis, I had a profound shift in consciousness.

I got the initial news from my doctor via cell phone while I happened to be walking on a busy street in Midtown Manhattan in the very neighborhood where I grew up. Just as she told me she was sorry she had to deliver bad news, I paused right in front of a building that used to house a restaurant where my parents always took me to dinner when I was a kid. It was like coming full circle in that one second; the birth-to-death cycle seemed more than a theory. I felt it. Life speeds by, and the next thing you know, it's over. Whatever *it* is . . . I got it in that second. Some people call it a psychic shift. The best way I can describe it is that, although I felt scared, I also felt incredibly liberated.

In one second, my entire life fell into much clearer perspective. My everyday worries suddenly seemed trifling. *So what if I don't get a job? So what if I don't pick up the phone when so and so is trying to reach me? So what if I don't make it to that funeral or that baby shower? So what if I want to sit on the beach all day reading magazines and eating popcorn and playing catch with my dogs?* The guilt and the sense of obligation that used to be my albatross suddenly unraveled and slipped away.

I went back to my therapist for a tune-up, just to make sure I wasn't having some kind of bizarre delusional episode. I explained to him that I was sort of perplexed over experiencing this euphoria connected to my diagnosis. He got it immediately.

"It can be very freeing," he explained. "Now, you really can do whatever you want to do for the rest of your life. And when somebody asks you to do something you don't want to do, you can say, 'Sorry, for health reasons, I can't do that.'"

I've come to learn that many people who've been diagnosed with cancer have had similar reactions. In a lot of ways, it was a "get out of jail free" card. Certainly, it was a "get off my back" card. For example, I knew that I loved giving my opinion on the issues of the day. That was always my passion. It probably goes back to my living-room debates with my dad. Also, Nancy Grace started asking me for my opinion while I was a daily guest on her show during the Jackson trial. That allowed me to burst out of my restrictive role as a straight, objective news reporter and put some spin on the ball. I absolutely loved it and, again, have Nancy to thank for helping me break out of my hard-news shell. Still, it was a risky leap to attempt to do commentary full time, without having a paid full-time gig with a news station. For the most part, people don't get compensated for being invited on as a guest to offer their opinion. It was because I had just experienced this brush with death that I became psychologically capable of taking the risk and following my passion. Instead of being fear-based and just taking any job that came along, I vowed that I would try to establish myself as a TV pundit.

In the weeks following, as I waited for my surgery, I experienced a few moments of profound sadness while contemplating my own mortality. I knew there are no guarantees when you're dealing with cancer. I was aware they could find something during the surgery that could be more serious than initially believed. I thought of all the people I'd miss. My family and friends . . . and Sandra. I thought of my dog of fourteen years, Baja, who has since passed away. I also hated the idea of leaving this world in the condition it was in, with all its cruelty and chaos, even as I knew I had precious little power to change it on my own.

In so many ways, the entire episode was a huge growing experience. After two surgeries and radiation, I was deemed healthy once again! In retrospect, none of this should have come as a big surprise to me. My father died of cancer and numerous studies have shown a connection between heavy alcohol use and breast cancer. In 2008, researchers at the University of Chicago reported their conclusions from one of the largest studies of its kind. The team, which presented its findings at the American Association for Cancer Research 2008 Annual Meeting, found women who have three or more drinks a day, are increasing their odds by as much as 51 percent.[2]

I'm sure my drinking was a major contributor. I also believe my plant-based diet will help me to stay healthy from now into the future.

How did this experience push me into action? It liberated me from the chains of my more mundane concerns, thereby giving me energy to focus on issues that go well beyond my own personal survival.

---

[2] *http://www.foxnews.com/story/0,2933,351208,00.html, accessed April 2009.*

Previously, I had been devoting too much energy to managing the minutia of my life—my IRA's, the market value of my home, my pension, my car's condition, my insurance rates, and other similar considerations. These things are important, but they're just not *that* important.

I'd had long been an activist. I'd long donated more than I could afford to causes and organizations that try to stop the ongoing carnage against the earth and its most helpless inhabitants. It was just that I had been a worried, neurotic activist, always fretting about how I could balance my passions with my purse strings. After my cancer experience, my level of concern about the practical and material aspects of my life diminished considerably. My level of concern about the state of the world also increased considerably. I began thinking, *I only have a certain amount of time to make a difference!*

I can assure any naysayers that, in my mind, the pressure to succeed and to maintain a certain standard of living has lightened considerably. I experienced, in a word, psychological relief. Ironically, my professional life took a very favorable turn once I stopped putting so much emphasis on it. When I let go and stopped trying to control the direction of my career, voilà, the task took care of itself. Certainly, I hope my news show *Issues*, which I began in late 2008 on HLN, is a long-running success. It's a blast to host the show, and I love when I can inject an environmental message into the conversation. But if—for some reason—it doesn't continue in the long run, that's the way it's *supposed* to be. My higher power must have another plan in the works for me. I've learned, to a certain extent, to let the currents of that higher power take me where it wants. *Thy will, not mine!*

The second lesson that my brush with mortality taught me was . . . I definitely can't take it with me. Part of the reason the pressure lessened on my psyche is that I began to ask myself, *What am I preparing for beyond the inevitable rainy day and—if I'm lucky—my old age?* Being childless, I have only myself to worry about. If I have any money to leave, it will be given mostly to charity. But I'd rather put it into action while I'm alive. When I was a kid, I would have this recurring dream that I lived alone in a small studio apartment. Oddly, the stark, simple, and humble lifestyle didn't bother me . . . in the dream. When I woke up, that was another story. I still grapple with my cravings for the things that make life softer. I love taking an exotic vacation every so often and staying in grand hotels. And I like to live in the center of the action, whether I'm in Manhattan or Los Angeles. But gradually, lots of burning desires have been stamped out as I've learned more about the painful reality behind so much of what we call luxury.

The other night I walked down Madison Avenue's so-called Gold Coast in Manhattan. Heading south from 72nd Street, I encountered one "luxury" store after the next. The stores were closed, but their display windows remained brightly lit. I marched past the diamonds, furs, leather boots, leather handbags, and various and sundry haute couture items for sale. All of it revolted me.

This is where the richest people in the world shop, I marveled. Presumably, that includes some of the smarter people around. And, yet, everything here was just a uniform to wear in a competition called "Look at me, see how rich I am. Aren't you jealous?" The answer, from me anyway, is no, I'm not jealous at all. I wouldn't want to be like the people who shop at these places. I pity them for feeling the need to display their wealth so ostentatiously, oblivious to the cruelty involved in producing their status symbols. Anybody who reads or watches the news knows that indescribable cruelty often forms the basis of high fashion. Yet, I'm left to marvel at the willful ignorance and heartlessness of so many.

When I walk on the streets of New York City in the winter, I wear a "no fur" button, and I shake my head at anyone I pass by who is wearing fur. I call this a different kind of hunting. I'm hunting for any sign of a conscience. Sometimes, I hunt all day without success.

How clueless do you have to be to walk your dogs while wearing fur? Yet, it happens all the time in Manhattan. I even ran into a woman who was wearing a fur coat and walking a little dog who was also wearing a fur. And, believe me, I could tell it was a real fur, not faux.

"Your dog is wearing a dog," I said to her. "Millions of dogs and cats are skinned alive in China for fur trim and small furs."

She began screaming at me. "You're ignorant! You don't know what you're talking about. This is eco-fur!"

What a sick joke. There is no such thing as eco-fur. Animals killed for fur are either skinned alive, trapped in the wild and killed, or raised in fur farms where they are kept in tiny cages before being anally electrocuted. I've watched all those videos, and sometimes I can't sleep thinking about them. But that woman doesn't want to know the ugly reality behind her make-believe story. She is willfully ignorant.

One of my activist friends has a video of a raccoon dog being skinned alive, which he stores on his iPod. When he enounters someone wearing fur, he plays it for them.

Of course, no one wants to see the video, their startled eyes speaking volumes: *Don't confront me with the truth! Don't confuse me with the facts!*

As I walked down Madison Avenue, I had no lust. Where I once saw sparkling symbols of wealth, I now see blood and anguish.

For the past two Christmases, I have made donations to causes as gifts to family members in lieu of giving them purchased, wrapped gifts. The only exception I make is for my great-niece, Nicole, because let's face it, Christmas is for kids. And she's a next-generation environmentalist who is so up on the issues that I would never dare to give her anything that wasn't totally PC.

I've asked my family not to buy anything for me. I explained to them that I could no longer bear participating in Christmas gift-buying rituals that were wreaking massive environmental havoc. Just the wrapping paper alone eats up huge swaths of forest. There are other ways to experience the fun of gift giving without buying a bunch of gifts that nobody needs or even wants. Also, there are environmentally friendly shopping sites where one can purchase relatively harmless gift items, if a gift must be given. Handmade soy candles, such as the ones I handed out one year, seemed to pass environmental muster. My sister, Gloria, had a great suggestion: Throw a white-elephant party. Everyone wraps (in old newspaper, of course) the least favorite gift they've ever gotten that they tucked away in a dark closet somewhere. It's fun to see who gets "stuck" with the kookiest, tackiest gift. That's our game plan for next Christmas. It's actually a lot more fun than the traditional wrapping-paper-and-cardboard-box orgy that most of us endure to, of all things, celebrate the birth of Jesus Christ.

What would Jesus think of how we massacre the environment and animals to honor his life? I think he'd be as angry as when he chased the money changers, the cattle buyers, and the dove sellers from the temple. He'd quite possibly be angrier, as today's destruction is so much greater. It's often overlooked that Jesus's outburst in the temple was aimed at the business of animal sacrifice. By chasing out those dealers and scattering their stock, he liberated the animals. Today, in America, Jesus would be called a radical environmental terrorist by the very people who claim to speak in his name.

A key tenet of spiritual practice is nonviolence. Violence usually doesn't occur when others are watching. As I've learned over three decades covering horrific crime stories, most murders are not caught on tape. The worst acts perpetrated by humans against each other and against animals are committed in secret. But often these acts of violence are carried out to satisfy the lusts of those who *see no evil and hear no evil*. We all want to remain far removed from the violence that is carried out to satisfy our cravings. We want deniability! *I didn't know!* Of course I did. I just *pretended* I didn't know.

I started this book by saying that I am defined by what I want. My slow and rocky evolution has primarily been about one thing: how my cravings keep changing. I think it's fascinating that—in the Four Noble Truths of Buddhism—the discussion of the origins and cessation of suffering centers around cravings.

The first truth says, among other things, suffering happens when we don't get what we want. The second truth says the origin of suffering is *craving* for sensual pleasures. The third truth says the end of suffering is connected to relinquishing and gaining freedom from *cravings* and lust. The fourth Noble Truth speaks of the Noble Eightfold Path as the way to end suffering: right understanding, right thoughts, right speech, right conduct, right livelihood, right effort, right mindfulness, right concentration.

What blows my mind is that the very principles embedded in that Noble Eightfold Path are the same principles contained in the Twelve Steps. *Right understanding* involves knowing yourself for who you really are and accepting life on life's terms. This sounds a lot like the first step, where we realize we are powerless over our addiction and accept the truth, that our lives have become unmanageable.

Right thoughts, right conduct, right livelihood, and *right effort* are about practicing—in thought, word, and action—nonviolence, honesty, and kindness. The Twelve Steps are all about undertaking a moral housecleaning of ourselves, admitting our wrongs, becoming ready to have our higher power remove these character defects, and coming clean with those we've hurt.

Right mindfulness and *right concentration* are about awareness and meditation. The Twelve Steps tell us to pray and meditate to improve our contact with our higher power so we can learn what we're here to do and how to carry that out. The Noble Eightfold Path is a guide to a cessation of suffering on the road to enlightenment or "awakening." The Twelve Steps talk about having a spiritual awakening and spreading the word.

When I was about thirteen, I read a book that had a profound impact on me: *Siddhartha* by Hermann Hesse. Siddhartha's journey to enlightenment has a lot in common with the historical story of Buddha. It was the book that taught me that life is a journey and that the outward terrain is not as important as the changes that occur within. Another wonderful book about a transformative journey, which I stumbled across as an adult, is *Way of the Peaceful Warrior* by Dan Millman. It's a story of the transformation that occurs as a young man who is looking for answers is severely tested. Ultimately, with the help of a spiritual guide, he finds those answers within himself.

These stories, and stories like them, have a common thread. The central figure goes out into the world seeking truth and meaning. He finds that he has to let go of certain things in order to get other, more intangible things. Likewise, the true story of Buddha takes him from a princely and pampered childhood to extreme self-deprivation. But then, it brings him back to moderation.

Buddhism urges us to find the Middle Way. Neither extreme self-indulgence nor extreme self-renunciation is the path to enlighten-ment. It is the Noble Eight Fold Path that helps us find this Middle Way. As I try to navigate my own "middle way" through this world, I certainly don't want to live a life of extreme renunciation. I don't have to. Despite all the changes I've made I can still exist in society and enjoy many of its delights.

I'm a vegan, but I can still eat delicious food. I'm an environmen-talist, but I can still shop by being careful about my choices. I'm an animal activist, but I can still have a mainstream career. I'm gay, but I can still find love. I'm a recovering alcoholic, but I can still have fun by dancing, biking, skiing, and even belting out a karaoke number . . . all sober. I've given up processed sugar, but I can still taste life's sweet-ness in a bowl of fruit or a dessert made with agave nectar.

I've really given up nothing and gained everything. A life free of addiction, a life of emotional sobriety, a life of honesty, a life of simplicity, a life that emphasizes kindness to all living things . . . that's not a sacrifice. It's an adventure.

I hope you join me on this adventure. We're so conditioned to believe that, since most people in our society live a certain way, that's the way we have to live too. There is no safety in numbers. Just as we are all naked under our clothes, we are all alone in the end. You, and you alone, are responsible for your choices. You, and you alone, must decide what you want.

Guess I am that all-American girl after all.

Recommended Reading and Websites

I n my sobriety, I've made every mistake imaginable . . . except two. I haven't had a drink, and I continue to work on staying sober. We only get one day at a time, so that's how I take it. If you have an addiction, whatever it may be, please take heart. You *can* conquer it. There was a time when I thought I would never be able to get sober. I believed I was going to remain a drunk for the rest of my life. I proved myself wrong.

I highly recommend the following books and websites. I hope they help you on your way. The first step is admitting that you have a problem . . . the next is imagining a life without that problem. If I could do it, so can you. Good luck!

Alcoholics Anonymous—Big Book 4th Edition
(Alcoholics Anonymous World Services, Inc., 2002)

This is the bible when it comes to sobriety. Its language is simple, its message profound. It's a must-read for anyone who has any sort of addiction. The personal stories are profoundly moving. I could read this book a hundred times and not get tired of it.

Facing Codependence: What It Is, Where It Comes From, How It Sabotages Our Lives by Pia Mellody (Harper & Row, 1989)

This book lays out codependence in a way that really shows you its roots and its consequences. It's essential reading for anyone who is living with an addict or alcoholic or who engages in any enabling or codependent behavior. Mellody is also the author of *Facing Love Addiction: Giving Yourself the Power to Change the Way You Love* (HarperOne, 1992)

Skinny Bitch by Rory Freedman and Kim Barnouin (Running Press, 2005)

This No. 1 *New York Times* bestseller helped me kick some of my worst eating and drinking habits by grossing me out with the truth, even as I laughed my arse off. *Skinny Bitch in the Kitch* (Running Press, 2007) has great recipes. There's also *Skinny Bastard* (Running Press, 2009) for the guys.

Mad Cowboy: Plain Truth from the Cattle Rancher Who Won't Eat Meat by Howard F. Lyman and Glen Merzer (Scribner, 2001)

This is the fascinating story of cattle rancher Howard Lyman and his courageous decision to expose the secret horrors of his industry after a life-changing personal battle. Howard opened my eyes to the truth, which is why I went vegan.

Farm Sanctuary: Changing Hearts and Minds About Animals and Food by Gene Baur (Touchstone, 2008)

This amazing book will change your mind about food and farm animals. It's an eye-opening journey through America's factory farms, as animals left for dead are rescued by caring people and brought back to health at Farm Sanctuary. A searing indictment of the institutionalized cruelty of factory farms, this book also traces the movement to grant these animals basic protections, like the right to turn around and lie down. After you read this book, you will want to join Farm Sanctuary. Visit them at http://farmsanctuary.org/.

Alcoholics Anonymous • www.aa.org: This website will tell you everything you need to know about getting on the path to sobriety. From the history of the Twelve Steps to where to go for help, this is the place to start your journey to recovery.

Adult Children of Alcoholics (ACA) • www.adultchildren.org: Adult Children of Alcoholics is a Twelve-Step program for people who grew up in alcoholic or otherwise dysfunctional homes. Members meet in a safe setting to share their common experiences and discover how childhood often impacts adult lives.

Al-Anon • www.al-anon.alateen.org: Al-Anon, which includes Alateen (for children and teens), offers help to those living with an alcoholic or in families affected by the disease of alcoholism.

Caring Consumer • www.caringconsumer.com: This is the website of choice to get a list of fabulous cruelty-free products from companies that practice compassion. Use it!

Farm Sanctuary • www.farmsanctuary.org: Visit this group to learn about a growing national movement to give billions of farm animals basic protections.

The Humane Society of the United States • www.humanesociety.org: This is the nation's largest and most influential animal-protection organization—backed by 10 million Americans, or one in every thirty.

PETA • www.peta.org: People for the Ethical Treatment of Animals is considered the most influential animal-rights organization in the world. It focuses on areas of the most intense animal suffering, including factory farms, laboratories, and the clothing trade.

The Peace Alliance • www.thepeacealliance.org: Learn more here about the campaign to establish a Department of Peace within the U.S. government and foster a culture of peace nationally and globally.

VegSource.com• www.vegsource.com: This main Internet hub of the vegetarian/vegan community offers everything from great recipes to great strategies for getting healthy and fit.

Glossary

Adult Children of Alcoholics (ACA)—a program for women and men who grew up in alcoholic or otherwise dysfunctional homes. Children of alcoholics experience trauma when they grow up with a person who really isn't present the way a sober person is. Often, these children have been traumatized by the excessive drama in the household brought on by the alcoholic's behavior, which tends to be one of the following: irresponsible, rageful, weepy, and/or detached. Children of alcoholics have a tendency to develop bitterness over their stilted relationship with the alcoholic parent.

Al-Anon—an organization that provides a twelve-step program of recovery for friends and family members of alcoholics. "It is estimated that each alcoholic affects the lives of at least four other people . . . alcoholism is truly a family disease." This quote is from the literature of Al-Anon, which—for more than half a century—has been helping families of alcoholics cope with their addicted loved one. If you're a spouse, a child, a parent, or even just a close friend of an alcoholic—and you're struggling to cope—this is where you can get help.

Alcoholic thinking—the alcoholic's state of mind, which has a tendency to be self-absorbed, grandiose, and self-pitying, all at once. Another term for this is "stinking thinking." Even when we get sober, we can still exhibit alcoholic thinking, unless we maintain emotional sobriety.

As sick as our secrets—a powerful Twelve-Step phrase that reminds us that there is a price to pay for lying, even lying by omission. Privacy is fine, but when you hide embarrassing incidents from your past and try to pretend they never happened, it creates a toxic tide of shame that grows and grows and eventually turns your soul rancid. So, the lesson is: share your secrets in a safe setting.

Attraction not promotion—setting a good example. The best way to help others who need help getting sober is by being a good example of sobriety yourself. That way, people will look at you and say, "Wow, she's cool. I want what she has." The wrong way to get people sober is to badger them and brag about how wonderful sobriety is. It just doesn't work. I've tried to drag people kicking and screaming into sobriety and never succeeded. But I've also had friends who suddenly got sober after I did. Perhaps, just perhaps, they noticed how I went from being a kooky lush to a happier, infinitely more responsible human being.

Being of service—an attitude adjustment that refocuses the world away from ego and toward being of service to other people, other creatures, and the world as a whole; a key to emotional sobriety. A drunk is self-obsessed and narcissistic to the point of malignancy, and when he or she dries out, the alcoholic mentality remains. Being of service is required to become emotionally sober.

Character defects—the aspects of our personality that were pumping iron while we were out there drinking and drugging. In sobriety, we are forced to confront these unpleasant aspects of our character and actually do something to change them. Step Five (of the Twelve Steps) involves admitting to our higher power, to ourselves, and to another human being the exact nature of our wrongs. Steps Six and Seven involve reaching out to our higher power to let these character defects go.

Chasing the high—part of almost every alcoholic and drug addict's story. There is an initial moment of euphoria that a drug brings. That is notable because it's the best high the addict will ever have. Often, recovering addicts will talk eloquently about that first time all their problems dissolved as they were enveloped by the high of their drug of choice. This is comparable to the first time one has sex and really enjoys it. Unfortunately, at least where drugs/alcohol are concerned, it's all downhill from there and the addict spends years, often the better part of their existence chasing that first blush of euphoric intoxication, never to recapture it.

Codependency—one of the hardest addictions to define because, in many ways, it's invisible. When you're drunk, people can see it. But when you're codependent, it may look like you're the kindest, most loving person in the world. Call it the invisible addiction. When you're hooked on someone else in an unhealthy way and/or enabling that other person's addictive behavior, then you're being codependent. Why are codependents so attracted to addicts? Because addicts are usually exciting. Their lives are filled with drama, unnecessary drama of course, but drama nevertheless. Sometimes negative excitement is better than no excitement at all. Where does love end and codependency begin? My answer: when I'm using my interest in another person as a drug to escape my own feelings. Sometimes, to win points with them, I'm simultaneously helping them get away with their bad behavior. That's called enabling.

Competitive consumption—a *keeping up with the Joneses* mentality that tells us if our neighbor has it and we don't, then they are better than us. This is one of the sick notions that fuels our overconsumption. Advertisers and major corporations encourage competitive consumption to keep us buying.

Consumption addiction—a national addiction. Even if you are not an alcoholic, drug addict, foodie, codependent, gambler, or debtor, if you're an American living in the twenty-first century, chances are you are a consumption addict. We are a consumer society. We are called consumers, and told this is the way we're *supposed* to live! The way out of this addiction is through counterintuitive behavior. It's become second nature to shop our way out of every problem, we need to start thinking of the consequences of our thoughtless daily habits.

Consumption inventory—a list of everything you purchase or use for a specified period of time, say three days or a week. This will open your eyes to the massive amounts of "stuff" devoured and discarded, much of it unnecessary. On average, each American throws away four to five pounds of trash a day. But when you actually see this—not as a statistic—but rather as *your life,* it can be a huge wake-up call.

Contempt prior to investigation—an unhealthy attitude adopted by people who need help with their addiction but refuse to get it due to false assumptions. For example, without actually checking out a recovery program, they may think, *Oh, those twelve-step programs aren't for me. It's all bull.* People like this would rather remain ignorant than learn the truth, because once they learn the truth, they might have to change (which people often resist).

Contrary action—after becoming sober, doing the opposite of what the brain advises. This is one of the most important principles in recovery. As drunks/addicts, we develop hideous habits and leanings. When we get sober, our instincts are still askew because many of those unhealthy habits are still ingrained within us. That's why we often need to do the opposite of what our still-addled brains are advising. So, if my mind tells me: "Oh, I don't have to work on my sobriety. I'm okay. Anyway, I'm really tired," that's a clear-cut signal that contrary action is needed. The more I don't want to work on my sobriety, the more I need to do precisely that.

Daily reprieve—renewing our spirituality on a daily basis, by working the Steps, praying, and taking other suggested actions. If we don't work it . . . it stops working. The quickest way to slip is to assume you're somehow cured. There is no "cure" for alcoholism—only a daily reprieve.

Drama addicts—people who continually cast themselves in the leading role of their own performance-art soap opera. Drug addicts and alcoholics are, by definition, drama addicts. Their inebriation wreaks all sorts of havoc and chaos and can be very exciting. That's why there's a whole class of people, called codependents, who are addicted to the drama-prone addict.

Drug of choice—a substance or behavior that one consumes or performs compulsively. Figure out what your drug of choice is. For alcoholics, that's easy. But for those who are not hooked on a drug of consumption, it can be a lot harder to spot your "drug of choice." For example, some people are hooked on exercise. They may get into great shape and then cross a line where they work out too much and injure themselves or become emaciated. In other cases, someone's drug of choice may be food. That's an easy addiction to spot since two-thirds of Americans are overweight or obese. Obesity is not a lifestyle choice; it's an addiction to food.

Dry drunk—an alcoholic who still exhibits alcoholic thinking and behaviors even though no alcohol is being consumed. For any alcoholic, it's vitally important to put down the drink. However, that's where the real healing begins, not ends. Underlying emotional, spiritual, and psychological issues that caused or contributed to the alcoholism still need to be worked out. Without working out whatever it was that caused you to get drunk, then—when you quit—all you get is dry . . . not sober.

EGO = Edging God Out—ego is the big toxin that creates most of the problems in this world. And it's really just fear inside out. When we have no fear, we have no need for ego, because we already feel safe. When we let go of our ego and our fear, we stop edging out that power that is greater than ourselves. When I'm in synch with a power greater than myself, I feel immensely protected and safe.

Emotional eating—eating not to appease hunger but to escape unpleasant or uncomfortable feelings. Often addicts who get sober begin using food as a drug. Recovering alcoholics often become obsessed with sugar, using it to alter their mood and get a rush.

Emotional packaging—ego-targeted messages used to advertise products to make consumers think they "need" the product to be whole, healthy, and/or happy. This is the great scam of modern times perpetrated on a public so conditioned to accept it that we never even question the outlandish assumptions behind it.

Emotional sobriety—a state of being we must maintain to avoid alcoholic thinking and behavior. Emotional sobriety involves doing the inner work that allows us to stay on the spiritual beam, where we concentrate on having the right intentions, taking the right actions, and being of service to others. This right thinking gives us an inner peace that translates into serenity, patience, and contentment.

Enablers—those people who allow an addict to continue his or her self-destructive ways, thereby helping them to remain mired in their disease. They act like friends and supporters, but because an enablers are so "helpful," they can be hard to pinpoint, like those shape-shifting characters in the movies who first appear to be the hero and then end up the villain. Most practicing addicts and alcoholics have enablers in their lives. Sometimes, the enabler is the drinking partner, who may also be an alcoholic. Sometimes, it's the sober spouse or lover. Sober enablers need to get help for their *codependency* and can do this by attending Al-Anon meetings.

Enabling—helping an addict carry out his or her addictive behavior. This can be a simple act such as bringing a quart of ice cream to the home of a compulsive eater. Or, it can be very subtle, such as covering up an addict's disease by pretending it's not happening or by minimizing or rationalizing it: "Oh, he just had too many to drink because he's upset over the stock market." Enablers are like public-relations hacks. Sometimes, though, enablers aren't codependent, but rather, are manipulating the addict for their own ends. A stoned artist is easier to steal from than a sober one.

False personas—practicing alcoholics often try to mask their underlying spiritual bankruptcy by putting on a phony front that radiates something that the alcoholic is not. For example, the boozer may be a wild partier by night. But because he doesn't want this reckless side to be discovered by his employers, he may act extremely proper at work, even putting on an act of being a stay-at-home bookworm.

Fast-food nation—the national "need" for speed when it comes to eating meals. When we rush to get our meals and finish them quickly, we tend to eat the wrong things, gain weight, feel miserable, and become ill. It would be smarter to take a little more time and care with our choices and save our health, our looks, and our sense of well-being.

Faux dairy products—non-animal alternatives to dairy products. I've heard a lot of people say, "Oh, I don't eat much meat anyway, but I could never give up dairy." I tell them that there are many alternatives—from sour cream and cream cheese to meltable cheddar and milk—on the market that are just fantastic. Tofutti and Follow Your Heart faux cheeses are two brands I really enjoy.

Faux meats—non-animal alternatives to meat. Today, you can get a faux version of any meat product you crave. This is a great way to practice substitution therapy. If you are having a craving for a burger, try a veggie burger. Really, what you are craving is the experience of biting into a bun lathered with ketchup and sprinkled with onions and lettuce and tomatoes and that other thing too. You have the exact same experience with a veggie burger without the guilt. A veggie burger has fewer calories and no cholesterol. It also has much less impact on the environment.

High bottom—the point at which a person realizes he or she has an addiction and wishes to seek help for the problem while not hitting bottom in the classic sense. There are plenty of people who don't have to descend into the literal gutter to realize they have an addiction problem. Alcoholics Anonymous is not even a century old. In the 1940s and 1950s—when my dad was drinking—AA was not the powerful force that it is today. Now, just about anybody with a pulse and a TV knows that there are recovery programs available if they have a problem. Fortunately, it's not so shameful anymore to admit to an addiction. This is why people are now getting sober at younger ages before they've lost everything. It's a fabulous trend!

High-functioning alcoholic—closet and/or controlled drunks and lushes who are able to function professionally despite their drinking problem. Because they've managed to control it all so well, they remain in denial, often long after the sloppy drunk has been forced to get sober.

Hit bottom—the point at which an alcoholic's life becomes so unmanageable that he or she is ready to seek lasting help for the problem. This is often what has to happen for an alcoholic/addict to really be ready to move toward lasting sobriety. Through the Twelve Steps, the addict who hits bottom first admits powerlessness over the substance and acknowledges that his or her life has become a mess or unmanageable. Since this predicament is where their best thinking got them, it's time to hand the steering wheel over to a higher power.

Identify with my story—the miracle of Twelve-Step sharing. Somehow, when you listen to or share your predicament with somebody who has the same problem, all the shame and judgment gets drained out of it. You learn that you're not alone and you can get ideas from the other person on how to get better. It's bonding and healing and all sorts of good stuff. It's very hard—nay, impossible—for alcoholics/ addicts to accept a message and/or direction from someone who is not addicted themselves. That's because when someone who isn't addicted tries to counsel someone who is addicted, the addict knows that "normie" talking to them has no idea of what it's really like to be overpowered by a craving. Therefore, the addict feels judged. However, when someone who is addicted speaks, the addict/alcoholic who is listening identifies with the story and learns from it, without feeling judged.

I do enough, I am enough, I have enough—a mantra that, to me, is miraculous. The first time I heard this phrase was from the lips of my longtime sober buddy, Debbie. When I'm overwhelmed or I'm trying my hardest but I'm still falling behind, repeating this simple phrase calms me and puts the situation into perspective. There is only so much any one of us can do, be, or have. Learning to accept ourselves as we are right now can be an enormous relief. It's like taking the weight of the world off of our shoulders.

In my disease—another way for an addict or alcoholic to describe the time when they were using drugs or drinking. Those of us in recovery need to have a lot of phrases to describe our previous usage because one crucial component of staying sober is to constantly remember what it was like "out there." Addicts have a tendency toward "amnesia" when it comes to their drug of choice and can easily start "romancing the drug."

Kindness inventory—a test that helps to eliminate cruelty and environmental waste when considering a purchase. One such test is "Was it tested on animals?" If the answer is yes, don't buy it. Another test: "Is it made of recycled materials?" or "Are the packaging or contents biodegradable?" Yet another is "Were the workers who made this product exploited?" That can be a tough one to determine, but there are ways to shop—especially online—to insure that you are buying products that were made by people who got fair wages and decent workplace conditions.

Less than—undervaluing oneself irrationally, especially compared with others. There's a saying that goes "Never compare your insides to somebody else's outsides." It will usually leave you feeling "less than."

Life on life's terms—accepting that, when it comes to life, it is what it is. This is our challenge in sobriety. Without the ability to escape through booze or drugs, we have to confront unpleasant situations, cruelties we wish didn't exist, the bad behavior of others, and sometimes our own self-destructiveness. Sobriety isn't always fun, but at least we're experiencing reality. In the end, that's called being alive.

Liquid meat—dairy products. Dairy cows produce calves, which are generally ripped away from their mothers almost immediately after birth. Some of them become veal calves. That means those baby boy calves are stuck in a dark crate, chained there so they cannot move—all to keep their flesh soft for consumption.

Living amends—in cases where a person cannot apologize or make amends to a person, creature, or institution she has harmed, she can do a "make up" that is in the general area of where she committed harm. For example, if you've stolen money from someone but cannot track them down to give it back, you could donate the amount you stole to a worthy cause.

Love addict—a person who is compulsively focused on a love interest in a manner that's unhealthy and self-destructive. Sometimes love addiction can seem very similar to codependency, but there are distinctions. Love addiction comes in many forms. Sometimes the love addict is so hooked on the high of courtship and early romance that he or she can never make it past the honeymoon phase.

Managing the gray areas—adapting a more nuanced approach and breakdown of an addiction. This is sometimes necessary because many addictions are not black-

and-white; the substance or activity must be confronted every day, and we can't just say no as we would to alcohol or drugs. Food is the most obvious example, but the dilemma also applies to other addictions such as work and spending. This is when an addiction must be broken down into gray areas. Some activities are light gray, some are dark gray. Instead of black-and-white thinking, we manage the grays by trying to keep our behavior in the light gray areas.

Moment of clarity—the moment when the lightbulb goes off in the addict's head and they, metaphorically or sometimes literally, look in the mirror and see themselves as others see them—for the drunk or druggie they really are. That brief instant of clarity can be utterly devastating and powerful. I had a few moments of clarity (MOC) before the final one that helped me get sober. Each MOC was horrifying as—in that instant—I looked at my behavior objectively and was disgusted with myself. That made me want to get better.

Normies—the so-called normal people—those annoyingly perfect people—who don't seem to be under the sway of weird or uncontrollable urges. However, normies can be the worst closet addicts with some of the most crippling addictions, namely the ones you can't see, hear, or consume!

One day at a time—this is all any addict or alcoholic has, one day at a time to remain sober. The worst thing a newly sober addict or alcoholic can do is say, "I'm never going to drink/use again . . . for the rest of my life!" Wow, what an impossible burden! However, when we say, "I'm just not going to drink today," it seems much easier. It's doable! We don't have to worry about the rest of our lives. We just won't use or drink today.

Overfunctioning—a cousin of perfectionism; taking a good thing to such an extreme that it becomes a bad thing. Addicts/alcoholics have a very hard time doing anything in moderation. In work, one is never fully, ideally, 100-percent prepared. There is always one more thing to do, one more article to read, one more call to make, and so on. You can drive yourself—and others—mad. Sometimes doing too much is worse than not doing enough. Being aware of this compulsion and having a label for it are very helpful because, when you start doing it, you can say to yourself: stop overfunctioning. Often workaholism is a manifestation of overfunctioning.

Peace begins on your plate—a phrase that brings the concept of nonviolence down to a level that's right in front of your face. I first heard this phrase from my dear friend and fellow animal activist Patty Shenker. A lot of people love to talk about peace and tell other people to be peaceful, when they themselves are not peaceful. If you confront the violence that goes to putting certain foods, like meat, on your plate, then you have to admit you are not being peaceful by eating those foods. A plate of organic vegetables is a peaceful plate.

People pleaser—a person who is so invested in being liked by others that he or she becomes terrified of doing anything that might displease anyone else. The emotional toll that this fear-based thinking exacts is enormous and psychologically crippling. The people pleaser tries to be everything to everybody and, consequently, ends up being nothing to anybody. People pleasing fosters inauthenticity, which is fancy way of saying people pleasers are big phonies who suffer from low self-esteem and a myriad of insecurities.

Pink cloud—an overwhelming sense of relief and euphoria that overtakes the newly sober alcoholic/addict when she realizes she is no longer a slave to her disease! (Ah, the pink cloud. I remember it well. *Freedom! Yipee!*) The pleasure of that freedom is almost indescribable. Remember, addiction is not a willpower issue. So many of us alcoholics spent years in an exhausting, frustrating crusade to get sober through willpower. It's like trying to push a giant boulder uphill by yourself. You may have the best of intentions, but that boulder ain't going where you want it to go. Sometimes, I reexperience the pink cloud when I flash on an image of my previous life as a drunk and realize—with supreme relief—I'm not that person anymore!

Pity party—luxuriating in the feelings of having been wronged and taking a hard-to-define pleasure out of the resulting self-pity. Pity parties are usually a party of one. When something doesn't go the way we want it to and we feel sorry for ourselves, it can be "fun" to wallow in the problem. We feel victimized, and this sick party keeps us in the problem when we need to get into the solution. This is a dangerous indulgence for alcoholics/addicts. There is a sober saying that explains why pity parties are perilous: "Poor me, poor me, pour me . . . a drink." The Twelve Steps show us how to take responsibility for "our part" in any situation, thereby allowing us to move past self-pity and into accountability.

Power greater than ourselves—a benevolent force greater than oneself. Many people have a hard time wrapping their minds around this concept. The word "God" is so loaded that for some it's a cure-all and for others it's a delusion. But remember, it's just a word—the idea behind the word is what's important. I prefer the phrase "power greater than ourselves" or "higher power." I can't tell you what this higher power is. I have my own understanding of it, which changes from day to day, and you can have your own understanding. That's what so brilliant about this open-ended spirituality. You get to define it! In fact, you get to say, "Gee, I can't define it, but I'll try to get in touch with it anyway, since it helps me so much." It's sort of like 9-1-1 operators. You don't know what they look like or where they are, but damn, when you need help, they're a power greater than you! All I know about my higher power is that I can get in touch with it by letting go of my ego and my fear. This is a power greater than myself. I believe this is a force for good. I try to get myself out of the way so I can be a conduit for this force.

Powerless—what an addict is when it comes to addiction. It's a dichotomy because the only power we have is the power to admit we are powerless. Once we do that, we can make a decision to ask some force more powerful than ourselves—a higher power—for help in fighting the disease. But nothing happens while we are still bargaining with our addiction. Getting over an addiction is like getting over a death. There are stages of grief and the final stage is acceptance. We need to accept that we are powerless over our disease, just as we are powerless over someone's death.

Present—being here. This is the tough part. It's why people drink and drug, so they can get out of "here"—at least mentally and emotionally if not physically. Life is weird. *Why are we here? What's it all about, Alfie? Why is there such evil and such suffering?* These existential questions plague most thinking humans. Suffering is an unavoidable part of life, and we are often powerless to stop it. Sifting through all of this when sober is challenging, but if we're stoned and drunk, we certainly can't make anything better. By being present and sober, we are more able to be of service.

Problem of perception—the skewed outlook of the alcoholic in her disease. How we view the world is completely twisted by the mood-altering substances we consume. You could also call them "perception-altering substances." This doesn't just apply to moments of intoxication. The alcoholic mindset leads to drama, even when technically sober. That's because the alcoholic perceives herself as the center of the universe, with everything revolving around her. When we get sober, we experience an attitude adjustment if we work our program of sobriety.

Pulled a geographic—literally moving to a new location for a "fresh start" without working on overcoming one's addiction; in other words, running away from the problem. Instead of confronting our illness, we decide it will all get better if we only get a fresh start somewhere else. The only problem is, wherever we go, we take ourselves and our addiction with us.

Rage-aholics—a person who is addicted to rage. Rage masks other emotions buried underneath, like sadness. It's easier for a lot of people to reveal that they're angry than that they're sad. Rage often comes in the form of "righteous indignation." It is said in the Twelve Steps that one luxury alcoholics can't afford is righteous indignation. That's because, when an alcoholic feels he's been wronged and becomes righteously indignant, he can also become very dangerous and even violent.

Relationship autopsy/inventory—breaking down and analyzing a failed relationship. This can help when you are trying to move on. It's a good way to learn what went wrong in your last relationship. An honest inventory involves acknowledging your part in it. Once you acknowledge your part, you are no longer a victim, but merely a participant.

Reverse pride—feeling guilty for things that are beyond one's control. This is a tricky concept, but boy, is it helpful for the guilt-ridden. Essentially, this concept highlights the egocentricity at the basis of so much unnecessary guilt, especially those of us with addictive personalities. We are not responsible for things beyond our control. So, to feel guilty for them is irrational.

Rigorous honesty—having a healthy relationship with honesty. This is what is required to stay sober, not just dry. You can be dishonest with yourself and still achieve white-knuckle sobriety. But to be really sober, in the full spiritual sense, you need to create a healthy relationship with honesty by being faithful to honesty 100 percent of the time. Mostly, it's just a matter of being honest with yourself and the ones you love.

Self-medicating—playing doctor with ourselves to escape emotional pain. When we can't deal with life on life's terms, we self-medicate. Bad day at the office? Write yourself a prescription: three martinis. Heart-wrenching breakup? A joint a day and a bottle a night. Unfortunately, this self-medicating only makes us sicker in the long run. The sicker we get, the more meds we need. That's why addiction is progressive.

Serenity Prayer—one of the most popular prayers for those living a life of sobriety because it reminds us to accept life on life's terms, but yet strive to be of service. "God grant me the serenity to accept the things I cannot change, courage to change the things I can, and wisdom to know the difference."

Sex addiction—an addiction to sex. Some people use sex as a drug, just as others use food, booze, or drugs. Sex is a great way to escape, forget, and alter your mood. The problem occurs when you use your partner to escape as opposed to sharing intimacy with that other person because you love them. Sex addicts often jump from person to person the way a junkie throws out an old needle before grabbing a new one. Any time you "use" anything or anyone for ulterior motives, you're entering dangerous territory.

Share—a practice in which you admit to certain feelings and/or behaviors. Although scary, it must be done to achieve emotional sobriety. Sharing is the best way to let out the tires of toxic shame. But it's best to do it with people who "share" your problem, who are less likely to judge you and more likely to listen. Listening to someone who is overcoming addiction share about the way they are doing it can be an inspiration and a great way to pick up some sobriety tips.

Soul sickness—a condition in which one is frozen emotionally and spiritually. This is what happens to the alcoholic/drug addict after a long period of consistent "using." When you're constantly escaping from everything and never dealing with life on life's terms, there is no emotional or spiritual growth. Spiritual growth often comes out of pain. If you're always putting yourself out of your own misery through booze or pills or some other addiction, then you never really experience the pain and you never grow from it, leading to spiritual bankruptcy.

Spiritually bankrupt—soul sickness at its lowest point. At a certain stage of the disease of addiction, there is no "there" there. Everything has been sapped by the craving, the efforts to fulfill the craving, and the remorse of what was done while stoned or drunk. For many high-functioning and/or financially independent alcoholics, the bankruptcy is manifested in toxicity: scheming, backstabbing, unnecessary drama, outbursts, and general viciousness. It's like rabies of the soul.

Stinking thinking—the irrational, often self-destructive thought process that can lead recovering alcoholics/addicts to make bad decisions in sobriety. The alcoholic belief system is toxic and often quite ingrained. So, just because somebody gets clean and sober doesn't mean their thinking automatically cleans up.

Stuffing my feelings—covering up one's uncomfortable feelings by using drugs, alcohol, or some other addictive behavior to mask them from oneself. Getting high is an easy way to avoid emotional pain. *Feeling blue?* Have a glass of champagne and act happy. Since it's an act, there's the need for another glass of champagne . . . and another. The reason addicts and alcoholics fear they will never have any fun again if they get sober is that relief from their unpleasant feelings is only through escaping with a drug or drink. Sometimes, even in sobriety, we'll use something else, like sweets, to stuff our uncomfortable feelings. Ultimately, however, our goal is to face the feelings and sit through them. That's how we grow.

Sugar substitutes, healthy (evaporated cane juice, brown rice syrup, tapioca syrup, agave syrup, molasses, beet syrup, barley malt syrup, date sugar or real maple syrup)—"good" sweets that won't give you a sugar rush the way white sugar does. With these substances, you can satisfy your craving for sweets without getting the jitters. Also, because they're natural, these sweets have nutritional value.

Surrendering the results—getting out of ego. This is one of the most powerful concepts in sobriety. I almost always pray for the power to get out of my own way so I can suit up, show up, do the next indicated thing, be of service, and stay out of the results. When I fail to do that, when I begin daydreaming of recognition, I don't get my work done and I screw up. Surrendering the results is akin to surrendering your ego-centered desire for glory.

Surrendering to my powerlessness—the key to it all when it comes to sobriety. When friends with a drug, alcohol, or codependency problem tell me the Twelve Steps are not for them, I say, "Well, look at where your best thinking got you. Maybe it's time to try something else. Perhaps it's time to admit *you* can't fix this thing and surrender to your powerlessness. That way, you open yourself up to alternatives, like the Twelve Steps, that actually work." Surrendering is the hardest part because it feels like an admission of defeat. Actually, it's a monumental relief to surrender. To me, it felt like the weight of the world came off my shoulders.

Terminally unique—viewing oneself as so special and unique that the rules that govern everyone else could not possibly apply to him or her. This is a very commonplace diagnosis where the alcoholic is concerned. It could also be called exceptionalism, a philosophy where the norms of society should apply *except* to those addicts who feel they are somehow exempt by virtue of their specialness. Sadly, this attitude often gets the alcoholic in trouble, as rules exist for a reason and constantly breaking them is dangerous and self-destructive.

The next indicated thing—the next step in a process. This is another very useful concept in recovery. When I'm given a big assignment that begins to overwhelm me, I remember to just *do the next indicated thing*. This allows me to focus and continuously move toward my goal, whether it's mastering the details of complex story or getting all the information on a breaking news story. I also use this concept in my personal life: if I'm faced with a problem, I try to approach the solution by simply doing the next indicated thing and taking the next logical step.

There's No Mess I Can't Clean Up—a sober saying that is a tremendous comfort to me because, let's face it, we all screw up from time to time. When I do something that I'm not proud of, this saying gets me thinking about the solution: how I can clean up the mess. For example, if I'm uncharacteristically terse with someone because I'm stressed out, I've learned that a card with a small gift can undo the hurt. Of course, I try to make that a card sent on recycled paper and a gift that's not hurtful to the environment.

Twelve Steps—A series of simple, but powerful instructions that can help you overcome addiction. Based on fundamental spiritual principles, the Steps are a path to sanity and serenity. (See page 268.)

Unmanageability—a state in which the alcoholic/addict has lost control of her life. Unmanageability is the final stop on the addiction train, and all addicts are headed there. Even if the addict's life still seems fine on the outside—she still has her job, car, lover, dog—she is nevertheless on an express train toward unmanageability. As our lives get messier through addiction, it can manifest itself differently. For some, their apartment becomes messy. For others, their relationships become messy. For still others, their work life becomes messy. At a certain point, for most addicts, everything becomes a mess: job, relationships, home. That's unmanageable.

User—a person who literally uses a substance, situation, behavior, person, or thing for escape. For example, when somebody goes shopping because they're depressed and need a pick-me-up, that person is a "user." It's vital to become aware of when you've stopped shopping for good reasons and started shopping for bad ones. Virtually everyone is a user in some way, shape, or form. That's why America can be correctly diagnosed as a nation of addicts.

Vegan—a whole-life practice based on the philosophy that animals are not here for us to use. It's a simple concept that is not that difficult to implement. Vegans do not eat animals, wear animals in the form of leather or fur, or use products that contain animal ingredients. I also take it to mean that we do not use products that were tested on animals. Becoming vegan will radically transform your life for the better. You will be healthier, save money, help save the environment, and definitely save the lives of many animals. Going vegan is really a spiritual journey.

Withdrawal—the emotional, psychological, and sometimes physical pain of giving up a drug during the craving phase. It doesn't matter what drug you're talking about, withdrawal is invariably emotionally, psychologically, and sometimes, even physically painful. The withdrawals don't last forever; the trick is to get through them and past them. You're trying to swim to shore, and withdrawal is a powerful undertow trying to drag you back out into dangerous waters.

Workaholic—a person who works compulsively. Work is used as a drug to avoid facing uncomfortable or frightening personal issues. This is a tough habit to break because our society encourages it. However, in the long run, a workaholic does not have a balanced life and therefore may not have the best judgment or perspective. Sometimes less is more.

The Twelve Steps
of Alcoholics Anonymous

1. We admitted we were powerless over alcohol—that our lives had become unmanageable.

2. Came to believe that a Power greater than ourselves could restore us to sanity.

3. Made a decision to turn our will and our lives over to the care of God *as we understood Him.*

4. Made a searching and fearless moral inventory of ourselves.

5. Admitted to God, to ourselves, and to another human being the exact nature of our wrongs.

6. Were entirely ready to have God remove all these defects of character.

7. Humbly asked Him to remove our shortcomings.

8. Made a list of all persons we had harmed, and became willing to make amends to them all.

9. Made direct amends to such people wherever possible, except when to do so would injure them or others.

10. Continued to take personal inventory and when we were wrong promptly admitted it.

11. Sought through prayer and meditation to improve our conscious contact with God *as we understood Him,* praying only for knowledge of His will for us and the power to carry that out.

12. Having had a spiritual awakening as the result of these steps, we tried to carry this message to alcoholics and to practice these principles in all our affairs.

Source: Alcoholics Anonymous—Big Book 4th Edition. *Alcoholics Anonymous World Services, Inc.,* 2002.